# Horizons of Justice

# Critic of Institutions

Roberta Kevelson
*General Editor*

Vol. 8

PETER LANG
New York • Washington, D.C./Baltimore
Bern • Frankfurt am Main • Berlin • Vienna • Paris

# Horizons of Justice

Edited by
J. Ralph Lindgren

PETER LANG
New York • Washington, D.C./Baltimore
Bern • Frankfurt am Main • Berlin • Vienna • Paris

**Library of Congress Cataloging-in-Publication Data**

Horizons of justice/
[edited by] J. Ralph Lindgren.
p. cm. — (Critic of institutions; vol. 8)
Includes bibliographical references and index.
1. Law—United States. 2. Law—Philosophy. 3. Justice.
I. Title. II. Series.
KF379.L56 340'.11—dc20 95-11862
ISBN 0-8204-2802-7
ISSN 1068-4689

**Die Deutsche Bibliothek-CIP-Einheitsaufnahme**

Horizons of justice/
edited by J. Ralph Lindgren.
- New York; Washington, D.C./Baltimore; Bern;
Frankfurt am Main; Berlin; Vienna; Paris: Lang.
(Critic of institutions; Vol. 8)
ISBN 0-8204-2802-7
NE: GT

Cover design by Nona Reuter.

The paper in this book meets the guidelines for permanence and durability of the Committee on Production Guidelines for Book Longevity of the Council of Library Resources.



Printed in the United States of America.

**In Memory of Jay Knaak**

**Teacher, Scholar and Friend**

# Contents

# Introduction

Since classical Greece the term "justice" has been used to denote those properties that distinguish practices and institutions that deserve the support and loyalty of peoples they affect from those in which that support is optional. It is in this sense that John Rawls proclaims that "justice is the first virtue of institutions."[1] For example, if a government is found to be just, subjects are held to be under obligation to obey its commands or laws.

This was the consistent use of "justice" for the two and one half millennia since Plato and Aristotle first cast the concept in that role. As we approach the third millennia of the common era the role of "justice" in our vocabulary is undergoing radical revision.

During the second half of the Twentieth Century recognition of diverse cultures has been in the ascendancy. Multiculturalism has taken hold so firmly in developed nations that holdouts are openly ridiculed. Whereas during earlier times according legitimate status to populations that support values systems that are incompatible with one's own had been condemned as a sure sign of moral bankruptcy, in our era it has one of the hallmarks of a sensible moral bearing. This change has profound implications for the role of "justice" in a multicultural world.

The essays in this volume explore different aspects of this changed role of "justice." Rather than attempt an overview of these contributions, an effort that, in any event, would be as presumptuous as it is premature, abstracts are provided to assist the reader in identifying which of the many themes developed here he/she wishes to explore first.

Chapter One, by John Brigham, addresses "Institutional Authority and Political Momentum: Constitutional Equal Protection in American Politics." Although recognized as pressing matters of public policy, the conditions under which much of black America lives—segregated and poor—have not been considered matters for constitutional scrutiny. From 1954 to nearly the present, the legal culture in this area has seemed fixed to the principles of non-discrimination announced in *Brown*. Now, there are signs of a change that can best be understood with reference to the emergence of the present paradigm. Some other possibilities were even suggested in the 1970s. In one, the appeal of *Gomperts v. Chase* in 1971, Justice William O. Douglas actually suggested that *Plessy v. Ferguson* had not been overruled with respect to de facto segregation. But equal protection jurisprudence turned away from the course that had been charted in the 1940s to a much more limited promise. The result was the current straitjacket of the *de facto/de jure* distinction as it has developed in constitutional law. With emerging critiques of the old standard we may wonder about the future of equal protection jurisprudence. This paper only suggests some of the possibilities. It does not attempt to predict the outcomes.

Chapter Two, by William C. Charron, is entitled: "Public Reason, Mediation, and Markets: Kant Against Rawls." A new proposal has been put into the political arena: that all future debates, decisions and votes on fundamental political issues be conducted within the limits of what is called *public reason*. This is the recommendation of John Rawls in his most recent book, *Political Liberalism* (1992). Behind his insistence on the need to respect the constraints of public reason is a disillusionment: Rawls has no hope that citizens of liberal societies can ever come to free agreement on fundamental religious and philosophical, including moral, theory. Rawls, however, is not satisfied to treat political life as an *n*-person bargaining game in which agreements are compromises subject to renegotiation as threat advantages shift within the society. What he is proposing is a sort of middle way between agreement by bargaining and agreement by demonstration of moral truth. He is advocating as the basis of public discourse and decision a new form of civility that observes the constraints of what he calls "public reason." By the proprieties of public reason, one always avoids any claim to the truth of one's own beliefs about religious, political or moral matters, and one sticks to "plain truths" widely understood and accepted by citizens and avoids scientific theories that are "elaborate" and "controversial." By so limiting discourse and decision, Rawls seeks to work up and secure the basis of a stable consensus of overlapping elements in otherwise divergent comprehensive systems and at the same time reconcile deep divisions within existing liberal democratic constitutions, especially that between the two liberalisms, classical and welfare. Although Rawls nominally ties his notion to Kant's notion of the *public use of reason*, it is not in the spirit of Kant in important respects and, thus, derives no legitimacy-by-tradition from its connection with him. Charron wants to show that Rawls's proposal for the new civility of public reason is excessively levelling and threatens to be repressive in its rigorous application in the current political climate, and that its underlying fault is that his approach to pluralism is too narrowly focussed: it casts questions of agreement and disagreement as questions to be settled only in political forums. I suggest a different approach, one which also has a Kantian (as well as Humean) bloodline: it respects and fosters a freer (less prohibited) use of speech in public forums, and it highlights market places as public forums in which differences of interest and opinion are impartially and impersonally respected and satisfied in a way that is mutually advantageous. In effect, it proposes moving away from an exclusively adjudicational approach to conflict resolution toward a mediational one.

Chapter Three, by Robert Ginsberg, considers "The Future of Past Injustices" The Dialogue explores the peculiar problem of doing justice to past victims who do not leave descendants. Symbolic commemoration is proposed as a way of making past victims count as well as a way of preventing future victimization. The development of a just historical conscience is beneficial when facing present injustices. Remedying the present takes precedence over rectifying the past. Yet some long-standing evils are concealed from our recognition by social presuppositions. Thus, the critique of history can bring us to new awareness of such evils. Self-concealment is constitutive of the problem of much systemic evil, such as racism and sexism. The common feature of such evils is in drawing lines to keep us apart from other groups of human beings whose full humanity is denied. The dialogue turns back and forth on the priority of treating pressing problems now vs. searching through history for undetected problems. Conscience and responsibility are linked in the imperative to discover the systemic evil in which we are unknowing participants.

Chapter Four, by Edward Keynes asks: "Personal Liberty and the Public Welfare: An Irreconcilable Conflict? Since 1923 the U.S. Supreme Court has developed a jurisprudence of personal liberty that conflicts with republican principles of the public welfare. In an effort to reconcile these competing values, Justices Sandra Day O'Connor, Anthony M. Kennedy, and David H. Souter attempted in *Planned Parenthood of Southeastern Pennsylvania v. Casey* (1992) to strike a new balance in the abortion context between individuals liberty claims and legislative authority to promote the public health, safety, welfare, and morals.[2] However, their analysis fails to resolve the inherent conflict between liberty, conceived as an indivisible right of individual autonomy and privacy, and the public welfare, viewed in utilitarian terms. This chapter concludes that as long as the Supreme Court treats privacy as a dignitary right, it must restrain public intrusions unless they advance a right that has a greater value in the transitive hierarchy, e.g., a person's right to life. Alternatively, the Court could adopt a utilitarian theory of rights, which would leave legislatures free to weigh "rights" as public goods in cost/benefit terms. This would undermine the Supreme Court's substantive due-process jurisprudence, since the legislature is responsible for making calculations of the public welfare in a republican society. The justices' role would be reduced to determining whether the legislature had followed constitutionally prescribed rules in distributing public goods. While this work should not be interpreted as an appeal for a utilitarian theory of rights, it does point to the Court's dilemma in attempting to balance individual liberty and the public welfare. The justices' current methodology simply does not permit a principled resolution of the controversy.

In Chapter Five, Jay Knaack discusses "The Illusions of Justice." This chapter looks at the ways in which claims for justice are constructed, or the way in which the norms, standards and rules of what is to be considered just are authorized, phrased and certified. An examination of these linguistic constructions enable us to look at justice as consisting in various sorts of illusions, (many of which are well known), and to also see justice as a matter of social discourse, that is, as part of social process, rather than as any sort of fixed state of social relations, end state of society, or single group of principles. Here various states or principles which are often viewed as basic for justice are considered to be part of the process of dialogue and dispute, construction and reconstruction.

In Chapter Six, Ralph Lindgren explores the "Implications of the Multicultural Turn for the Practice of Morality." What are the minimum adjustments that must be made in the practice of morality to accommodate the implications of deciding to recognize the existence of a plurality of cultures? The first section of this paper examines the form of moral practice that tends to prevail where people do not acknowledge the status of other cultures—moral monism—pointing out one of the dangers inherent in it. The second section argues that two strategies which attempt to salvage monism fail. The ever popular mega-culture approach founders on the incompatibility of diverse cultures, while the universal module approach recently sponsored by John Rawls founders both on grounds of cultural bias and the arbitrary commitment to the centrality of moral consensus. In the next two sections Lindgren defends the view that we don't need a normative consensus to support stable, cooperative relationships among diverse peoples and that we do not need moral justification to establish the legitimacy of social institutions, especially in a democratic society. The closing section identifies the weakest adjustment to the practice of morality that would survive the multicultural turn. The analysis presented here urges a more pragmatic and a less pretentious form of morality for a multicultural setting. The clear implication of these conclusions is that the recoginition of a plurality of incompatible cultures requires that justice relinquish the position as the first virtue of institutions to the more pragmatic quality of workability. In a context of value pluralism, justice cannot be the primary concern.

In Chapter Seven Joseph Margolis considers "Rawls on Justice—Once Again" In *Political Liberalism*, John Rawls attempts to bring his well-known *A Theory of Justice* to bear on formulating a philosophical justification for preferring liberalism. The argument depends on supposing that one can distinguish between the "objective truth" of moral claims and their "objective reasonableness" in the absence of establishing their truth. Margolis argues that there is no viable strategy for justifying the seemingly weaker claim that does not implicitly invoke the stronger claim at some point or does not, on politically realistic grounds, inevitably compromise the apparent reasonableness of political liberalism itself. Rawls faces a dilemma which he cannot resolve. The point of pursuing the issue rests with the fact that Rawls has offered what may be the most scrupulous and sustained defense of political liberalism, on the assumption that the truth of moral norms is not accessible. Liberalism, therefore, is an inherently flawed and irredeemable thesis or, alternatively, it is a cryptic version of the moral realist's position that it means to elude.

Margolis takes Rawls's puzzle to lie at the heart of Western moral philosophies and, because of its indefensibility, to encourage moral skepticism. In particular, he attempts to show that the concept of justice, like the concept of thought itself, must be historicized. Several constraints on a defensible model of justice suggest themselves: first, in accord with Isaiah Berlin's claim (which Rawls accepts), it is not possible to construct a political order in which no "Great Goods" will not be sacrificed; second, against Jürgen

Habermas's misplaced criticism of Rawls, what is morally or politically reasonable is, in some measure, an artifact of historical perspective. With regard to the first issue, we must avoid skepticism without falling into the excessive claims of moral realism; with regard to the second, we must grasp the irrelevance of the contrast between the "monologic" and the "dialogic" in admitting the essentially interested nature of normative values. On both counts, there can be no Kantian-like universalizing of the sort Rawls favors. The upshot is that a so-called "reflective equilibrium" regarding justice—Rawls's proposed strategy—yields a "constructive" theory of justice, but one that is not universalizable or objectively neutral. The ultimate reason for this is simply that reason itself is a changing artifact of our historical life. Admitting that curbs our overly sanguine expectations about moral philosophy, but it also permits us to avoid moral skepticism.

Chapter Eight by William Murnion is entitled: "Natural Law or Social Contract? The Foundation of Rights in Hobbes and Locke." Both Hobbes and Locke utilized a dialectic between natural law and social contract to construct their theories of natural rights. But Hobbes's theory was positivistic, Locke's naturalistic. For Hobbes was concerned with legitimizing the absolute power of a monarch to protect the right to life of his subjects, while Locke was intent upon prohibiting a monarch from interfering with a people's rights to life, liberty, and property. Thus, from similar premises they arrived at contrary conclusions.

From a social context in which an absolute sovereign seemed the only alternative to anarchy Hobbes described the state of nature as a state of war. A commonwealth under the aegis of an absolute sovereign seemed the only practicable means to protect human rights. Thus Hobbes's conception of rights is conventionalist: they are the product of laws promulgated by an absolute sovereign within a commonwealth. Locke, living in a situation in which an absolute monarch seemed to threaten the exercise of human rights, portrayed the state of nature as a state of peace. Life, liberty, and property, flourishing in the state of nature, needed only the collective will of a people in a civil society, together with a government to carry out its will, to be safe and secure. Thus Locke's conception of rights is naturalistic: they are the functions of human rationality.

While Hobbes's conception of rights may seem more realistic insofar as Hobbes gives full weight to human depravity and the prevalence of violence,

Locke's may actually be more realistic insofar as he trusts human nature and respects the rule of law.

Chapter Nine by Michel Rosenfeld is entitled: "Restitution, Retribution, Political Justice." In pluralist societies, there is a clash between legal justice and moral and political justice. This clash is exacerbated in the aftermath of radical social and political change, such as that brought about by the recent transitions from socialism to democracy in East Central Europe. In particular, these transitions have given rise to claims of restitution and retribution. Because they require crossing the boundaries between different social and political systems and different ideologies, restitution and retribution afford a privileged vantage point to examine the most vexing problems confronting the scope and limitation of justice in contemporary settings. Moreover, restitution and retribution cannot be assessed independently from other forms of justice, such as distributive, compensatory and procedural justice. Accordingly, consideration of restitution and retribution makes for a fruitful reexamination of the relationship between the various forms of justice as they emerge in the context of the radical changes such as those involved in the transitions from socialism to democracy. Placing restitution and retribution in a broader context that encompasses the other forms of justice reveals that all of them are interdependent, but that they undermine one another as much as they complement each other. This leads to the conclusion that in a pluralist society comprehensive justice is at once necessary and impossible. Justice's impossibility does not call for despair, however, but for an incremental approach in search of the best possible approximation. Consistent with this, Elster's all or nothing approach to restitution and retribution in East Central Europe as well as other approaches that do not embrace comprehensive justice must be rejected in favor of a contextual approach. And applying comprehensive justice contextually justifies some restitution and some retribution in East Central Europe.

Chapter Ten, by George Teschner, addresses "The Concept of Justice in Computer Managed Telecommunications." The goal of this chapter is to analyze the nature and language of justice in computerized communication environments of the kind that are called "Bulletin Board Systems." The article begins by looking at how computerized communication differs from other forms of communication. It is argued that computerized communication is unique in that it combines mass communication with interactivity and is an institutional structure with social and political implications different from any seen before in human civilization. The chapter then turns to an analysis of computerized communication as a unique semiotic environment. Because the message is both an enunciative event as well as a written text, unique hermeneutical possibilities arise that cause the message to have properties of oral as well as written communication. The chapter finally shows how from Aristotle's account of the principle of equality and inequality, it can be argued, that in the context of computerized communication, there is less likelihood of disputes over matters of justice and injustice.

## Notes

1. John Rawls, *A Theory of Justice*. Cambridge, MA: Harvard University Press, 1971, p. 3.

2. See their joint opinion in *Planned Parenthood of Southeastern Pennsylvania* v. *Casey*, 112 S.Ct. 2791 (1992).

# Chapter 1: Institutional Authority and Political Momentum: Constitutional Equal Protection in American Politics[1]

**John Brigham***

> "Through our history, it seems that the black robes have been more devastating than the white sheets." Jesse Jackson, June 3, 1994[2]

There are signs of a change in the legal paradigm on racial equality and the Constitution that has dominated the United States since the ruling in *Brown* v. *Board of Education* in 1954. The early 1990s saw a spate of movies bringing life in the urban black community into the mainstream, like *Boyz N the Hood* and *Crooklyn*. The resignation of Justice Thurgood Marshall and the nomination of Judge Clarence Thomas to replace him focused attention on the diversity of the black community and the politics of constitutional jurisprudence. The acquittal of the police officers filmed beating Rodney King in Los Angeles led to devastating riots that made it hard for white America to ignore certain facts of city life. Finally, the prominence of Louis Farrakhan on the college lecture circuit and his acceptance by traditional civil rights groups like the NAACP challenges the presumptive validity of the old legal equal protection model.[3]

These events call attention to the relationship between social life and the law, particularly constitutional law. We have long seen the conditions of life for urban blacks in terms of policy failures, but seldom as having implications for constitutional law. Unlike the drinking fountains and schools in the South a generation before, the riotous conditions so characteristic of urban America today, have been seen as unfortunate but not illegal. Now, the constitutional connections are being asserted, as the above quote from Jesse Jackson suggests. This paper considers how that has come to pass and suggests a way to look at decisions of the Supreme Court that is more political than legal. The focus is the life of the *de jure/de facto* distinction as a part of constitutional ideology that reaches beyond the Court into our conceptions of what is appropriate. This law is embedded in a semiotic web that to a greater or lesser degree connects legal institutions to the culture in which they function. In the case of the replacement for Justice Marshall, the candidate was seen in the light of Marshall's life, since after winning as a litigator in *Brown* v. *Board of Education*, Marshall went on to fashion civil rights law from his seat on the Supreme Court. In the case of the distinction itself, the Latin legalisms draw authority from ordinary experience.

## Inventing De Facto

The doctrine that equal protection of the law only applies to *de jure* conditions appears to parallel the idea that the ghettos of America are "natural" rather than the consequence of state or government action. This perception is a new development in constitutional practice that gives conventional thinking a constitutional patina. This limitation on equal protection doctrine reflects a transformation in the ideals of equality since the height of the Civil Rights Movement. The ways of understanding equal protection have a distinctive relation to conventions or what Americans ordinarily think. In this case, the perception that ideas can be separated from reality is crucial to the appeal, legal and political, of an otherwise archaic tradition in law.

Until relatively recently, *de facto* as a term of art in the law had little relation to equality. This apparently elegant Latin term, and its companion, were concepts in international law. They developed from the "law of recognition" where the issue was sovereignty and the need was often for taking account of the actual state of affairs, such as a revolutionary government, whether or not the government was legal in the traditional sense. The international law quality of the dichotomy goes back at least to *Blackstone's Commentaries*.[4] It was particularly evident after the Revolution and the Civil War. In 1877, Justice Stephen J. Field wrote an intricate treatise on the legal status of the Confederate States in *Williams* v. *Bruffy*, a case concerning the obligations to the confederate state of Virginia. For Field, "[A] *de facto* government enjoying belligerent rights, has control over the territory it holds, and its laws are binding...." "[T]he test of such *de facto* government is the number of the population adhering to it...."[5] To Field, the confederate government was not a *de facto* government. Rather, "Whilst it existed, it was simply the military representation of the insurrection against the authority of the United States...."[6] For jurists in this period, convention was the limited perspective of the public and in international law the Latin formulations served to legalize practices where that seemed appropriate to the interests of the state. While the terms *de facto* and *de jure* were seldom applied to equal protection, the arguments in *Plessy* v. *Ferguson* break down according to a majority refusing to face the reality of domination and the lone dissenter bringing forth the now embarrassing "reality" of the inevitable domination of White over Black.

*De facto* brought a sort of common sense into the law, but it was initially transformed into a legalistic exercise to serve various interests. During this period, judicial interpretation of the Constitution was influenced by the sort of cultural phenomena we have become familiar with in constitutional law, where an idea like privacy or equality becomes part of an exchange between the judiciary and the culture in which they function. The ordinary understanding that there should be little public responsibility for the way people live became a matter of constitutional doctrine through interpretation by the justices of the Supreme Court. In the period of its rise as an aspect of equal protection doctrine, the distinction between *de facto* and *de jure* drew both Northerners and southerners into its semiotic web providing opportunities as well as pitfalls to both.

For years after the Civil War, the "State Action" Doctrine separated government conduct from private action. Protection in the Fourteenth Amendment had not extended to private conduct abridging individual rights since the *Civil Rights Cases*.[7] Responding to the Civil Rights Act of 1875, the Court split between a majority holding that congressional authority under the Civil War Amendments reached only to state action, and Justice Harlan in dissent who believed this view "entirely too narrow and artificial." State action comes from the distinction between actions taken as a matter of law and conditions that simply arise from choices made in society, the *de jure/de facto* distinction. Thus, state action, though logically reflecting the distinction between *de jure* and *de facto*, had the historic effect of keeping *de facto* concerns from the law of equality. In *Shelley* v. *Kraemer* (1948) the Supreme

Court transformed the state action doctrine "...into an instrument for prohibiting private racial discrimination"[8] by striking down provisions in deeds that restricted sale to certain groups, called restrictive covenants. For over twenty years from this ruling the Court did not retreat behind the state action doctrine to deny relief in matters of equal protection. Although it had been available to the jurists for nearly 100 years, by the time the law ceased to comprehend separate as conceivably equal the justices had stretched the doctrine of state action to implicate action where it depended on the state in any material way.[9]

The judicial role in the development of constitutional doctrine on state action had been superseded by the momentum of the civil rights movement and the Civil Rights Act of 1964. The Warren Court could do little else but uphold the Act as it did in *Heart of Atlanta Motel, Inc.* v. *United States* (1964). Ultimately, state action becomes subsumed under a notion of *de jure*. Beginning with a "legal strategy against segregated education"[10] exemplified by the political change that would begin in the South, sweep North, be rebuffed and then return South in a variety of rhetoric and moves in and around the definition of the fundamental law on race. This is the law of equal protection, and it revolves around what was meant by discrimination and the consequences of that definition for segregation. While "separate but equal" was the doctrinal issue, separate and unequal schools were the fact of social life presenting America with its "dilemma."[11]

There is no explicit mention of *de jure* v. *de facto* discrimination in *Brown*. However, attention to the legacy of *Plessy* v. *Ferguson* (1896) led to a doctrine that turned away from "equality" under separate schools in order to bring the psychological effects of separation under law. When the Court, in *Brown*, says "minors of the Negro race" have "...been denied admission to schools attended by white children under laws requiring or permitting segregation...," the central concern is lawmaking to segregate. Later in the opinion the 14th Amendments protection is defined "...as proscribing all state-imposed discriminations against the Negro race." The opinion puts aside the issue of inequality, holding that the schools in question have been found to be substantially equal. The emphasis is clearly on segregation of schools with the sanction of law.[12]

With nearly total resistance in the South after *Brown*, little more was said by the Supreme Court about the nature of discrimination for nearly six years.

One artifact of this period, the opinion by Judge John J. Parker in *Briggs* v. *Elliott* (1955), best characterized the constitutional route of southern resistance. While southern resistance decried "the law" in the face of their reality or black and white as separated by hierarchical boundaries, Judge Parker created a formulation that would provide wiggle room up North. Parker articulated southern strategy when he held that *Brown* did not call for integration, merely an end to segregation.[13] The move away from total resistance foretold where subversion of the ends in *Brown* would come from.

In *Cooper* v. *Aaron*,[14] scholars are beginning to point out, the Supreme Court claims for the first time that "the federal judiciary is supreme in the exposition of the law of the Constitution."[15] The claim for "...the responsibility of this Court as ultimate interpreter of the Constitution" also appears in *Baker* v. *Carr*[16] and then again in *United States* v. *Nixon*. The elevation of judicial interpretation in this field made the Courts a focal point, but all alone, momentum and convention played a role in how we came to talk about equal protection.

For the jurists of the Warren period at the Supreme Court, the public was held in nearly as great disdain, and the attack on *de jure* drew from the formalism of the first stage. Off the Court, the 1963 civil rights March on Washington and Martin Luther King, Jr.'s "I Have a Dream Speech," expressed the vision of a world in conformity with the aspirations of integration. In King's speech, the world of imagination is set against reality. Attention is drawn from who is responsible for the conditions of segregation and directed at a society without racially identified worlds. Its immediate impact in law was on the 1964 Civil Rights Act but it also expressed the vision an inevitable integrated future that we see expressed in interpretation of constitutional equal protection. The speech has become a significant icon in the language of equal protection. With its dramatic image of little white and little black children walking hand an hand in some future time the speech emphasizes integration.[17] King turned to the theme often, as when he wrote

> The natural bloom of flowers is a composite of many colors and shapes which are pleasing to the eye, as well as to the sense of smell. Man in his many forms and colors presents the same concepts of beauty.[18]

This society is, of course, presented in stark contrast to the one that exists.

The equal protection standard was changing in 1964.[19] From the Supreme Court and Congress to the lunch counters in the South, the politics of the period expanded the expectations and visions associated with equal protection. Debate in Congress over the 1964 Civil Rights Act began when the bill was submitted to Congress by the President and although it may well have been the assassination of John F. Kennedy, the ascendancy of Lyndon B. Johnson to the presidency and the most dramatic struggles of the Civil Rights Movement that led to its passage, Kennedy's words are worth noting in assessing the kind of discrimination which the Act was attempting to reach.

> The Negro baby born in America today, regardless of the section of the nation in which he is born, has about one-half as much chance of completing high school as a white baby born in the same place on the same day, one-third as much chance of completing college, one-third as much chance of becoming a professional man ... a life expectancy which is seven years shorter, and the prospects of earning only half as much.[20]

The emotional content of the words is infused with the tenor of past and future events. Its vision confronted the facts of life for black America. And, its logic drew on the emerging constitutional interpretation of equal protection. While public attention focused on defiance, a more strategic accommodation in the South began to limit the reach of *Brown* by focusing on its *de jure* qualities. As the North became attentive to its neighborhoods, community became a countervailing force against the need to eliminate a segregated society. *De facto* reality here joined northern and southern resistance in the alliance of politics and convention that ended doctrinal development.

Congress was reluctant to define discrimination too precisely. Political reasons had to do with passage of the legislation and hope that administrative discretion would also be advantageous to those proposing the legislation. Debates at the time struggled over the pace and scope of integration with early concern about racial balancing finding its way into the Act as a limit on busing. In particular, the issue of meaning for equal protection perceived in Congress oscillated around the *de jure/de facto* distinction. Debate over the 1964 Civil Rights Act became central to the Brennan opinion in *Regents* v. *Bakke*. On the defensive in 1978, liberals tried to hold the line by embedding their decision in understandings from a decade and a half prior. According to Brennan, "We agree with Mr. Justice Powell that, as applied to the case before us, Title VI goes no further in prohibiting the use of race than the Equal Protection Clause of the Fourteenth Amendment itself..... " It was clear to Rep. Cellar that Title VI "... was not placing new substantive limitations upon the use of racial criteria but rather was designed to extend to such facilities 'the existing right to equal treatment' ...."[21] As Justice Brennan pointed out in *Bakke*, "Many questions, such as whether the Fourteenth Amendment barred only *de jure* discrimination or in at least some circumstances reached *de facto* discrimination, had not yet received an authoritative resolution."

President Nixon's statement of March 24, 1970 provides a full review of legislative, judicial and administrative opinion on the matter of desegregation. Titled "Desegregation of American Elementary and Secondary Schools," this policy statement began with reaffirmation of a "personal belief that *Brown* was right."[22] The President called attention to the 1964 Civil Rights Act provision prohibiting busing for racial balance and went on to say, "I am advised that these provisions cannot constitutionally be applied to *de jure* segregation. However, not all segregation as it exists today is *de jure*."[23] Citing the *Briggs* opinion as a way to hold the line on *Brown* the statement goes on to indicate how the *de jure* standard can be used to limit expansion of the *Brown* mandate to residential neighborhoods. Nixon had thrown down the gauntlet to the liberals on the Supreme Court.

## The Politics of Distinction

The interpretation of equal protection would remain wedded to providing remedies for past "purposeful" discrimination, in the North and in the South. Although by the early 1970s, "a considerable number of lower courts had assumed that *de facto* discrimination was a constitutional violation," according to Gerald Gunther, this was about as far as judicial authority went.[24] The emerging position on the judiciary was beaten back with a public appeal to home and neighborhood as beyond the reach of judicial remedy.

Douglas and Powell, in the midst of the Court's struggle with equality, 1970–1973, reflected an effort to break down the formalism and merge law with social life — Powell to save the South, Douglas to give law a fuller meaning and hold the public responsible for its juristic creations. The opinion in chambers of Justice William O. Douglas in the case of *Gomperts* v. *Chase* (1971) was a sort of judicial gasp. Douglas was serving as Circuit Justice for the west coast and writing from his summer home outside of Yakima, Washington, expounded on *de jure* and *de facto* segregation before denying a motion for a preliminary injunction. The case involved a school district in the San Francisco Bay Area comprised of six predominately white high schools and one overwhelmingly black school. Douglas did not find "the classic" *de jure* segregation, by which he meant the southern kind where laws, and signs and color lines announced the will of the government. He did, however believe there was a new or broader kind of *de jure* segregation. He found state action and state responsibility in creating the segregation because the state built a freeway that separated the black school from the others and because realtors licensed by the State, banks chartered by the State and restrictive covenants enforced by the state fostered residential segregation. Douglas' analysis of what fits under the cover of *de jure* anticipated a legal strategy that would appear the next year in *Keyes*.[25]

Douglas also proposed that "there can be *de facto* segregation without the State's being implicated in the actual creation of the dual system." He wrote that this kind of discrimination would be unconstitutional under *Plessy* v. *Ferguson*. Because, reflecting the prevailing view, *Brown* applied to *de jure* segregation, Douglas held that it had not been overruled for schools segregated due to residential patterns that were unequal. Douglas found evidence that Ravenswood High School, the predominately black school, was an inferior school and wondered about possible remedies. He indicated that he could "...see no answer to the argument that school boards can rectify the situation among the races by designing a system whereby the educational inequalities are shared by the several races."[26] This was clearly one of the boldest salvos in the short lived struggle over implications for desegregation of a distinction between *de jure* and *de facto*.[27] The decision came on September 10, 1971, barely three weeks before the new term of the Court would begin. It was in that new term, the October Term, 1972 that the influence of the Civil Rights movement on constitutional interpretation by the Supreme Court began to wane.

In *Keyes* v. *School District* (1973), *de jure* was equated with discriminatory intent and a basis was established for finding such intent in the North where the history of state mandated segregation did not exist. Justice Brennan's majority opinion read constitutional promises as applying to northern districts without a history of explicit legal mandates to segregate. The case from Denver came with a ruling by District Court judge William Doyle based on *de facto* segregation and the fact of inequality in the schools. *Keyes* is a turning point for the political momentum of *de facto*. The opinions are the beginning and the beginning of the end for an expanded equal protection of the laws.[28]

Justice Douglas' concurrence in *Keyes* holds there to be no constitutional difference between *de jure* and *de facto* segregation.[29] Focusing on the state action proposition evident in his *Gomperts* opinion, Douglas moves back from the implications he held out for *Plessy* in the Goose Prairie opinion. Perhaps back in Washington, D.C. he was a bit more circumspect. In any case, his *Keyes* opinion still contains more of the egalitarian vision than any of his brethren showed. Douglas' reason for discarding the distinction is that in effect his colleagues need to be focused on the reality of governmental responsibility for the things we call "neighborhoods." His opinion here, like the one in *Gomperts* contains an argument for a "strong" *de jure* standard. It does, however, turn away from the even more dramatic view that constitutional equal protection under a still authoritative *Plessy* standard incorporates a *de facto* claim that is weak in the sense that it does not incorporate intent.[30] Moments such as this in constitutional interpretation can only be understood in terms of what is possible at the time and this involves conceptual leaps suggested by what is being said as well as political choices colored by realities of power.

Justice Lewis Powell had come to the Court two years before. He came as a southerner and acted like a southerner — not a red neck, which we had come to think epitomized the South, but a proud, civil, southern gentleman. He didn't come very far, from Richmond, Virginia to Washington, D.C., and he didn't leave his sensibilities behind. The southerner in him exploded in *Keyes* and produced a very interesting commentary on *de facto* and *de jure*. Powell's decision takes on the *de jure/de facto* distinction with regard to the failure in the country as a whole to integrate. This failure, he says, was due in part to a distinction which Powell believed was rather gleefully aimed at the southern states. Noting some progress in the South he says "No comparable progress has been made in many nonsouthern cities ... because of the *de facto/de jure* distinction nurtured by the courts and accepted complacently by many of the same voices which denounced the evils of segregated schools in the South."[31] Although Gerald Gunther cites Powell here in asking "Do the far-reaching demands for eliminating past discrimination make the distinction between *de jure* and *de facto* segregation increasingly unjustifiable...?,"[32] it is not clear that Justice Powell and Professor Gunther had the same thing in mind.[33]

In his opinion, Justice Powell appears to want to eliminate a distinction that would narrow *de jure* to "legislative actions"[34] and perpetuate a view that the classic violation is southern.[35] He goes on to write "...if our national concern is for those who attend [segregated] schools, rather than for perpetuating a legalism rooted in history [that is, castigation of the South] rather than present reality, we must recognize that the evil of operating separate schools is no less in Denver than in Atlanta."[36] Powell's view is that a national doctrine would not use the stereotypical Southern case as its framework. The doctrine would move from the guilt implicit there to a neutral standard providing that segregated schools establish a prima facie case of constitutional violation which would impose a burden on the "duly constituted public authorities" to "demonstrate they nevertheless are operating a genuinely integrated school system."[37] Thus, the equal protection right without the *de jure/de facto* distinction would be the right "...to expect that once the State has assumed the responsibility for education, local school boards will operate integrated school systems...."[38]

Though odd, it may be appropriate to see the Douglas and Powell opinions as more expressive of the egalitarian vision of the Civil Rights Movement while the other opinions, the majority and Justice Rehnquist's dissent, exemplify the Supreme Court's retreat from the Civil Rights commitment. Ultimately, however, Powell's fails to adhere to the progressive implications of his opinion in *Keyes*. For instance, he fails to side with dissenters in *Milliken* v. *Bradley* in 1974, where the implications of segregation in Detroit were so great but where the majority could find no *de jure* angle on the segregation. After *Keyes* the characterization of residential segregation as *de facto*[39] employs an elegant Latin phrase to naturalize the neighborhood school concept and absolve northern resistance of responsibility much less racism.[40] The politics of this period are a powerfully reactionary struggle directly related to the movement of the Supreme Court to the right with the elections of Richard Nixon, Ronald Reagan and George Bush. The convention is neighborhood as "fact" with the emerging development of discrimination as talk, attitude or affect.[41] But the implications went far beyond the issue of segregated neighborhoods and the formulation of a lack of constitutional responsibility for the "facts" of social life influenced a variety of cases.[42]

## Socio-Legal Argument Today

Our attention to race is mediated in the press, in the news and in political discourse with opportunity (for black actors, directors), with choice (of Clarence Thomas in 1991 to be on the Supreme Court), and with concern (for progress in education, quality of housing).[43] A focus on ideals and opportunities keeps the reality of these conditions under raps and out of sight. Only at the margins does discussion come close to home,[44] generally the talk has served as a surrogate for the fact of summer in the cities for the last fifty years. The reality, the actual conditions of a very comfortable European-American community and a much less comfortable African-American community, although sometimes perceived, is shielded by law. The *de facto/de jure* distinction adds a formal barrier from critical inquiry into segregated conditions the sense that justice only applies to purposeful, intentional discrimination, the kind epitomized by the Jim Crow signs over restrooms in the South or Sheriff Bull Connor attacking black protestors with police dogs.

We can see the contemporary rhetoric of the distinction by looking more closely at its use by the Chief Justice in his majority opinion in *Board of Education* v. *Dowell* announced on January 15 of 1991 and Justice Marshall's final plea to a brooding presence already much diminished by 20 years of decline. Chief Justice Rehnquist established almost immediately that the issues from which the litigation stems are *de jure*, that is, the 1961 suit by "black students and their parents" led to a finding that "Oklahoma City had intentionally segregated both schools and housing in the past, and the fact that Oklahoma City was operating a 'dual' school system — one that was intentionally segregated by race."[45] Thus the distinction appears with force and has implications reminiscent of *Plessy* v. *Ferguson* where the social world was beyond the reach of the law.

Justice Marshall worked in one of his last dissents to get what he could from the stingy doctrine now widely accepted as separating intentional from unintentional segregation. He describes the exploitation of residential segregation "...that had been created by legally enforced restrictive covenants."[46] He calls for recognition of "...the threatened reemergence of one-race schools as a relevant 'vestige' of *de jure* segregation" and would have the Court hold "...that formerly *de jure* segregated school districts take all feasible steps to eliminate racially identifiable schools."[47] Always operating within the dominant *de jure* context, this noble dissenter, this litigator of *Brown*, in his last term on the Court teaches us to forget the aspiration of two decades prior. His very presence makes a connection between *Brown* and the impoverished interpretation of the equal protection clause. Although the movement of which *Brown* was a part promised an end to the separation sanctioned in *Plessy*, the result has become a jurisprudence that sanctions separation under the banner of *de facto* and links this to a jurisprudence so comprehensive that even Justice Marshall's dissents had little effect on their standing. This was certainly a factor in why he left the Court.

Hypersensitivity to quotas, a particular kind of explicit discrimination, and analogous special treatment, is the conventional ground for the move to characterize the ends of the Civil Rights struggle as merely the removal of formal legal barriers. Justice White, writing for the majority in *Washington v. Davis*, in 1976, drew from the cases beginning before *Brown* in considering the claims of black applicants to the D.C. police force that a test for admission was discriminatory where four times as many blacks as whites failed the test. White placed special emphasis, however, on *Keyes* and the delineation of unconstitutional state action as having the "purpose or intent to segregate." Justice White left open the possibility of that a discriminatory intent might be inferred from data on impact, but this the jurisprudence of such inferences failed to develop. Increasingly, complex realities were considered outside the narrow frame of constitutional protection.

As the second post-Warren Court decade progressed and the conservatism of the Supreme Court became more consistent, equal protection doctrine raised the standard by which intent to discriminate had to be established. Where the earlier approach had set the law against the practice, Justice White's description of the Salmon canning operations in Wards Cove, the town and the case, is laced with vivid pictures of the environmental and social distinctions that produce and justify a racially stratified work force while the reach of human intention seems less and less substantial.[48] The facts are a limit on the reach of equal protection and the obligations of employers. In *Wards Cove* the issue was the "disparate impact" theory of liability in Title VII of the 1964 Civil Rights Act where a "facially neutral" employment practice may be judged illegal "without evidence of employer's subjective intent to discriminate." This brings us to the present national debate on civil rights.

The debates over the 1990 and 1991 Civil Rights Acts reflect the struggle over the legacy of equal protection. The first bill came out of committee in the summer of 1990, was branded as a "Quota Bill" by Republicans in the fall of 1990, and vetoed by President George Bush. The bill was designed to modify or reverse a series of conservative Supreme Court decisions[49] which made it harder for minorities and women to win job bias suits and also expand monetary damages for the victors in those suits. The second was passed by the House in the early summer of 1991 and considered in the Senate as that body began to consider the nomination of Judge Clarence Thomas to succeed Thurgood Marshall on the Supreme Court. The 1991 Act was not precisely about desegregation — the standards are different — but rather about the distinction between discrimination against which there is protection and discrimination that is beyond the reach of the law is paramount. There is little law Latin here, but the *de jure/de facto* distinction has a bearing on the debate.

Discussion of quotas employs a distinction similar to that between law and fact examined thus far. Thus, those who have framed the debate hold out merit as an abstract consideration arrived at formalistically, usually this is by emphasizing tests or cumulative evaluations. On the other side, the picture is of preference where characteristics like sex and race are taken into account — usually through a link to social conditions of oppression or discrimination. In a letter to *The New York Times* prompted by the Thomas nomination,[50] Russell Nieli writes that five Gallup polls, beginning in 1977, showed that over 80% of respondents "favor a strict meritocratic system... over a system in which women and members of minorities" are given preference. Merit is a standard, in this analogy, on the same order as law or ideals and it stands against conditions or characteristics. Merit, in the conventional debate today, is drawn parallel to *de jure* and affirmative action, or the opposite of merit, is drawn as operating in a *de facto* condition. This is not inevitable; the ideal of affirmative action reflects the logic of a high period of equal protection analysis twenty years ago. But, today merit, no matter how idealized it may seem, is widely set off against preference, a system driven by condition and operating against not in terms of the natural order of things.

In the culture we have distinctions that reinforce the *de jure/de facto* distinction in constitutional interpretation. The formal treatment, by conservatives, of Clarence Thomas as simply a man that could do a job, rather than in any important sense a black man, is a political construction removed from "reality." In the place of the explicit delineation of a racial line, as in the tradition of segregation, the political move here denies the relevance of reality in a sort of *de jure* color-blindness. At the same time (and by the same groups), the reality of Thomas' rise from poverty in Pin Point, Georgia, where he was born in a house without electricity or plumbing, to the threshold of the Supreme Court, was posed as a reason to see the nominee as a representative of his race even though in political terms he had been allied with white conservatives more than the majority of his race. Under the title "From 'Hatred and Love' To a Successful Career," — drawing on a quote from

Thomas, "I am a child of the marshes, a son of this soil. I am the product of hatred and love." — *The National Law Journal* juxtaposed the condition of "[g]rowing up poor and black in the segregated South of the 1950s and 1960s" with his nomination and called it "...the stuff of American folk legend."

While one might have seen the Horatio Alger quality of this construction in much the same way as the denial of a racial designator under the ideology of the autonomous individual, the vivid immersion in the bootstraps world of crab picking, rural poverty and the mid-60's south of Jim Crow segregation[51] was a reality check on the national scene. For conservatives the emphasis is on escape from poverty and escape becomes a consideration more important than the actual conditions. The steps taken leave a world of want behind.[52] Still, once called to mind, once a part of the governing picture, this world has an evocative power and this world is very much a part of public consciousness recently.

In Spike Lee's 1989 movie, *Do the Right Thing*, the choice that constitutes the framework for the film is between the dream of Martin Luther King, Jr. and the violence or at least the saber rattling of Malcolm X. The movie is ambivalent in its direction but the end is violent, a sort of inevitable reality where the "right thing" was left to the imagination. In the tradition of an ideology that operates at some distance from reality, President Bush, in his nomination of Judge Thomas claimed to be "doing the right thing." The parallel with the movie should not be to the violence with which it concludes but to the ambivalent and slightly hopeful message given by the title. The challenge for liberal opponents of the Thomas nomination to the Supreme Court is to confront the reality of condition in the discursive world of ideas.

The distinction between reality and myth, fantasy, ignorance and misinformation was also evident in Singleton's *Boyz N the Hood* in 1991. With this movie, reports of the opening at a theatre on the edge of South Central Los Angeles were basically about the lack of violence. The suggestion is that the gangs respected the theater and the turf it occupied. The story ends with a quote from a black man who supervises youth programs in a neighborhood park. He was pleased with the accurate and sensitive portrayal of the people in the neighborhood and concluded that the film, "...was not entertainment .... This was reality."[53] Driving home the realism in attention to race by reporting from the neighborhood in which the movie took place, this article drew from one of the main characters who says at the end of the film "They don't know, don't care and don't show what goes on in the hood." The violence in the film and the violence associated with its screening, is symptomatic of the dichotomous way America has treated the conditions in which most African-Americans live, and the very limited conception of equal protection it entails.

**Professor of Political Science, University of Massachusetts, Amherst*

# Notes

1. This chapter was originally prepared for the panel "Non-Judicial Interpretation of the Constitution," at the American Political Science Association Convention, Washington, D.C. August 27–September 3, 1991. I have benefited from comments by Christine B. Harrington, Louis Fisher and Jeff Wright.

2. Ronald Smothers, "Jackson Tours to Tell Blacks of New Threat," *The New York Times*, June 5, 1994, p. 24.

3. Alex Kotlowitz, "Benjamin Chavis: A Bridge Too Far?" *The New York Times Magazine*, June 12, 1994, p. 41.

4. Vol. 4, pp. 77–78.

5. *Williams* v. *Bruffy* 96 U.S. 176 (1877) p. 181.

6. Ibid at 191.

7. 109 U.S. 3 (1883); See also *NCAA v. Tarkanian* 109 SCt 454 (1988).

8. David O'Brien, *Constitutional Law and Politics* Vol. II (Norton, 1991) p. 1258.

9. *Burton* v. *Wilmington Parking Authority* 365 U.S. 715 (1961).

10. Mark V. Tushnet, *The NAACP's Legal Strategy Against Segregated Education,* 1925–1950 (UNC Press, Chapel Hill, 1987).

11. Gunnar Myrdal, *An American Dilemma* (1944).

12. Kristin Bumiller *The Civil Rights Society: The Social Construction of Victims* (Baltimore: The Johns Hopkins University Press, 1988); Alan Freeman (1978) "Legitimizing Discrimination through Anti-Discrimination Law: A Critical Review of Supreme Court Doctrine," *Minnesota Law Review* 62: 1049–1119.

13. *Briggs* v. *Elliott* 132 F. Supp 776 (1955); See also Peltason, J.W. *Fifty Eight Lonely Men* (Champaign: U. of Illinois Press, 1961) p. 22.

14. 358 US 1 (1958) at 17.

15. Susan Burgess, "What's New About the 'New Institutionalism'? Legal Rhetoric and Judicial Supremacy," American Political Science Association, 1991.

16. 369 US 186 (1962) at 208.

17. In a 1962 article, King referred to the movement as the "integration movement." King, Martin Luther Jr. (1962) "The Case Against 'Tokenism,'" *New York Times Magazine*, August 5.

18. Charles W. Fisher, *Minorities, Civil Rights and Protest* 2d Ed. (Dickenson, 1967) p. 27.

19. See Brennan *infra* on the relevance of the 1964 context to the 1978 decision in *Bakke*.

20. Theodore C. Sorensen, *Kennedy* (Bantam, 1965) p. 530.

21. *Regents of the University of California* v. *Bakke* (1978) p. 16; See 110 Cong. Rec. 6050, 6544, 12677, 13820.

22. Weekly Compilation of Presidential Documents, Vol. 6 (1970) US Government Printing Office.

23. At 427.

24. Gerald Gunther, *Constitutional Law* (Foundation, 1991) at 729; A related combination of statutory and interpretive developments in *Griggs* v. *Duke Power* (1971) where the Court interpreted Title VII, the employment discrimination provisions of the 1964 Civil Rights Act, to limit tests given to applicants for jobs to those that were related to job performance.

25. *Keyes* v. *School District* 413 U.S. 189 (1973)

26. *Gomperts* 404 U.S. 1241.

27. It is also, in some sense, an attempt to introduce seemingly compelling law Latin as an effort to dictate to the lower classes much as the Normans had dictated to the Anglo-Saxons some time before. See David Mellinkoff *The Language of the Law* (Boston: Little, Brown, 1964).

28. The 1972 Term was the first with the four Nixon appointees behind the bench.

29. See also his dissent in *Milliken* v. *Bradley* 418 U.S. 717 (1974).

30. In *Milliken* he would recognize that the tide had turned and that along with *San Antonio* v. *Rodrigues*, 411 U.S. 1 "...there is no violation of the Equal Protection Clause though the schools are segregated by race and though the Black schools are not only 'separate' but 'inferior'."

31. Ibid. at 218–219. Powell places *de facto* first in labeling the distinction though most of the time, in this same opinion and in most others, the order places *de jure* first.

32. Gunther, 1991: 729.

33. Powell is reported in *The Brethren* as being offended by the tone of Brennan's opinion concerning the South (at 263). Certainly the meaning of the query by Gunther in 1992 is very different that it was when made by Powell in 1972.

34. At 217.

35. Douglas called in classic in his opinion. Political Scientist Walter Dean Burnham calls it "easy" (as opposed to "hard") in his text *Democracy in the Making* 2Ed. (Prentice-Hall, 1986) p. 132.

36. At 219.

37. At 224.

38. At 226; for a detailed analysis of the context in this case as they influenced constitutional strategies see Wilkinson, *From Brown to Bakke* (Oxford, 1979). Wilkinson had been a clerk to Justice Powell.

39. See Wilkinson for an excellent discussion of the integration efforts in Denver, prior to federal court involvement (1979: 202).

40. See Peter Fitzpatrick, "The Innocence of Law."

41. John Brigham, "Bad Attitudes: The Consequences of Survey Research for Constitutional Practice," *The Review of Politics* (1990) 582–602.

42. See *Washington* v. *Davis* 426 U.S. 229 (1976).

43. Although most dramatically chronicled in the cities, the separation of the races gives an edge to romantic summer portrayals of rural America as in a *New York Times* story on Centerville, Tennessee where the black part of town is "...referred to casually around the square simply as Nigger Ridge" (July 26, 1991).

44. Such was the case in 1989 when discussion centered around Spike Lee's *Do the Right Thing* and in the summer of 1991 the violence of the ghetto threatened to spill over into movie theatres during the screening of John Singleton's *Boyz N the Hood.*

45. *Board of Education of Oklahoma City* v. *Dowell* 111 S.Ct. 630 (1991) at 633.

46. Ibid at 639.

47. Ibid.

48. *Wards Cove Packing Co.* v. *Atonio* 109 S.Ct. 2115 (1989).

49. The most prominent of which were *Patterson* v. *McLean Credit Union* (1989); *Wards Cove Packing Co.* v. *Atonio* (1989).

50. July 24, 1991.

51. *The National Law Journal* reports Thomas attending an all white boarding school, the St. John Vianney Minor Seminary in Savannah. It is not clear how it could have been all white if he was there (7–15–91).

52. Some aspects of Thomas' rise, like his founding of the Black Student Union and his attraction to the Black Muslim movement in the 1960s while at Holy Cross College seem particularly challenging to the nominee's conservative advocates. Although ideologically they may be similar, Clarence Thomas and Dan Quayle are quite different in fact.

53. Reinhold, Robert "Theatre by Gang Area Features Respect," *The New York Times* July 15, 1991.

# Chapter 2:
# Public Reason, Mediation, and Markets: Kant Against Rawls

**William C. Charron***

*Einig zu seyn, ist göttlich und gut; woher ist die Sucht denn Unter den Menschen, daß nur Einer und Eines nur sie?*

Hölderlin, "*Wurzel alles Übels*"

A new proposal has been put into the political arena: that all future debates, decisions and votes on fundamental political issues be conducted within the limits of what is called *public reason*. This is the recommendation of John Rawls in his most recent book, *Political Liberalism* (1992).[1] Behind his insistence on the need to respect the constraints of public reason is a disillusionment: Rawls has no hope that citizens of liberal societies can ever come to free agreement on fundamental religious and philosophical, including moral, theory; there is no reason to expect a comprehensive consensus on moral principles and their foundational reasons among disparate groups in the free modern societies where state power does not enforce uniformity of expression. Rawls, however, is not satisfied to treat political life as an *n*-person bargaining game in which agreements are compromises subject to renegotiation as threat advantages shift within the society.

What Rawls is proposing is something without precedent in political philosophy: a sort of middle way between agreement by bargaining and agreement by demonstration of moral truth. Under the rubric of what is "reasonable" procedure, Rawls is advocating as the basis of public discourse and decision a new form of civility that observes the constraints of what he calls "public reason." By the proprieties of public reason, one always avoids any claim to the truth of one's own beliefs about religious, political or moral matters and makes no use of reasons peculiar to those beliefs; one refuses to consider or reconsider any issues which have been taken off the public agenda because they are deemed incompatible with a liberal political order; and one sticks to "plain truths" widely understood and accepted by citizens and avoids scientific theories that are "elaborate" and "controversial," when questions of fact are at issue. By so limiting discourse and decision, Rawls seeks to work up and secure the basis of a stable consensus of overlapping elements in otherwise divergent comprehensive systems and at the same time reconcile deep divisions within existing liberal democratic constitutions, especially that between the two liberalisms, classical and welfare.

Although Rawls nominally ties his notion to Kant's notion of the *public use of reason*, it is not in the spirit of Kant in important respects and, thus, derives no legitimacy-by-tradition from its connection with him (Kant 1784, 55–57). Because of Rawls's notable influence on the legal profession of this country, it is important that a hard critical look at this novelty be made from many quarters. I want to show that Rawls's proposal for the new civility of public reason is excessively levelling and threatens to be unnecessarily repressive in its rigorous application in the current political climate, and that its underlying fault is that his approach to pluralism is too narrowly focussed: it casts questions of agreement and disagreement as questions to be settled only in political forums. I suggest a different approach, one which also has a Kantian (as well as Humean) bloodline: it respects and fosters a freer (less prohibited) use of speech in public forums, and it highlights market places as public forums in which differences of interest, taste, and opinion are impartially and impersonally respected and satisfied in a way that is mutually advantageous. In effect, it proposes moving away from an exclusively adjudicational approach to conflict resolution toward a mediational one.

## The Problem

With empire comes the illusion of vision *sub specie aeternitatis*. With the illusion of vision under the form of eternity comes the idea of a universal, rational, and final adjudicational principle — an ultimate rule which determines, for any mix of individual preferences, at any point in history or space, a correct social ordering that is rationally compelling. The Roman Empire was the natural home of the Stoic mind, which claimed command of the correct social ordering from the universal point of view, the point of view of the *logos*. The logostic social ordering, presumed to be evident to the intelligence of the sage, was claimed to be, not only *universal* and *rational*, but also *motivating* and *eudaemonic*: satisfaction of its demands guaranteed well-being and anyone who properly understood the ordering would be motivated to comply. The Stoic idea continued, essentially unmodified, until the break up Christianity in Europe in the sixteenth and seventeenth centuries. The idea of the *logos* had been incorporated into the Christian consciousness under the rubric of natural law, when Christians came to the realization that the end was not at hand and that for the indefinite future they would have to organize themselves and the barbarian invaders of what remained of the Empire and its Holy Roman successor.

With the widespread rejection of a centralized moral authority and the multiplication of conceptions of the good life following the Reformation, the mixing of cultures through global missionary effort, colonial expansion, and world marketing, came disillusionment; moral pluralism became an unavoidable and disrupting fact of life. Something of the Stoic idea would have to be amended: the claim of universality, rationality, or autonomous motivation, or the eudaemonic promise. Fully aware of the situation as so described, Kant articulates the disillusionment and begins the line of revision in which Rawls situates himself.

## Kant and the Public Use of Reason

With his eye on the then recently translated work of Cicero, Kant launched a revolutionary revision of Stoic thinking about morals and political philosophy, attempting to accommodate the new pluralism and conflict of religions and conceptions of the good life.[2] Kant's new, liberal theory of reason and its public use can be represented as four revisions on the original Stoic idea of universal reason.

1. In the new spirit of liberal enlightenment, Kant denounces anyone's or any institution's pretension to the role of sage: there is no sage. In current cant, he de-centers the locus of the subject of reason. Reason in the pursuit of knowledge requires free communications and debate and its end and test is the free agreement of inquirers: in the search for knowledge, "reason's verdict is always simply the agreement of free citizens, of whom each must be permitted to express without let or hindrance, his objections or even his veto" (Kant 1787, A738/B766). As an actuality to be achieved in history, the free agreement definitive of knowledge implies "the right of each individual to submit openly for discussion one's thoughts and doubts ... and to do so without

being decried as a troublesome and dangerous citizen." As a participant in the universal human reason, each individual has, then, an "original right ... to have his say" (Kant 1787, A752/B780). This is the right of the free use of public reason; one exercises it "as a scholar addressing the real public (i.e., the world at large) ... speaking in one's own person," rather than in one's role as the holder of political or religious office (Kant 1784a, 57). At the same time, although it is the right of everyone to think and speak for oneself, it is also one's duty to take account of the claims and arguments of everyone else, "in order, as it were to compare one's judgment with human reason in general and thus escape the illusion that arises from the ease of mistaking subjective and private conditions for objective ones" (Kant 1790, 190). Kant advocates, then, a project he locates midpoint between two extremes: "passivism" — the habit of uncritically conforming one's thinking to the say-so of another — and "logical egoism" — the habit of confident satisfaction with one's thought without the benefit of the effort to render it communicable and testable against the judgments of others (Kant 1798, 10ff). Through the former, agreement can be achieved, but only at the price of heteronomy; through the latter, one maintains a type of autonomy, but without the self-control that makes possible a check against illusion through public argument. Kant had no doubts that the free agreement of participants who thought for themselves and considered the claims of everyone else would be knowledge (*wissen*), since the content of the agreement would be "enforced by proofs" freely acknowledged before one another, after a consideration of arguments for and against. The free agreement that defines the achievement of knowledge is not only not extortion, it is not submission without argument and evidence (Kant 1790, § 33, 149). On this understanding, the pursuit of knowledge is a project of open-ended debate. Knowledge itself, if it is achieved, is a collective, not an individual, accomplishment — an accomplishment of humanity, as it were, for it recognizes no political or sectarian boundaries. In words strongly reminiscent of those of the Averroist, Dante, Kant remarks: "In man,... those natural capacities which are directed toward the use of his reason ... can be fully developed only in the species, but not in the individual" (Kant 1784, 42).[3]

2. Pursuit of knowledge so understood is not a proper mechanism in situations calling for immediate decision, as in the sphere of politics and economics. Questions of knowledge must be distinguished from questions of the polity. Questions of knowledge are born out of a desire for *truth*, which is

to be educed through open debate and identified in the emergence of a free consensus. Questions of polity are born out of *fear* of harm at the hands of one's fellows humans. At its best, the polity is the regulator of strife and the guarantor of individual security through immediate decision and coercive power. Since no one is obligated to wait to learn from hard experience of the other's contrary disposition, yet general aggression is mutually defeating, everyone must be coerced by everyone into a civil order guaranteeing in advance the equal security of one's freedom (Kant 1795, 98n; 1797, 121–24). Here again Kant reduces rationality to a sort (although a different sort) of consistency or agreement: whereas reason in the pursuit of knowledge is defined in respect of an historical agreement of *inquirers*, reason in the establishment of right political order is defined in respect of an hypothetical agreement of *contractors*. The appropriate device for representing this agreement is the idea of an original contract (*contractus originarius*): according to this idea, every individual within a people is imagined to give up lawless freedom in order to take it up again as a member of an ideal commonwealth (republic) in which each is a member. The laws of this ideal commonwealth would be just those that everyone (*omnes et singula*) would agree to as free, equal, and independent contractors, interested in freely advancing one's own interests — one's own conception of happiness — in a world of scarce resources. In most general terms, the contractors would call for a constitution allowing the greatest possible human freedom in accordance with laws by which the freedom of each is made consistent with that of all others (Kant 1787, A316/B373).[4] The idea of the hypothetical original contract and the agreement it envisages is to function as both a model constitution for any reform of historical constitutions and as a criterion of the rationality of the actual legislation of any state. From the side of the government, every legislator is obligated to attempt to formulate laws in such a way that the whole people could possibly have agreed to them as individually free, equal, and independent members of the ideal republic (Kant 1793, 79). From the side of the citizen, each has the right and the obligation to make public use of reason in the critical assessment of actual legislation and governance: each citizen is to be "completely free as well as obligated to impart to the public for its judgment all one's carefully considered, well-intentioned thoughts on what one considers to be mistakes and what one thinks would be a better arrangement" on matters of public rules and institutions

(Kant 1784, 56). The public use of reason in the polity, then, is to be critical, not decisional; disputatious not decretal: "Argue as you will on what you will, but obey!" Of course, no polity could wait upon a consensus generated through the public use of reason as the basis of political and economic decision. Yet, without the freedom of citizens to make public use of reason in matter of politics, no polity can be expected to make steady progress in bringing itself to ideal of the hypothetical original contract of equal, free, and independent negotiators.

3. By the third Kantian revision of the traditional theory, there is no longer the pretension that compliance with right social order is a guarantee of happiness. The eudaemonic promise of the Stoic is not reasserted. Justice is dissociated from expediency, and the right is given priority over the good. The problem this entails is understanding how the idea of social order untied to happiness can be motivating of itself. Although Kant maintains that a rational social ordering is intrinsically motivating (although it is effective only if one freely incorporates it into one's character as one's dominant incentive), he insists that as a matter of fact humans have chosen not to be so motivated. Beneath the veneer of our custom- and law-enforced civilities is the will to do evil. "Universally, human nature is depraved": in every individual is a readiness to engage in some kind and level of force or fraud, when circumstances permit and the opportunity costs of fairness are too much. To operate in the real world on the assumption of strict compliance in dealing with any populace is, then, culpable folly. Quoting Robert Walpole, Kant warns: "Every man has his price!" The maxim of everyone, "even the best," has the form: Be moral, provided the cost is not greater than *Q*. The value of *Q* varies, of course, from individual to individual and is the measure of one's corruption (Kant 1792, 27–34). Here, obviously, is a version of the Augustinian idea of original sin, reaffirmed in Luther before Kant and after in Burckhardt and in Baudelaire, Eliot, Camus, Frost and other "poets of pessimism." Kant is the last of the great philosophers to take imputable evil seriously.

4. From this third revision of comes a fourth. For this world of imperfect moral motivations, Kant adds a qualifying condition to the ideal of a constitution of the greatest possible equal freedom. It is this: "In order to organize a group of rational beings who together require universal laws for their survival, but of whom each is secretly inclined to exempt himself, the constitution must be so designed that, although the citizens are opposed to one

another in their private attitudes, these oppositions must be related in such a way they inhibit one another and the public conduct of the citizens is the same as if they did not have such evil attitudes" (Kant 1795, 112–113). To this end, Kant reinforces his advocacy of the ideal of a politically and economically liberal constitution. Essential to social stability in an imperfect world are (1) civil liberties, including especially free public use of speech, and (2) citizen representation in the legislature of the government, as well as (3) the right of private property, including ownership in the factors of production, and (4) markets with broad freedom of entry and exit. The first pair of institutions is essential to bringing the responsibility the costs (and not just the benefits) of political decision to the decision maker (Kant 1795, 100). The second pair reduces rivalry by directing differences of interest into "mutual self-interest" (Kant 1795, 114). Furthermore, history suggests that these institutions are not independently possible. The past gives evidence of causal connections between political and economic liberties. As Kant notes, when the economy of a society has become market oriented, civil liberties (including free public use of reason and free association) and, thereby, autonomous thinking spread. Thus, upon the beast of commerce, enlightenment enters society. The connection seems to be this: for efficient production and distribution decisions a market economy requires extensive, continuous, and unfettered communications and movement. "Civil freedom can not be infringed without disadvantage to all trades and industries, and especially commerce" (Kant 1784, 50–51). Buyers and sellers must all find each other and freely coordinate in order to make mutually advantageous exchanges. "If the citizen is deterred from seeking his personal welfare in any way hc chooses which is consistent with the freedom of others, the vitality of business in general and hence also the strength of the whole are held in check. For this reason, restrictions placed upon personal activities must be relaxed." With the growth of civil liberties, "although folly and caprice creep in at times, *enlightenment* gradually arises" (ibid.). And with enlightenment comes the first step in the development of reason: critical thinking (Kant 1790, 160–61).[5]

## Rawls and Public Reason

Kant's liberal modification of the traditional conceptions of rational political (and economic) order is an attempt to accommodate the diversity of modern conceptions of the good life. Intending to respect each individual as a free, equal and independent agent, Kant identifies rational political order with principles of cooperation that all could freely agree to, while fully recognizing the motivational limits of human nature in respect of compliance with any such principles. The particular set of principles that he nominates finds itself now at the classical end of a growing array of liberal schemes backed by a diversity of philosophical arguments. Rawls is responding to this higher level conflict among deeply divided liberalisms. Rawls further modifies the Stoic conception by giving up the idea of universality: we must, he says, take our start from ideals and values "implicit in the public political culture of [our] democratic society" if we are to find valid principles (43); we cannot speak for any society not having a similar political culture. Despite the surrender of universality, a vestige of the notion of the unity of reason remains in his notion of public reason. He insists on the idea of a *single* public reason that demands from all its users a *belief* in a single, ideal set of correct, if not true, liberal political principles.

Public reason, as Rawls constructs the notion, is an ideal characteristic of a democratic people insofar as they engage in political advocacy and decision making in the public forum when matters of basic justice and constitutional essentials are at issue. Its opposite, "nonpublic reason," is the class of the varied sorts of rules of reasoning appropriate to particular institutions and associations in the civil society; these include the different rules of evidence and argument found in scientific societies, professional groups, universities, and religions. As with any concept of reason, the ideal of public reason imposes certain limits on the conduct of those who submit to it.

## Scope of Application.

The limits of public reason apply only to debates and decisions on certain topics and to persons operating in certain capacities and circumstances. To be specific, (a) the limits apply only to constitutional questions and questions of basic justice, both political and economic, debated and decided in the public sphere. Thus, they apply to questions such as: who is to have the right to vote, who is to be assured fair equality of opportunity, and who is to hold property (214). Extension of the ideal of public reason to all matters over which the state exercises power — taxation, laws regulating property use, defense spending, national parks and preserves, grant funds, and so on — might be "highly desirable," but for now (at this stage in the promotion of the idea of public reason) only issues of fundamental justice are covered (215). (b) The limits of public reason apply to citizens only when they engage in debates in the public sphere, including campaigning and party politics, and when they cast their votes on fundamental matters. The limits also apply to government officials in their capacity as legislators speaking on the floor of parliament, executives in its public acts and pronouncements, and as judges in passing judgment and making judicial review (215f).

## Content of Public Reason.

Persons are to argue and vote only of the basis of "a political conception of justice" formulated from certain ideas latent in the public political culture of our democratic society and uncovered by a sagacious examination of our "political institutions ... and the public traditions of their interpretation (including those of the judiciary), as well as historic texts and documents that are common knowledge" (13–14). The revealed political conception of justice is "liberal" in character: specifically, it specifies basic political rights, liberties, and opportunities that are familiar in democratic regimes; it assigns them a special priority in respect of any other political or economic claims and values; and it affirms for all citizens the "adequate all-purpose means [including economic ones] to enable them to make effective use of their basic liberties and opportunities" (223). Such a conception of justice is "political" insofar as "it is presented independently of any wider comprehensive religious or philosophical doctrine" (223). In other words, one is to avoid argument or voting on the basis of the "whole truth" as one sees it from within one's comprehensive doctrine (216). In its role as the ultimate principle of argument and decision in the public use of reason, the liberal political conception, then, is to be entirely "free standing" (10).

The liberal political values latent in the political culture, which are to be the basis of public justifications, cannot, however, be expected to be beyond dispute. Despite agreements about the more general features of a liberal political order, liberals honoring the prohibitions of public reason would still differ on the relative priorities and combinations of admissible principles and values. The longstanding struggle between classical and welfare liberals — between liberalism in the tradition of Locke and that of Rousseau — is a fact of history and a force in contemporary and foreseeable political life. Accordingly, the ideal of public reason cannot be taken as requiring the acceptance of the very same principles of justice, if it is not to make arbitrary exclusions among liberals. In the un-ideal world of real liberal dispute, honoring the ideal of public reason can only be taken to require of each liberal practitioner the satisfaction of three conditions: that each

(i) *give* overriding weight to the ideal of public reason, whatever one's view of the whole truth as seen from within one's comprehensive doctrine (214);

(ii) *believe* that public reason is one and complete on questions of basic justice, so that "some combination and balance of political values alone reasonably shows the answer" (ibid.); and

(iii) *be sincere* in advocating and acting only on a particular liberal view one believes others as free and equal citizens could reasonably endorse, were they to see matters correctly (ibid.), and yet be willing to listen to others and to be fairminded in deciding when accommodations to their views should reasonably be made (217).

Satisfaction of the first condition would require enlarging or, possibly "bending," one's comprehensive view of the whole truth to accommodate liberal principles and values, including that of public reason, as "theorems," which are derivable, as it were, from the "axioms" of that view (242n). However, the supporting axioms which one's comprehensive view provides these liberal theorems are never themselves to be advanced as reasons for it in the public forum. Admittedly, then, the public discourse under the prohibitions of public reason "can seem shallow because it does not set out the most basic grounds on which we believe our view rests" (242). For anyone with a taste for paradox, here again is a demand for prohibition and purification under the banner of liberalism.

By insisting on satisfaction of the second condition, Rawls relocates himself within the tradition of the idea of the unity of reason, despite his disillusioned acceptance of reasonable pluralism among doctrines making comprehensive truth-claims. Rawls would have us think that, whereas there are "many nonpublic reasons," there is "but *one* public reason" (220). Although public reason does not guarantee a final comprehensive truth, it does contain a final and correct liberal political conception. Honoring the one public reason requires the liberal belief — to be counted among the dicta of the "reasonable faith" — that ultimately there is one complete and reasonable answer to all questions about basic justice, despite the (inevitable) emergence of disagreements even among liberals operating under the same discursive constraints of the public use of reason (101, 172, 241).

The third condition — the sincerity condition — requires that one only advance that combination and relative weighting of liberal principles and values that one honestly thinks the others can reasonably be expected to accept as citizens committed to doing the same. But sincerely thinking that others can reasonably be expected to accept one's view would require, in turn, that one have, and be ready to explain, a "criterion" of such reasonableness. Since one is prohibited from appealing to the truth of one's comprehensive view, the liberal must have ready some test such as the device of the original position, showing that one's liberal views follow from it. But again, it cannot be expected that there will be consensus on such devices and tests: as Rawls admits, "Many will prefer another criterion" (224). Presumably, Kant's idea of the original contract, which generates principles on the classical end of the liberal spectrum, would be such a test. "The idea is that we must have such a criterion and this alone already imposes very considerable discipline on public discussion" (227). Or does it? I return to this point in the final sections of criticisms.

## General Beliefs and Methods of Public Reason.

The ideal of public reason also puts strong levelling constraints on the sort of factual claims and the methods of reasoning and computation one may employ in applying liberal principles and arguing for particular policies and laws. Only "plain truths" — currently accepted general beliefs and forms of reasoning found in common sense and in science when these are not controversial or elaborate — are to be allowed in the public forum. "We are not to appeal ... to *elaborate* economic theories of general equilibrium, say, if these are in *dispute*" (224–25 emphasis added). Apparently, Rawls is concerned not only to exclude controversial claims but also ideas, arguments, and computations that are beyond the sophistication of the general run of citizens. Although he acknowledges an educative and informational role for public reason, that role extends only to enlightening others about the liberal political conception and assuring them of one's willingness to uphold it (86, 163). His reference to general equilibrium theory is telling: if the theory as demonstrated by Debrue

(1959), for instance, is to be excluded from the public forum on the grounds that it is controversial, then it may be wondered whether every theory is not to be excluded. Although there is question among economists as to the scope of its relevance, there is no significant controversy about the soundness of the demonstration of the theory among those who can follow the argument. If, on the other hand, the theory is excluded because of its complication and sophistication, then one must have great faith that all fundamental problems of justice are simple. Indeed Rawls seems to have that faith: "[A]pplying liberal principles has a certain simplicity,... [free from] elaborate theoretical calculations," he avers (162).

### *Motivational Assumptions.*

Unlike Kant, Rawls is only interested in identifying principles of social ordering for citizens assumed to be motivated to be strictly compliant. On this condition social order would be an equilibrium — that is, no one would be motivated to unilateral defection, no one tempted to free-ridership at the expense of one's fellows. Is this utopian? Rawls thinks not, apparently on the strength of the experimental research and theorizing of Kohlberg who moves in the line of moral learning theory of Rousseau and Piaget. The basic idea is that an adequately motivating sense of justice is the natural outgrowth of a liberal system that fully appreciates our social nature.[6] Although Rawls recognizes the controversial state of moral learning and moral motivation theory, he is willing to let an optimistic assumption about human nature stand as a piece of "reasonable faith" (172, 86f). But, as Kant recognizes, the question of the content of acceptable rules of justice is not independent of the question of compliance, and historical evidence undermines much optimism. Rawls's reply — "History is full of surprises" — only highlights one of the important grounds of the deep divide among liberals (87). Where the welfare optimist trusts, the classical pessimist profoundly fears any concentration of power: hence, the pessimist's strong resistance to allotting to government — an institution of coercion by definition — any work that can be done through voluntary cooperation in the market.

## *Arguments for the Limits of Public Reason.*

There are two levels of argument here. The first addresses liberals as "reasonable" persons: it purports to show why those who already have a desire to justify their actions to others on grounds the others can endorse must also accept the limits of public reason. The second argument addresses all agents as holders of different comprehensive doctrines: it purports to show why it makes sense for each to adopt liberal ideals, including the desire to justify one's actions to others on grounds they can accept as free and equal citizens. Both arguments, I think, fail. The argument to liberals for public reason as a necessary condition of satisfying the liberal desire for reasonableness simply does not go through. The second argument, although it claims to demonstrate liberal ideals as the basis of an overlapping consensus of different comprehensive doctrines, can be no more than attempt to mediate a negotiated settlement. To treat it as more is to endorse pandering and disingenuousness. Take the arguments in turn.

***Argument* I:** Rawls infers that a reasonable person must accept the constraints of public reason, including the avoidance of asserting or acting on the whole truth as one sees it, from a definition and a fact: the definition is that a *reasonable* person is one who is willing to act publicly only on the basis of principles one sincerely thinks all could accept as free and equal citizens who are willing to do the same, provided such principles are found; the fact is the *unresolvable pluralism* of comprehensive religious, philosophical, including moral, doctrines that are themselves reasonable in the sense of being internally consistent, value ordering, stable, and forswearing of any right to forceable imposition through the coercive power of the state (59–62).

But this inference goes through only if it is supplemented by the claim that just two options are available: "insisting" on the truth of one's claim, thus being unreasonable, *or* avoiding the statement of the whole truth as one sees it in compliance with the constraints of public reason. But the disjunction is false: Not insisting on the truth of one's beliefs does not require avoiding truth claims, provided one observes the prescriptions of the Kantian notion of the public use of reason: by that rule, a reasonable person is willing to assert what one thinks and at the same time to accept criticism and to make arguments for one's position (Kant 1790, 160–61). Certainly, anyone must think that each thing one believes is the truth, but at the same time, one may believe that at least some of what one believes is not true. Hence, it is rational to be open to criticism and to put one's self under the obligation to make one's case, while claiming the truth of what one believes. "Reason," although it must be free in its assertions, "must [also] in all its undertakings subject itself to criticism,... each one must be permitted to express, without let or hindrance, his objections or even his veto " (Kant 1787, A738–39/B766–67). Of course, the process of public reason so understood is open-ended. When the time comes for decision, there might be no agreement on what constitutes justice, just as there is none on what constitutes a good life. Part IV considers both political and nonpolitical procedures and mechanisms for determining what is to be done in the absence of agreement on principles of justice.

***Argument* II:** The second argument for political liberalism addresses all citizens as holders of different comprehensive doctrines: it purports to show why it makes sense for each to adopt liberal principles, including the ideal of public reason. The argument for the liberal political conception is not that it is *true*: the respect for intractable pluralism rules out such a claim (94). Nor does Rawls want to argue for the conception merely as a *mutually advantageous* compromise point for the parties in conflict, although it presumably would have that character. Yet, he wants to argue for the liberal political conception as *reasonable*. But given the fact of pluralism, the liberal political conception "is not reasonable unless in a suitable way it can win its support by addressing each citizens' reason, as explained within its own framework" (143). By implication, the liberal political conception must be shown to be *correct*, not in any absolute sense, but relative to the differing comprehensive doctrines. Different citizens would have different reasons for endorsing of the political conception: the conception would be correct for citizen 1 for religious reasons A and B, and for citizen 2 for philosophical reasons C and D, and so on (127–27). "All those who [come to] affirm the political conception start from within their own comprehensive view and draw on the religious, philosophical, and moral grounds it provides. The fact that people affirm the same political conception on those grounds does not make their affirming it any less religious, philosophical, or moral, as the case may be, since the grounds sincerely held determine the nature of their affirmation" (147–48).

There is no general argument for political liberalism. Any liberal advocate interested in justifying political liberalism to others so as to develop an "overlapping consensus" of comprehensive doctrines finds itself in a remarkable situation (153): assume one were concerned to promote liberalism as an agreed basis of political life. As a liberal committed to "the work of reconciliation by public reason," one could not advance ones own reasons for liberalism (157). If anything in the way of the development of consensus were to be done, one could appeal only to reasons implicit within the other's comprehensive doctrine, if such there be — reasons one might think are not good one's and could not accept for oneself. But this sort of constraint would reduce the promotion of liberalism to pandering, when it is anything more than an exercise of showing the implications of assumptions one is not ready to make. Furthermore, the liberal in using the other's reasons to argue for liberal principles (including the ideal of public reason) would thereby be arguing that the other is *not* to use those very same reasons in advocating and acting in the public forum; such would be a violation of civility. Here, then, is a new twist on Frost's liberal: "... so altruistically moral / I never take my own side in a quarrel" (1949). Under the new dispensation of public reason, the liberal can argue for its own side, provided the other's reasons are used.

What if there is not sufficient reason implicit within the other's comprehensive doctrine to generate an endorsement of political liberalism? Obviously, in the absence of a general argument for liberalism, bringing others to the free acceptance of liberalism could only be an exercise of the *political arts*: bargaining and trading. But, of course, that would be the sort of *reason as individualistic bargaining* that Rawls wants to avoid or get beyond. It might require "making changes in the principles of justice," and excessive changes would be the abandonment of liberalism. "I do not pursue this inquiry," says Rawls, "but assume, on the basis of a number of considerations, that the case for the stability of justice as fairness, or some similar conception, goes through" (66).

## Votes and Markets as Mediators

The idea of a collective mind, a consensus on adjudicatory principles in the correct settlement of our remaining differences, is at the heart of Rawls's political philosophy. His thinking is that only such a consensus could secure for a society a political order that was both non-repressive and stable. As the *overlap* of *different* comprehensive doctrines, it would avoid the repression of a single doctrine being imposed over an unresolvable pluralism and effect mutual tolerance. The implied constraints of public reason would subtract from public debate any arguments for the truth of one's position, if there could be no agreement because of the differences in comprehensive doctrines. As a general *consensus*, and especially as one in which the public use of reason were the practice, social stability would be secured. It would fix, once and for all, the content of certain basic rights, "taking them off the political agenda" and putting them beyond political contest. Further, the use of public reason would (help) solve the assurance problem facing any citizens. As both reasonable and rational, citizens would be ready to do their part, provided there is assurance the others will do theirs. Through the use of public reason, citizens would see in each other's constraint in debate the sort of respect for principles of justice that would give evidence of each other's intentions (163). Or so Rawls argues. But is the type of social unity Rawls prescribes either necessary for social stability or desirable?

## Is it necessary?

In fact, without the unity of mind and the constraints on reason Rawls deems necessary for social stability, the constitutional arrangement of this country — now the oldest continuous broadly liberal constitution in the world — has demonstrated a remarkable degree of stability. It has the ability to the moderate rivalry, despite different conceptions both of the good life and of justice and right. The system has the force of a convention, as Hume (1740, 490) defines the term: it reflects a compromise coordination that citizens prefer to support on the condition that each expects the others to do the same. As a compromise, the arrangement is somewhere between what each would ideally prefer. The force of the convention is the interest each has in the achieved coordination, compared with unmoderated rivalry. Of course, every party is sometimes tempted to reconfigure the convention more to its own liking by rebellious threats; but that is a dangerous game all can play.

Citizens are conditionally motivated to continue in their support of the constitutional convention because the constitution is an embodiment decisional institutions that accommodate and even promote cooperation and diversity, without agreement on either conceptions of the good life or on deep principles of justice and right: namely the republican vote and the market. As Kant had predicted, the combination of these two institutions has had great power to moderate rivalry. Neither the vote nor the market presumes the sort of unity of mind Rawls thinks necessary to stability. Although Rawls is aware of pacifying power of the vote, he gives no recognition to the mediating role of the market. Consider the different ways each mechanisms accommodates disagreement and diversity.

## The political vote.

Whereas the market decentralizes choice, the vote by aggregating individual values into a single collective choice centralizes it. The institution of majority vote is a means for determining what is to be done among alternatives in the absence of consensus; it ends stalemates of disagreement. But voting is zero-sum: there are winners and there are losers. From the point of view of the losing minority, which must accept an unchosen alternative, there is in this respect little difference between collective choice of a majority and the fiat of a dictator. An important factor contributing to the stability of the mechanism of the vote is a certain sort of *intransitivity* over time. As long as the losing faction has the hope of reversing the collective choice on some future round of voting, it is has reason to support the constitutional system. Were that hope to vanish — were majorities not merely temporal and were political decisions consistently to reflective a single political view — minorities would have reason to look for opportunities for subversion or rebellion.[7]

The constitutional convention is structured to protect the minority from the political majority by certain "constitution guarantees" that make it more difficult to remove certain subjects from the scope of majority voting or other political decision. Freedom of religion, speech, and press, and security against searches and seizures, political deprivation of life, liberty, or property without due process of law and the taking of private property for public use, without just compensation are all to be "taken off the political agenda," as it were. In so doing, any constitutional guarantee defines a private property right (a right of ownership and control) and protects free marketing in the property right in question. Thus, the separation of church and state in the First Amendment takes religion off the political agenda and, at the same time, enables free marketing among the producers or consumers of religion. And with the market comes invariably the diversification of offerings to fit the variety of individual demands in religious goods. The same holds for the constitutional guarantees of speech and press and the implied recognition of private property and market rights in speech and communications.

## The Market.

Three features of the market account for its power to mediate rivalries: its transformation of difference into mutual advantage and the marginalization of the winnings and losses of competitors, its impersonality and consequent impartiality, and its dispersing and counterbalancing of powers.

(1) In decision making by political voting, to repeat, there are non-overlapping sets of victors and vanquished: one candidate, party, or issue wins; all the others lose. On the other hand, in decision making through market mechanisms, the buyer and seller are both winners (on the condition of no force or fraud), for otherwise they would not enter into an exchange. Furthermore, the pecuniary winners and losers in the competition among sellers (or among the buyers), unlike that among candidates, parties and issue proponents, is not an all-or-nothing win or loss: in the market, individual decisions, unlike aggregate voter decisions, are made at the margin, where it is always a question of more or less.[8]

(2) Free markets tend to be impersonal: buyers and sellers insofar as they seek the best deal are indifferent to each other's person. Thus, the free market separates cooperation and mutual advantage from irrelevant differences such as politics, race, religion, and gender. For the most part, one does not know the politics, race, religion, or sex of most of those involved in the providing the goods exchanged. Furthermore, between buyers and sellers, anyone wanting to discriminate on any basis other than the best trade possibility, must pay for one's discrimination by settling for a less-than-best trade. In this way the tendency to impersonality in the market fosters a mediating impartiality.[9]

(3) Markets, together with private ownership of natural resources and the means of production, decentralizes the exercise of power. We need not go as far as Kant by assuming radical evil as the correct description of human nature. But the lesson of history is that power tends to corrupt the powerful, and it would be a mistake to think that powerful individuals because they are in political positions are always or usually effectively motivated by the same values to which they are verbally committed as political officials. The entrepreneur is "less corruptible" — though at base no differently motivated — as a business person than as a politician: that is, as the former, one is a trader and as such must cater to the interests of consumers to generate or maintain one's wealth; as the latter one can ignore those interests and seek rent through advantageous redistribution or market privilege through political

decision. The same is true of the average citizen as a consumer and as a voter: as the former one must give to order to receive; as the latter takings without compensation are an ever present temptation.[10]

To date the constitutional convention has kept the mechanisms of political decision from absorbing completely those of the market. This has enhanced liberal stability because reliance on government rather than markets always substitutes coercion for voluntary cooperation and tilts the balance of power to government, all of which exacerbates destructive rivalry and zero- (or negative-) sum transfers. A strong market sector has been the best counterbalance to the necessarily coercive powers of government — themselves necessary within the constitution to define property rights, prevent force and fraud among citizens, enforce market agreements, promote market competition, and overcome market externalities.

## Is it Desirable?

To begin to answer this, imagine what would happen were a population of typical liberal citizens to attempt to exercise the civilities of public reason. As Rawls is painfully aware, liberalism itself is a deeply divided tradition. The ideal of public reason requires that liberal citizens conduct their fundamental discussion in light of principles and priorities each "in good faith" regards as a political conception of justice the others can reasonably be expected to endorse and each is, in good faith, prepared to defend as such a conception. Denied the privilege of giving reasons from one's comprehensive doctrine, each liberal adherent of the ideal of public reason must then have, and be ready to explain, a *criterion* of the particular conception one "sincerely believes" other citizens may reasonably be expected to endorse — a neutral test such as the device of the original position. But is it not quixotic to expect that "this alone would impose very considerable discipline on public discussion" (227), when one considers the proliferation of such "devices of representation" among liberal advocates: Harsanyi's (1975) original position of "equi-probability," Ackerman's (1980) "constrained neutral dialogue," Habermas's (1990) "ideal community of communication," and Gauthier's (1986) "morals by agreement," and so. Then too, how sincere could many ever be about the reasonableness of any such devices? Would not many sincere, but conscientious, liberals have, then, nothing to say in the public forum? Would not the obligation of sincerity constrain them merely to listening to the arguments and claims of those who had enough confidence — if nothing else — in their own principles and criteria to think them fit for everyone's endorsement?

The auditorial etiquette of public reason requires that one be willing to listen to others and to make accommodations to their views that seem reasonable — at least to those who are like-minded in respecting the ideal of public reason (217). But what about the treatment of those who insist on making truth-claims on the basis of their comprehensive doctrines or who refuse to refrain from arguing in terms of complicated or controversial scientific theories that go beyond "the plain truths now widely accepted, or available, to citizens generally"? Since the constraints of public reason are to be taken as moral constraints, does it not follow that non-compliant behavior is to be publicly identified as such and support or approval denied? Would it not, then, be consistent (or necessary) for those committed to the ideal of public reason to use accusatory identifications and to attempt to isolate or shun those who insist upon arguing from (or for) the truth-claims of a comprehensive, controversial, or complicated theory in the public forum? Would not the new civility of public reason usher in a new "political correctness"?[11]

## What then?

Public reason in the pursuit of knowledge is, as Kant recognized, an open-ended project, a project not of any individual or political body, but of the species. This pursuit requires the give and take of open debate, without the prior protection or exclusion of any consideration. Free agreement is its hoped-for outcome, not its starting point. But humans are embodied intelligences. Political and economic decisions have to be made "now": they cannot wait for free agreement in the pursuit of knowledge defined by that agreement. At best, such decisions may rest on an agreement to disagree and to let political and economic mechanisms determine what is to be done, but without agreement on the fairness of the outcome. In its political role, public reason is the right and obligation of each citizen to engage in public criticism and suggestion: (to repeat) "to impart to the public for its judgment all one's carefully considered, well-intentioned thought on what one considers to be mistakes and what one thinks would be a better arrangement" (Kant 1784, 78).

To restate, free agreement is the ultimate aim, not the condition, of this public use of reason in political life. Rawls, by contrast, aims to make agreement the condition of political discussion. He perpetuates an attenuated notion of the common group mind in the ideal of a general overlapping consensus in which all individuals think and desire as constitutive parts of one whole, by limiting their public debate within the limits of a constrained notion of public reason. Just as nineteenth century liberal theology tried to fortify religion by minimizing its content, so Rawls would try to fortify liberalism by eliminating what is controversial or complicated, in forging a consensus.[12] He would subtract from public political debate that advancement and consideration of reasons for thinking something to be true by which debate is an exercise in critical reflection — in the Kantian sense of that term. It would retain only liberal notions of justice as "free standing" principles, however individual citizens privately connect them in their various comprehensive belief systems, and those "plain truths" about the world that are currently accessible to "citizens generally." As limiting and sparse as the practice of public reason would be, it is not clear that in the end it would do what it is intended to do, namely, to reduce controversy and stabilize consensus. And it is not clear that it leaves much, in the name of reason, worth having. Since more than one liberal political conception may be worked up from the fund of shared political ideas, rival conceptions will be in competition. One might well fear the addition of a new, liberal wing on the Tower of political Babel, as each in attempting to satisfy the sincerity condition generates a new way to explain to others why it thinks its version of liberalism is one all could accept as free and reasonable citizens.

What, then, would we have gained in the way of promoting and stabilizing consensus by the proscriptions of public reason on the public assertion of the whole truth as one sees it? What would we have lost? I'm afraid the answers are, respectively, *little* and *much.*

**Professor of Philiosophy, Saint Louis University, Saint Louis, Missouri*

# Notes

1. For earlier references to "public reason" and the "publicity condition" see Rawls 1971: § 34; 1980: 535–43; 1985: 230–31; 1987: 8, 14; 1993: 66–67, 139, 153, 161–62, 216–20, 226, 241. All references to Rawls, *Political Liberalism* (1993) are given simply as page numbers, without author and date notations. Thanks to Donna Card Charron and Richard Dees for their criticisms and comments.

2. Kant's *Grounding of the Metaphysics of Morals* (1785) is a direct attack on the program of finding a social choice rule satisfying Stoic requirements. The immediate target of Kant's attack is Cicero. In *De Officiis* (44 BC), which Kant read in the recent German translation of Garve, Cicero is at pains to argue that the universal and rational rule of social order is also eudaemonic: in his words, he claims to show that acting honorably was also expedient for the individual. (For an extended discussion, see Reich 1939) Kant's critique is, in effect, an attempt to demonstration an impossibility theorem: there exists no rule that is at the same time universal, rational, and eudaemonic. Universal rationality and eudaemonia are only by an act of faith united (a faith that Kant, unfortunately, embraces in his desperation). This is the point in the Antinomy of Practical Reason of the sceptical argument of the antithesis against the stoical claim of the thesis.

3. Responding to Kant's claim that reason and knowledge are properly attributed to the species, Herder was the first to peg Kant as an Averroist – certainly a malignity since Bayle's treatment of the subject in the *Dictionnaire* (1697). Kant's response was not to reject the charge, but to challenge Herder "to provide the world with a [better] model" (Kant 1785a, 220). In the high Middle Ages, the Averroistic doctrine of the unity of the intellect was assimilated into Western philosophy. As the first in a line of "political Averroists," Dante reconstructed the single possible intellect of Averroes as a community – the universal community of human kind (*universalis civilitas humani generis*). Where the individual stands to a single and separate being in Averroes, it stands to a universal community of reason in Dante. On this collectivist theory of reason, the aim of reason is to develop over time the total (speculative and practical) capacity of the possible intellect through the contributions of generations of individuals. Since no single individual or particular community can by itself realize the capacity of the possible intellect of humanity, mankind has to be composed of a multitude through which this entire potentiality can be actualized. And just as the tranquility of leisure is the basis of individual intellectual development so a perpetual and universal peace is the condition of the development of the possible intellect of the universal human community. But, argues Dante, only with Empire can there come to be the required universal peace (Dante 1313). Kant, as we will see, has other ideas about world government.

4. Given the freedom, equality, and independence of the contractors, three limits on what would be agreed to and, hence, made law would be met: (1) Given the *freedom* of the contractors, the laws would compel no one to be happy in accordance with the conception of welfare of anyone else. Hence freedom of religion, for instance, would be necessary. (2) Given the *equality* of the contractors, the laws would not exempt anyone from its requirements. Everyone would have equal protection of rights in relation to everyone else. From this ideal of equality, it also follows that the laws would permit every member of the commonwealth to attain any level of status to which the member's talents, effort, and luck may being one. (3) Given the independence of the contractors, the laws would reflect only the votes (preferences) of those individuals who are self-sufficient in the sense of having property (including any skill, craft, fine art or science). Thus, essentially dependent individuals, such as children, women, and service people, although subject to the law, would not be its legislators (Kant 1793, 73–79).

5. Kant also considers, but rejects, the Dantean call for world government as the guarantor of the peace necessary for the full development of universal human reason. Fearing that a "universal monarchy" would be a "soulless despotism" ultimately destined to "lapse into anarchy," Kant instead calls for a federation of autonomous republics, economically connected in a cosmopolitan system of free trade. Kant's prediction is that wars among such republics would cease and a mutually profitable peace would reign; this is to be expected primarily because of the shared commercial interests and the continual free expression and self-criticism of the public use of reason characteristic of liberal states (Kant 1795). So far the prediction has been supported by the facts.From a study of the 575 wars since beginning of politically and economically liberal states, Michael Doyle (1983) shows that though such states have become involved in numerous wars with nonliberal states, they have not engaged in war with one another. Beginning with three, the number of politically and economically liberal states has grown to around 50 in this latter part of the 20th century.

6. For his thoughts on moral psychology and compliance, Rawls references *A Theory of Justice* (1971 §76), which makes use of Kohlberg's work discussed in §69. For a report of the unhappy results of Kohlberg's experiments in social organization without enforcements, see Christina Hoff Sommers (1984, 381–389). In his own admission, Kohlberg (1978, 14–15) writes: "Some years of active involvement with the practice of moral education at Cluster School has led me to realize that my notion that moral stages were *the* basis for moral education, rather than a partial guide to the moral educator, was mistaken.... [T]he moral educator must be a socializer teaching value content and behavior, and not only a Socratic or Rogerian process-facilitator of development. In becoming a socializer an advocate, the teacher moves into `indoctrination,' a step I originally believed to be philosophically invalid."

7. Arrow's (1951) demonstration of the General Possibility Theorem has been taken to imply the irrationality of the majoritarian vote, given the possibility of inconsistency. In the direction of what is being suggested here, James M. Buchanan (1954, 114, 118) has argued that "the negative results of Arrow's analysis as applied to voting represent established and desirable features of the decision-making embodied in constitutional democracy." Specifically, "the fact that [majority voting] may be formally inconsistent provides one of the most important safeguards against abuse through this form of the voting process."

8. For this and other comparisons of voting and market decisions, see Buchanan 1954a, especially 339–40; 1984, 18–19.

9. See Friedman, 1962, 108–118.

10. For elaborations of this point, see Von Mises 1932, 10–12.

11. One sees this sort of treatment of non-conformist styles of argumentation in the workings of a policy setting body, such as a boards of directors of the American Civil Liberties Union. Members of the national or local boards are to determine policy on basic civil liberties questions. All can be assumed to be committed to the protection and promotion of civil liberties: this is signified by one's voluntary membership in the organization. Certainly the members have their own reasons for thinking it important; but these are unimportant. To bring them into the policy discussions is unnecessarily complicating and to pry into them can be taken as an invasion of privacy. Major differences among members emerge when a particular case or policy decision brings into play several civil liberties values which under the circumstances imply opposing courses of action: for instance, a case treated as a privacy issue prescribes one course of action; but treated as a free speech issue a contrary one. The question is then: Which civil liberty consideration is weightier, privacy or free speech? Anyone who attempts to argue either side by appeal to broader political or philosophical considerations is often met with a wall of silence. Preferences for one or the other consideration are frequently set and unaffected by continuing argument. There is no procedure for settling the disagreement and achieving consensus; there is only an agreement on procedure for determining what is to be done when disagreements cannot be settled: the vote. But, of course, a vote establishes nothing about the correctness of anyone's view: only a Rousseauean dreamer could think otherwise. Pre-vote bargaining and threats of resignation are, necessarily, part of the process. Effectiveness in winning others to one's side by any of these maneuvers is always a function of one's importance to the organization or to the concerns and interests of those whom one would threaten or offer a trade. Membership in the ACLU is, of course, not essentially the same as membership in society: one is voluntary in a way the other is not. Thus, the appropriateness of refusing to listen to wider sorts of arguments in the ACLU is not an (nor Rawls's) argument for its appropriateness in the public forums.

12. In reflecting on Rawls's minimizing strategy for fortifying the liberal consensus I am reminded of Santayana's (1900, 4) comments on the attempt of Protestant liberals to fortify religion by minimizing its content. It is not clear that religion's impoverishment helps it escape its problems: "[Religion] cannot become science by being reduced in bulk, but it may cease, as mythology, to be worth having." Nor, I want to say, can public debate become rational or stable by the purifications Rawls would have us exercise.

# References

Ackerman, Bruce. 1980. *Social Justice in the Liberal State*. New Haven: Yale University Press.

Arrow, Kenneth. 1951. *Social Choice and Individual Values*. New York: John Wiley & Sons.

Baier, Kurt. 1989. Justice and the Aims of Political Philosophy. *Ethics* 99: 771–90.

Bayle, Pierre 1697. Averroes. In *Dictionnaire historique et critique*. Amsterdam.

Buchanan, James M. 1954. Social Choice, Democracy, and Free Markets. *Journal of Political Economy* 62: 114–123.

_____. 1954a. Individual Choice in Voting and the Market. *Journal of Political Economy* 62: 334–43.

_____. 1984. Politics Without Romance: A Sketch of Public Choice Theory and Its Normative Implications. In *The Theory of Public Choice* - II. Edited by James M. Buchanan and Robert D. Tollison. Ann Arbor, MI: University of Michigan Press, 11–22.

Charron, William. 1980. Convention, Games of Strategy, and Hume's Philosophy of Law and Government. *American Philosophical Quarterly* 17: 327–34.

Cicero. 44 BC. *De Officiis*. Translated by Walter Miller. Loeb Classic Library. Cambridge, MA: Harvard University Press, 1913.

Dante, Alighieri. 1313. *De Monarchia*. In *Monarchy, and Three Political Letters*. Translated by Donald Nicholl and Colin Hardie. New York:

Noonday Press, 1947.

Debreu, Gerard. 1959. *Theory of Value: An Axiomatic Analysis of Economic Equilibrium*. New Haven: Yale University Press.

Doyle, Michael. 1983. Kant, Liberal Legacies, and Foreign Affairs. *Philosophy and Public Affairs* 12: 205–35, 323–53.

Friedman, Milton. 1962. *Capitalism and Freedom*. Chicago, IL: University of Chicago.

Frost, Robert. 1949. The Lesson for Today. In *Complete Poems of Robert Frost*. New York: Holt, Reinhardt and Winston.

Gauthier, David. 1986. *Morals by Agreement*. Oxford: Clarendon Press.

Gewirth, Alan. 1980. Introduction and Appendices to *Defensor Pacis*, by Marsilius of Padua. Toronto: University of Toronto Press.

Habermas, Jürgen. 1990. *Moral Consciousness and Communicative Action*. Translated by Christina Lenhardt and Shierry Weber Nicholsen. Cambridge, MA: MIT Press.

Harsanyi, John C. 1975. Can the Maximin Principle Serve as a Basis for Morality? A Critique of John Rawls's Theory. *American Political Science Review* 69: 594–606.

Hume, David. 1740. *A Treatise of Hume Nature*. Edited by L. A. Selby–Bigge, rev., P. H. Nidditch. 2nd ed.; Oxford: Clarendon Press, 1978.

Kant, Immanuel. 1787. *Critique of Pure Reason*. Translated by Norman Kemp Smith. New York: St. Martin's Press, 1968.

_____. 1784. Idea for a Universal History with a Cosmopolitan Purpose. In *Kant's Political Writings*. Translated by Hans Reiss. 2nd ed. Cambridge:

Cambridge University Press, 1991: 41–53.

_____. 1784a. What is Enlightenment? In *Kant's Political Writings*. Translated by Hans Reiss. 2nd ed. Cambridge: Cambridge University Press, 1991: 54–60.

____. 1785. *Grounding for the Metaphysics of Morals*. Translated by James W. Ellington. Indianapolis, IN: Hackett Publishing Company, 1981).

____. 1785a. Reviews of Herder's *Ideas on the Philosophy of the History of Mankind*, Part II. In *Kant's Political Writings*. Translated by Hans Reiss. 2nd ed. Cambridge: Cambridge University Press, 1991: 201–220.

____. 1790. *Critique of Judgment*. Translated by Werner S. Pluhar. Indianapolis, IN: Hackett Publishing Company, 1987.

____. 1792. *Religion Within the Limits of Reason*. Translated by Theodore M. Greene & Hoyt H. Hudson. New York: Harper & Row Publishers, 1960.

____. 1793. On the Common Saying: `This May be True in Theory, but it does not Apply in Practice.' In *Kant's Political Writings*. Translated by Hans Reiss. 2nd ed. Cambridge: Cambridge University Press, 1991: 61–92.

____. 1795. Perpetual Peace. In *Kant's Political Writings*. Translated by Hans Reiss. 2nd ed. Cambridge: Cambridge University Press, 1991: 93–130.

____. 1797. *Metaphysics of Morals: Doctrine of Right*. In *The Metaphysics of Morals*. Translated by Mary Gregor. Cambridge: Cambridge University Press, 1991.

____. 1798. *Anthropology from a Pragmatic Point of View*. Translated by Victor Lyle Dowdell. Carbondale, IL: Southern Illinois University Press,

1978.

____. 1800. *Logic*. Translated by Wolfgang Schwarz. Indianapolis, IN: The Bobbs-Merrill Company, 1974.

Kohlberg, Lawrence. 1978. The Methodology of Moral Education. *The Humanist* 39: 381–89.

Rawls, John. 1971. *A Theory of Justice*. Cambridge, MA: Harvard University Press.

____. 1980. Kantian Constructivism in Moral Theory. *The Journal of Philosophy* 77: 535–43

____. 1985. Justice as Fairness: Political Not Metaphysical. *Philosophy & Public Affairs* 14: 2230–51.

____. 1987. The Idea of Overlapping Consensus. *Oxford Journal of Legal Studies* 7: 1–25.

____. 1993. *Political Liberalism*. New York: Columbia University Press.

Reich, Klaus. 1939. Kant and Greek Ethics (II), *Mind* 48: 446–63.

Santayana, George. 1900. *Interpretations of Poetry and Religion*. Cambridge, MA: The MIT Press, 1989.

Sommers, Christina Hoff. 1984. Ethics Without Virtue: Moral Education in America. *The American Scholar* 53: 381–389.

Von Mises, Ludwig. 1932. *Socialism*. Translated by J. Kahane. Indianapolis, IN: Liberty Classics, 1981.

# Chapter 3: The Future of Past Injustices

**Robert Ginsberg***

Making up for past injustice is sometimes asserted as a priority for the present implementation of justice. Indeed, what would appear as an unfair imbalance in present-day treatment of some people may be justifiable as compensatory action for past injustice done to others. The past is insisted upon as inseparable context of the present so that our steps toward the future must be guided by it. To simply start our consideration of justice in present terms is to commit the grave error of blindness toward the often sorry story of how we have gotten to the present.

With our benefit of hindsight we can see that injustice on a massive scale occurred in the past. We can identify groups of people as victims. While other groups might be identified as perpetrators of the evil, more likely is that the social and legal system as a whole was at fault and should recompense those today who suffer the lingering effects of that practice.

If no one alive today suffers such ill-after-effects, then justice does not require that we do anything, other than symbolic acts of commemoration that pay tribute to the past victims. Let us explore the case for doing symbolic justice. While doing it sounds easy and it is quite inexpensive, it takes a lot of work and is a considerable social investment. As a first step, the present society must come to full consciousness of the past irreparable injustice. That consciousness must overcome the escapist sentiments, "So what? Too bad, but what does that have to do with me? That's just a thing of the past," in order to discover that the thing of the past matters to us. We are morally troubled by what happened.

The second step is to do something about it. "What can we do about happened? You can't change history." But we can change history by our interpretation and judgment of it: we are doing something with moral and social significance to the supposedly given features of the past. History is always being redone. In the case of extensive injustice we make a symbolic gesture, such as the memorial park in Portland, Oregon, dedicated to the Japanese-Americans unjustly deprived of rights during World War II, that recognizes, that regrets, but that also prevents.

While we cannot prevent the past from happening, we can prevent the past from happening again in the future. There is the lesson of doing symbolic justice in history, to history, with history. We insist that the same kind of injustice not be done, once we know about it and have judged it. And by our act of commemoration, we insist that others keep this lesson in mind. Often the warning to not let history repeat itself has a general application. If this was done to Japanese-Americans, then it might be tried sometime on Chinese-Americans, Mexican-Americans, African-Americans. So even if the injustice left no survivors or descendants, seeing to it that symbolic justice is done safeguards others from injustice.

Symbolic justice does something for those who do it. It expands the reach of what matters to us. Thus, though we may not be Japanese-Americans, nor have had any interest in their plight, we become attached to their experience. We are with them. For this could have happened to us and shouldn't have happened to anyone. We lose indifference. We make greater room for justice within ourselves.

While much of the injustice of the past comes with the extra injustice of our not being able to do anything about it, yet we may make amends symbolically and thereby we hopefully become more just. Character-building occurs in coming to grips with what seemingly cannot be changed. We redeem history by improving ourselves. Do not close the book, then, on the irremediable injustices of the past. Keep opening the book, looking for unnoticed injustices so that we may respond to them. Always read history as a judge.

But that is endless work! you protest. Indeed, it is. In the generally available histories are more than enough tales of injustice to keep us busy for a lifetime of symbolic gestures. The history of humanity, alas, is a history of inhumanity. And what if we were to seek out the little-known histories and initiate research to compile the Complete World History of Injustice? That project should not be limited to victimization of groups, but it would make us aware of every documented individual on earth who ever was the victim of grievous injustice. A billion case studies would be needed.

Of each case we would say, "This was wrong, this should not have been permitted to happen, we regret that it happened, we sorrow for the person, we resolve that this kind of thing shall not happen to others."

For humanity to come to grips with its history on such a scale may sound like an impossibility. But we can do it if we will to do it. The Church of Jesus Christ of Latter-day Saints (popularly known as the Mormons), engages in the practice of retroactive baptism for the deceased, which is assisted by enormous research activity in genealogy. Following such an example, we should be able within a few decades to computerize the records of all deceased human beings for whom accounts exist. The United Nations might sponsor the research network that would produce the world casebook of uncompensated deceased victims. Each country should have its Ministry of Past Injustice to carry out this function within its borders, although international monitoring is advisable since part of the problem in such injustice was (and may still be) the lack of recognition within that society that such things constitute injustice.

The principle behind this global project is: Every person counts. That any person anywhere suffered uncompensated and hitherto unrecognized injustice matters to humanity. That victim, who is gone, shall not be forgotten. We make the effort to commemorate the victims. Their names will be written on stone, or in the book of honor. We will not be content to shrug off a case with the words, "But that belongs to the past." Just as we usually conduct a forensic investigation if we unearth evidence of a local murder having been committed a century ago, because we want to set the record straight, so we will want to be sure that no murder at any time or place is dismissed as belonging to the past. The past belongs to us. Such research is not a matter of idle curiosity; it is a moral challenge to exercise our judgment.

The Vietnam Veterans Memorial in Washington has shown how moving can be the care for the individual in commemorating group losses. The names of 58,191 persons who died in the American War in Vietnam are inscribed on a wall. Notice that the memorial is named for the Veterans, the survivors rather than those killed. This is a national gesture of reconciliation for those who lived to return from an unpopular and illegal war. They count, if we make the effort to show that their fallen comrades counted.

This mode of commemoration was followed in the recently unveiled National Peace Officers Memorial in Washington, which lists the names of American law officers who lost their life in the line of duty. Unlike the

Vietnam Memorial, the Peace Officers Memorial is designed to be continuing. Plenty of space is available. That produces a chilling experience. The memorial is not just a gesture toward the past; it is open for further use right now and in the indefinite future.

The earth has enough stone for the names of a billion victims. They could be inscribed by laser on the Rocky Mountains or even on the Great Wall of China (a large percentage of the names will be Chinese). And if stone is not used, then the honor roll may be printed as books. I have seen a book with nothing but a million dots in it. A thousand of those books would contain a billion dots. The project is feasible.

But should it be done? Will it not overwhelm us, throwing humanity into despair over the magnitude of its inhumanity? The horror of it should strike us numb. We need the shock of recognition. To despair over our inhumanity may be prerequisite to taking action on behalf of our humanity. Better to be overwhelmed by doing good deeds than by suffering the repetition of bad deeds. As moral beings, we will find the will to respond. "This is horrifying, it is impermissible, it must not happen anymore," are the judgments that make possible our taking the next step: doing something about the past cases and about preventing future cases. We dedicate ourselves to redemption.

Such care for the past has a protective value for our own lives. It inhibits the inclination of any parties today who would victimize us, calculating that the crime would not be known until another generation. If we all become conscientious investigators and judges of history, then injustice will out. Some of our dignity will be redeemed in the future despite our hopeless victimization at present.

You may object that this preoccupation with past injustice keeps our nose buried in history, with the records of the dead, whereas what counts most for the betterment of humanity, and of individual human beings, is the move toward the future. We should create a just future for ourselves and our posterity rather than muck around in the past with its sorrow, dimness, and doubtfulness. The only thing we can do about past injustice is symbolic, whereas we can invest considerable constructive effort to making a just life for all in the future. Efficacity should be decisive.

That argument is quite right in placing value upon what we may do for a more just future. If rectifying the past were to lead to future injustice, then we would be wasting our time. But if rectifying the past contributes to a mature moral sense, a broader recognition of the worth of human beings, a thorough awareness of how we may go fatally wrong, and a will not to let any injustice get past us unnoticed, then such activity is valuable for shaping the world of the future. What future will we have, if we ignore the past? Hold back that future—I want to get off—unless we share an understanding about our history. Santayana's pithy remark that those who do not learn the lessons of history are condemned to repeat its mistakes, may be revised this way: Those who do not make amends for the evils of history allow such evils to launched in the future.

But the case against redemption of history does call for setting priorities in order. The problem with being human is that the legitimate demands for action that fall upon us at any moment always exceed our resourcefulness in responding to them. If you think that you are doing your moral job by facing the appropriate problems, then wake up to new levels of problems that you didn't know were for your moral action as well! A billion new problems await your discovery.

While I am obliged to make up for all of human history, commemorating the one billion persons to be identified, I also have to see to it that the future will be just for everybody, and I even have to attend to my day-to-day obligations. The Kantian claim about the logic of morality that ought implies can turns out not to fit the existential situation of human beings. The can-do ethics collides with the cannot-do humanity. That we cannot do everything which we should do is no excuse for accepting despair and doing nothing. The human predicament of being moral means that we must choose.

But how are we to choose? What makes a just choice when faced with ranking some justice-making activities over others? The temptation is to choose against choice: to say, "To hell with justice, past, present, and future. I just want to live my life fully!" But a full human life requires a good effort at supporting justice between human beings. To refuse to make that effort is to insist on living in a world that is not committed to justice. The commitment to living in a just world requires our effort to make it more just. So moral choice comes back to us as constitutive of our humanity. "Well, then," you might concede, "go ahead and devote yourself to your chosen field of advancing justice, say, for the ancient Patagonians, but isn't that an arbitrary choice, when the modern Kurds are being killed off?"

True, an arbitrary choice is blind. In the example mentioned, it would be unjust to choose symbolic commemoration of the dead while neglecting those whose lives are at stake. To do so would only allow more victims to join the dead. Here we have a principle to serve as arbiter of our choices in matters of justice: Always give priority in treatment to those currently suffering grave injustice over those who suffered it in the past.

"Ah, that makes sense. The present takes precedence. I have always thought that justice has to do with those who are now alive, including we survivors of murder victims. Its spirit is protective rather than retroactive. Your talk about doing justice in history goes against that spirit. But we won't really have to bother about history, because of the principle of choice that you have proposed. We have so much injustice afoot, or about to break out, that we will have to choose against working on the past. All that, I'm afraid is past. Now is the time to come to the aid of those crying out for justice."

"I accept your judgment that the present must always outweigh the past in seeing that justice is done. But we may still re-introduce the past in dealing with the present. Not to do so, remaining blind to history, is to miss the nature of injustice today."

"Don't burden me with history when the task is doing justice now."

"Won't you acknowledge that two kinds of injustice are at hand: (1) that which just began, its proximate origin evident and not long standing, and (2) the other which goes back in history, with a systemic or cumulative effect, continuing until today?"

"What we still have to judge in both instances is the severity and scope of present injustice."

"Agreed. But if we are given a long-standing injustice and a recent injustice which otherwise are equal, shouldn't we give priority in treatment to the one that has lasted longer?"

"That sounds plausible. But why is it so, if, as you say, the cases are equally unjust? How does it really differ if one party is victim, say, of recent racial discrimination, while another party has lived under such discrimination for a lifetime? Perhaps priority should be given to the fresh evildoing, to stop it from becoming long-lasting, while the long-standing ones can be let stand a little longer since they have so far been endured. Why should longevity matter?"

"Because it has imposed an extra layer of indignity, the burden of living much of one's life under injustice. If injustice should be nipped in the bud, as you suggest, then current evils with an extensive past should have been nipped long ago. Long-standing injustice compounds injustice through neglect. It sends the message to the victim that the victim does not count. A second kind of consideration dictates that long-standing cases be given priority, the principle of legal triage: cases should be considered in the order they arise, other things being equal. This principle of ordering befits a system of justice. It minimizes waiting while suffering, and it eliminates undue preference or discrimination."

"But when we take into account the long-standing nature of a present case, we are still dealing with the present, with what is present before us as a case. The history is not researched for its own sake. It is brought in, where appropriate, attached to the present case. You might say that every present injustice has its history. Our obligation in seeing that justice is done is to look into the bearing of that history. Looked at this way, we are relieved of the obligation to redeem history itself, that mad impossible project you were pushing a few moments ago. Don't address history; you will get lost in it. Address the case before us; you will find whatever history is relevant to it. We don't have to be moral historians."

"We do. Though you have correctly analyzed how we should proceed in dealing with cases whose history of injustice is clear or can be easily researched. Part of such cases are their history. We get to understand and act on such injustices when we see them in their historical nature. Fair enough. But a second kind of long-standing injustice may also exist whose long-standingness is not evident and in which the injustice itself might not be evident."

"Contradiction. Long-standing injustice means something wrong that has been around for a long time and therefore is more noticeable. If it isn't noticed, though it has been around, then it can't be a major problem. Hence, it should not take us away from confronting noticeably major problems that pop up today."

"Some injustices go back a long way, are major, and yet are unnoticed. What adds insult to injury is the very condition of being unnoticed, hence of secondary importance, thus, not rectified. Such historically unnoticed injustice perpetuates itself."

"That's serious business, but how can it go unnoticed?"

"Because the process of its concealment from society is linked to the mode of inflicting the harm and serves to protect the responsible party from self-discovery."

"Who is responsible, then?"

"We are."

"What! Are you calling me a thief or a murderer? Don't try to unload someone else's guilt on me."

"I wouldn't think of it. I'm confident that you are not guilty. But nonetheless we are responsible. The *we* is all of us, society as a whole, because as a society we have harmed others gravely while concealing the fact from ourselves that such harm has been done."

"But if we—society—has practiced this mysterious concealment from ourselves, then how can we know that we are, as you assert, responsible?"

"By the critique of history."

"What on earth is that?"

"Just what we have been discussing: the critical investigation of the past, especially as it is extended into the present, in order to uncover hitherto undisclosed injustices. Without such a critical survey we will remain blind to much continuing injustice, and therefore we won't do anything about it, symbolic or otherwise."

"But if we do not see long-suffering victimization right in front of our eyes, how would we better detect it by looking backward?"

"Very troubling point. Insofar as historical investigation is shaped by current perspectives which miss what is at stake, we will likely miss it as well in looking at the past. That is why a just historical conscientiousness requires that we positively seek out injustice. The old attitude we learned in college was that we turn to history to become informed: the past as record which we read. Now we should teach that we turn to history to judge: the past as challenge to our conscience. By cultivating our critical sense of the history of injustice, we can get to detect victimization close to home. We come upon the systematically concealed injustice from the backdoor. This practice is an art of undeceiving ourselves."

"What roundabout activities you require in the name of justice! This backward-looking attitude would be acceptable had we world enough and time. But life presses upon us from every direction with problems of justice. We should devote our energy and sensitivity to what we may find by flinging open the front door of injustice."

"I applaud your passion for justice, your willingness to step forward to set things straight, and your impatience with any distraction from that goal. 'Show me injustice!' your heart says, 'and I will rectify it!' But if you don't see it, you won't do anything about it. Hence, the requirement of finding of what lies in front of your nose. The new formulation of the categorical imperative is, 'Find ways of detecting the injustice that you are concealing from yourself, and then rectify it.' We have the moral responsibility to see that justice is done. The extra responsibility is to see that we discover the injustice being done. Thus, the need to look in the recent past for victimization that continues right up into the present but which we have hitherto not noticed."

"But why haven't we noticed it, if it is such a big and long-standing problem? How do we conceal it from ourselves, especially if we have a passion for justice? What kind of injustice is this that is so unapparent? *Where* is it?"

"It is all around us. It is part of the unquestioned presuppositions of society. We grew up with it. Hence, we don't see it as problem. We shrug it off if called to our attention. We are not stung to action by it. This built-in injustice may not have a name until people awaken to its presence. Then we call it, say, racism or sexism. We stigmatize the evil. We protest against it. We take action. While we are correcting society we are also correcting ourselves, for we had been insensitive participants in the social system which victimized others. Not that we are guilty, but we take responsibility for changing the system in which we are participants. If having recognized the evil, we did not act to change the ways things are, then we would be guilty."

"Racism and sexism keep appearing in our discussion. They are the hot topics in today's discourse on justice. Racism is surely stigmatized. If something can be identified as racism then everybody would condemn it. No one wants to be called a racist. Including racists. Sexism is different. What constitutes it is not entirely clear. Though many people would not like being called a sexist, yet they might not think the charge a serious one. Sexism is often laughed off as a non-existent evil."

"That is part of the problem of sexism. Sexism is a grave evil adversely affecting half of humanity, yet it is not, as you indicate, fully recognized as evil. Too many people dismiss the term as empty polemics, and hence of no relevance to their responsibilities and actions. They just don't see sexism. If they did, then they would see *that* they didn't see it. Such a reversal stimulates people to detach themselves from sexist practices and to take action against the social evil. We are in the process of discovering sexism. This is an exciting time for justice-seekers. We may revolutionize consciousness and expand conscience. Since people find it hard to detect sexism all around them, the study of the past should help their discovery, which involves their self-discovery. Thus, we can shift from the question of the political or economic equality of women today to such questions as, in the American context, how come no women have served as President of the United States? When did women first join the Cabinet or the Supreme Court? When were women allowed to vote? When did women have the right to own property, enter contracts, enter professions, etc.? The driving point behind such inquiry is find out why and how women were denied their full humanity. The system of exclusion is to be analyzed, revealing its essential feature of self-concealment. Women by nature are unfit for these tasks, so ran the cultural presupposition, therefore no harm is done in preventing them from engaging in such tasks. Indeed, the harm would consist in allowing them to do what they shouldn't do! Thus, people acted in good conscience in supporting a system which only later we would come to see as evil. Moving up from the recent past to the present, things look good, but sexism has hardly ceased to exist. Even in areas where it is no longer permitted by law, the after-effects of legal sexism act to the disadvantage of women. To kill sexism requires further work in changing the system."

"So what are the lessons that we are to draw from the case of sexism?"

"Our historical conscience shows: (1) sexism was a systemic evil not recognized as such. (2) It is becoming recognized as such and its therefore being combatted. (3) Yet it also remains embedded in the social system and is not recognized widely enough. (4) Since sexism eluded detection of goodwilled persons in the past as well as the present, then other evilisms are likely to be eluding our detection at this very moment; hence, we ought to periodically review every feature of life in the social system to see what we have been missing as evil."

"And will other systemic evils take the same form of sexism and racism? Do such isms have a structure for which we should look?"

"Systemic evilisms take on the form of the exclusion of a recognizable category of human beings from full status as human beings. There's the injustice. History teaches us that the traditional exclusion has been of other tribes, people of other nationalities, or, as we say today, ethnic groups. These were outsiders, foreigners, strangers, even when they lived within a society. They were the perfect scapegoats that everyone loved to hate. They were called wops, spicks, kikes, micks, krauts, chinks, geeks, frogs, dagoes, polacks, greasers, . . ."

"Wait, I can't recall who some of those were!"

"History will refresh your memory. Note how the short syllables make the groups sound like animals. Racial discrimination reinforced such dehumanization of ethnic groups as well as offering new grounds for group exclusion. Religious discrimination, also going back a long way, did likewise. Consider the history of anti-Semitism as it variously attacks a nationality, a race, or a religion. Sexual exclusion we have discussed in terms of sexism as discrimination against women, but human sexuality has been used to target many groups for evil. Thus, homophobia, or heterosexism, discriminates against homosexuals. Adults who engage in sexual life outside marriage have been targeted. And adults who consensually engage in specific sexual acts in private, even as married partners, have been labelled degenerates and lawbreakers. The history of sex is the story of evil being done to people on the grounds that they are evildoers. Another way of drawing the line for the sake of discrimination is in terms of age. The elderly, once thought of as having retired from full human worth, are regaining respect for their rights, especially in the workplace and the field of health care. The rights of children, once thought of as not yet human beings, are becoming recognized by society so as to protect the humanity of such persons against abuse in the family and workplace. While the class system seems to have withered away in America, in many parts of the world division by class still operates in a discriminatory fashion. Geographical discrimination, common throughout the world, remains evident in American society, for whether you came from Boston or Arkansas, Brooklyn or California may be decisive in job interviews. But this distinction too will wither away as ease of travel and communication make a more homogenous society. A big division everywhere has always been language, and it will continue to be so. How one speaks the official language and the approved dialect may be the shibboleth for success or exclusion."

"What of the handicapped, both mentally and physically? They were scorned or neglected as less than human beings, but now we are awakening to their human rights."

"Handicappism disabled the 'disabled' from reasonable participation in life. We may now speak of this group as the differently-abled, thereby drawing them within the circle of those who count and upon whom we may count. We have to still to recognize the enormous number of ways that we count people out because of some feature that deviates from what we take to be the standard for human beings, including body shape, weight, and height, or the color, texture, and quantity of hair. If you would give it some thought, aided by history, you would see that short people, fat people, 'blonds,' and bald persons may all be harmfully stereotyped. I am waiting for left-handedness to be discovered as an unjust grounds for harming millions of people."

"Ha, ha, that's a good one. You would replace the evil of 'handedism' by an even-handed inclusion of lefties and righties!"

"Laughter is the last resort of self-concealment. It means, 'there's no real problem here. This is a hollow complaint. We even lack a name for it.' I could tell you a tale of woe about the emotional suffering that left-handers undergo in this world, the social disadvantages they face, and even their economic hardship, but you would be more receptive of the story if we approached it in dispassionate fashion by looking at history. History as heuristic. In any case, other evilisms exist at this moment which you and I are unknowingly perpetuating. They have no names, though in future they will. Human beings, it seems, will never run out of ways to categorize others for the sake of diminishing their humanity. In the next century, the historians of injustice looking back at us will remark, 'How could such goodwilled and sensitive people miss the evil all around them which they would have corrected had they been aware of it?' We will be an object/abject lesson for history."

"Well, if we don't know our shortcomings which will be known to the future, so be it. Let our successors in justice-making make up for our shortcomings, while we direct our energies to correcting what we are aware of. Always work on what is at hand—that's the imperative of justice."

"But since we have become aware of the very likelihood of our not being aware of what we should be aware, then we may take steps to become aware of it, thanks to critical history. We can discover ourselves, our shortcomings as well as our responsibilities. By putting ourselves in the perspective of the future, we may look back on ourselves now and change before it is too late. Injustice has a history, a life, a continuity. It not only began and developed, but it goes on. The categorical imperative of justice is to consider the possibility that we are engaged through our social system in injustice, and then to enlighten others so that we may change the system. Always work on expanding our recognition of what is unjust—that's the imperative."

"You know, we share a sentiment, a drive, a concern, though you speak so much of the past, while I insist on the present. We both see justice as future-oriented, as something to be introduced, to be cultivated, to be made more secure. Justice is not a deductive answer to an abstract puzzle. It is a human contribution to life on earth. The signs and symbols and systems for it should not obscure that it is a shaping, a doing, a re-doing, an extending, a judging, . . ."

". . . A making better. Yes, justice is the creative project of a being born into a universe that does not judge and into a society that, no matter how just it may appear, practices evilism. As human beings we insist on justice. Thereby we become more just."

"Just so. Justice is as much what we make of ourselves as of our world. It is the rectification of wrongdoing, but it is also our transformation into righteous living. Permit me a further question, before we go our ways in this world of injustice which we both seek to make better: *Who are you?"*

"I am your conscience. The inescapable critical second thoughts that you have had as you ponder doing justice in the world. I have called you back temporarily from action in order to grasp the historical context in which actions occur. I have called for recognition of the new categorical imperative which should guide doing what is right by discovering what is wrong."

"Then who am I?"

"You are my responsibility. The inescapable insistence upon responding by action to the injustices of our world. You have irrepressibly emerged in these pages to point to that world as I was turning backward and inward in intellectual exploration. You stand for the commitment that to know what is right is not enough without doing what is right."

"We're partners, then, who have much to work on together. I hope that we meet again."

"I am sure that we will"

*Professor of Philosophy, The Pennsylvania State University, Delaware County Campus*

# Chapter 4:
# Personal Liberty and the Public Welfare: An Irreconcilable Conflict?

**Edward Keynes***

## Introduction

Since 1923 the U.S. Supreme Court has developed a jurisprudence of personal liberty that conflicts with republican principles of the public welfare. A line of decisions beginning with *Meyer* v. *Nebraska* (1923)[1] illustrates the difficulty, if not the impossibility, of reconciling the Court's views of justice and legislative determinations of the general welfare. Beginning with *Eisenstadt* v. *Baird* (1972)[2] and *Roe* v. *Wade* (1973)[3] either a majority or a plurality of justices has advanced a theory of individual autonomy in the area of reproductive liberty that has intensified the conflict between judicial conceptions of liberty and legislative determinations of the public welfare. In an effort to reconcile these competing values, Justices Sandra Day O'Connor, Anthony M. Kennedy, and David H. Souter have attempted to strike a new balance in the abortion context between individuals' liberty claims and legislative authority to promote the public health, safety, welfare, and morals.[4] However, their analysis fails to resolve the inherent conflict between liberty, conceived as an indivisible right of individual autonomy and privacy, and the public welfare, viewed in utilitarian terms.

## Substantive Due Process: The Jurisprudence of Liberty and the Police Power

The Supreme Court's jurisprudence of liberty rests on a substantive interpretation of the Fifth and Fourteenth amendments' due process clauses, which Justices Stephen J. Field and Joseph P. Bradley first developed between 1873 and 1887. Beginning with their dissents in the *Slaughterhouse Cases*, Field and Bradley argued that due process imposes substantive limits on legislative authority to interfere with the individual's economic liberty, i.e., right to make economic choices.[5] While acknowledging that the Louisiana legislature could limit individuals' liberty of contract to promote the general welfare, they denied that establishing a monopoly in the slaughterhouse business had anything to do with the public health and safety. The slaughterhouse monopoly was nothing more than an unjustifiable use of the state's power to advance one economic interest to the disadvantage of another.[6] Their opinions were anchored in nineteenth-century police-power jurisprudence, which recognized that individuals' property rights and economic liberty were subject to general regulations that advance the community's welfare, as distinct from partial legislation that furthers the interests of a distinct class.[7] Thus Field and Bradley recognized that liberty and property rights are conditional rather than absolute.

By 1887, in the *Minnesota Rates Case*, a majority of the Court accepted Field's and Bradley's views that the Fourteenth Amendment protects individuals' property rights and economic liberty against partial or class legislation.[8] Within a decade, however, the Supreme Court transformed the argument into a more general protection of liberty of contract.[9] In a line of decisions between *Allgeyer* v. *Louisiana* (1897)[10] and *Adkins* v. *Children's Hospital* (1923)[11] the justices developed an unenumerated liberty of contract from the due process clauses. While numerous authorities have claimed that liberty of contract is without any constitutional foundation,[12] constitutional jurisprudence prior to the Civil War as well as the Fourteenth Amendment's framing suggest that it protects a core of economic rights that included the Freedman's liberty to make labor contracts. In fact, the Amendment's authors understood civil rights largely in economic terms -- the right to acquire, use, enjoy, and dispose of property, the liberty to contract one's labor, and the right of equal access to the courts in order to vindicate every other constitutional right.[13]

As Justice Rufus Peckham described this liberty in *Allgeyer* it

> means not only the right of the citizen to be free from the mere physical restraint of his person, as by incarceration, but the term is deemed to embrace the right of the citizen to be free in the enjoyment of all his faculties; to be free to use them in all lawful ways; to live and work where he will; to earn his livelihood by any lawful calling; to pursue any livelihood or avocation, and for that purpose to enter into all

> contracts which may be proper, necessary and essential to his carrying out to a successful conclusion the purposes above mentioned.[14]

In *Lochner* v. *New York* Peckham argued that liberty of contract is instrumental to realizing other rights that are fundamental to the orderly pursuit of happiness in a free society.[15] Only legislation that has a direct and substantial relation to the public welfare could justify intruding on the individual's economic liberty, i.e., freedom to make economic choices. While numerous critics have pilloried Peckham's opinion,[16] there is evidence to demonstrate that the New York bakery law, limiting the workweek, was partial legislation that favored the interests of large bakeries over small, independent entrepreneurs. In condemning *Lochner*, most critics have ignored the class character of New York's law.[17]

## The Fourteenth Amendment, Unenumerated Rights, and Personal Liberty

Although the Supreme Court has abandoned liberty of contract, it adheres to the concepts of liberty and unenumerated fundamental rights that informed such decisions as *Lochner* and *Adkins*. Long before the Court turned away from the protection of property rights and economic liberty in 1937–38, it adopted the reasoning of *Lochner* in protecting other personal liberties from the states' burdensome policies.[18] Beginning in *Meyer*, Justice James Clark McReynolds, a bête noire of New Deal liberals, carved out an area of liberty, under the Fourteenth Amendment, that encompasses many aspects of marriage, the family, child rearing, and procreation.[19] Turning directly to the line of economic liberty decisions, McReynolds added the rights "to acquire useful knowledge, to marry, establish a home and bring up children, to worship God according to the dictates of [one's] own conscience, and generally to enjoy those privileges recognized at common law as essential to the orderly pursuit of happiness by free men."[20] Despite Justice Hugo Black's funeral oration for *Lochner* in *Ferguson* v. *Skrupa* (1963),[21] Peckham's and McReynolds' views continue to animate the Supreme Court's decisions in the areas of contraception and abortion.[22]

Just two years after Black pronounced substantive due-process reasoning dead, the Supreme Court invoked the Fourteenth Amendment to expand the meaning of personal liberty. In *Griswold* v. *Connecticut* (1965)[23] a majority decided that the due process clause protects a married couple's decision to use contraception. Without a compelling interest, reasoned Byron White (concurring), the state cannot burden a married person's unenumerated right to make procreative choices.[24] In 1972 the Court extended *Griswold* to encompass an unmarried person's decision to prevent conception. Writing for a majority in *Eisenstadt*, Justice William Brennan asserted that the right to make reproductive choices may inhere in the marital relationship but a woman, as an autonomous individual, has a fundamental right to decide whether to bear children.[25] For the first time, the Supreme Court detached procreative liberty from marriage and the family, institutions the Court previously had acknowledged as essential to the preservation of society, democratic government, and the constitutional order.

One year later, the Supreme Court extended its reasoning to abortion. Speaking for a majority, in *Roe* v. *Wade* Justice Harry Blackmun acknowledged that a woman's right to decide whether to have an abortion is not absolute.[26] But he insisted that the state would have to demonstrate a compelling interest in regulating the medical profession, protecting women's health, or promoting potential life when restricting the performance of abortions.[27] In the first trimester of pregnancy, Blackmun argued, a woman must be free to make this decision, in consultation with her physician, without the state's interference. Because the performance of abortions is safer than carrying to term, he reasoned, until the end of the first trimester there is virtually no justification for intruding on the exercise of this right. At later stages the states may impose regulations that protect women's health or, at the point of viability,[28] preserve potential life. However, the states cannot impose regulations that compromise a woman's life or health.[29]

Since much ink has been spilled over Blackmun's trimester analysis, there is little need to examine his argument in great detail. Moreover, in *Casey* the plurality abandoned his trimester framework.[30] But there are several important points about the Court's due-process reasoning from *Meyer* to *Roe* that are worth emphasizing. Unlike earlier economic due-process decisions, which demanded that the state show a rational or, at most, a substantial and direct interest in limiting economic liberty, recent decisions involving procreation require the state to demonstrate a compelling interest. In other words, the Court has increased the states' burden substantially by subjecting legislation to close scrutiny and the most demanding standard of judicial review. The

Warren and Burger courts consciously manipulated the standard of review to make it virtually impossible for the states to justify most regulations of contraception and abortion.

In addition to detaching these personal liberties from marriage and the family, institutions that the Court had recognized as fundamental to and predating the constitutional order,[31] recent decisions rest on the theory that society is composed of autonomous persons who possess rights that are inimical to republican interests. Therefore, a majority of justices has set up an irreconcilable conflict between liberty and the public welfare. The Supreme Court's abortion decisions leave little room for legislation expressing the community's interests in preserving the family, marital relationships, or preserving potential life. While the Court has rejected these conceptions of individual autonomy in the economic realm, it has deified autonomy in the realm of procreation. Unless there is a justification for distinguishing among various unenumerated rights, there is little rationale for granting greater protection to individual's procreative choices than their economic one's.[32] Indeed, there is considerable evidence to support the argument that the framers of the Fourteenth Amendment viewed economic rights as core liberties that they sought to protect in the privileges or immunities, due process, and equal protection clauses.[33]

## Procreative Liberty and the Public Welfare

As the Supreme Court's abortion decisions suggest, prior to *Casey* the majority created an irreconcilable and, perhaps, unnecessary conflict between individual liberty and the public welfare. While there is a link between *Roe* and earlier liberty-of-contract decisions, there are some important differences. In *Lochner* Justice Peckham conceded that individuals exercise property rights and liberty interests subject to the public welfare. The test of an appropriate exercise of the police power is whether, in fact, legislation advances a public purpose or merely promotes a particular group's interests. Although the legislature has the primary responsibility for deciding questions of policy, Peckham noted, a mere assertion of the public welfare would not deter the Court from determining whether the facts support the legislation's ostensible purpose. In deciding these questions, Peckham asked whether there was a substantial and direct relation between the regulation and the stated purpose. Looking beyond the stated purpose, he concluded that the New York law was a form of class legislation. Therefore, it was an unjustified intrusion on the individual's autonomy to make personal economic decisions because there was no valid public purpose.[34]

While one can criticize Rufus Peckham as myopic, for failing to recognize the connection among working long hours, the incidence of respiratory disease in the bakery business, and the public's interest in sanitary conditions, *Lochner* leaves the legislature room to adopt regulations directly related to the public health. Undoubtedly, New York could have enacted inspection laws, mandated periodic health examinations, and required owners to install adequate ventilating equipment. The Court subjected the New York law to careful scrutiny, but did not presume that the legislation was facially invalid. The majority's analysis did not oust the legislature from the field.

Unlike *Lochner*, *Roe* deals with an absolute prohibition rather than a regulation of conduct. The State of Texas had virtually prohibited the performance of abortions at any stage in a woman's pregnancy. Thus the law struck at the core of Norma Jean McCorvey's decisional liberty.[35] Perhaps, under these circumstances, it was appropriate for the Court to require the State to show a compelling interest in prohibiting abortion altogether. However, every subsequent abortion case has involved state regulations governing the performance of abortions. By applying a strict-scrutiny, compelling-interest test, the Supreme Court consciously narrowed the scope of the states' legitimate authority to protect maternal health, marital and family relationships, and potential life. The Court's analysis contains a presumption of invalidity, which the states can not easily overcome. The Supreme Court also limited the states' authority to regulate medical practice and the operation of hospitals and clinics in the abortion context.

Beginning with *Doe* v. *Bolton* (1973),[36] the companion case to *Roe*, the justices began the arduous task of delineating acceptable from burdensome regulations of abortion. During the next decade the Court confronted state laws that required: (1) married women either to inform spouses or obtain their consent, (2) dependent minor women to obtain their parents' or guardians' consent before obtaining an abortion, (3) physicians to recite a statement of all the potential risks of abortion to patients, and (4) women to wait a fixed period before obtaining an abortion.[37] In deciding whether these laws advanced the states' ostensible purposes of protecting maternal health, potential life, and regulating the medical profession, a majority or a plurality generally applied a compelling-interest standard of review. Predictably, most state regulations did not survive Justice Blackmun's rigorous test.

Although Justices Byron White and William Rehnquist denied that the due process clause encompasses an unenumerated right to obtain an abortion, their argument presumes that the Fourteenth Amendment contains a fixed set of liberty interests. Their theory of "originalism" is attractive, but the Amendment's authors did not fix the boundaries or enumerate the liberties that are protected. Justice O'Connor also has been critical of the Court's jurisprudence; however, she accepts the view that a woman's right to choose in such personal matters as childbearing is part of the liberty that the due process clause comprehends. She has directed her criticism at Justice Blackmun's trimester analysis and compelling-interest standard, which, as she argues, fails to account for the states' legitimate interests and leads to unnecessary conflict with representative, republican institutions.

Sandra Day O'Connor has attempted to strike a new balance in the abortion controversy. Beginning with her dissent in *Akron* v. *Akron Center for Reproductive Health* (1983),[38] Justice O'Connor has urged judicial self-restraint in evaluating the states' regulation of abortion. As Justice O'Connor articulated her approach in *Akron*, *Thornburgh* v. *American College of Obstetricians & Gynecologists* (1986),[39] and *Webster* v. *Reproductive Health Services* (1989),[40] trial judges should evaluate abortion policies in two stages. In the first stage, a trial judge should ask whether the governmental policy (regulation or prohibition) challenged burdens or impinges on a right that is fundamental, i.e., unenumerated, but constitutionally protected. If the answer to this threshold question is 'no,' the court's inquiry should cease, because the policy is within the legislature's constitutional discretion. Should the people find the policy uncommonly foolish or politically unacceptable, they can reject the legislature's judgment in the polling booth.

If a trial court finds that an abortion law implicates a woman's reproductive freedom, it must then determine whether the regulation or prohibition either destroys or severely burdens the liberty interest asserted. At this second stage, the trial court should make a factual inquiry into the nature of the burden. Is the policy only minimally burdensome or is it unduly burdensome?[41] In order to guide state and federal trial judges, O'Connor has prodded the Court to develop explicit standards for measuring just how burdensome specific regulations are in relation to the individual plaintiff's claims. As Justice O'Connor argued in *Akron*, an unduly burdensome statute is one that either destroys or interferes substantially with a woman's right to decide in favor of abortion. In the context of the Supreme Court's recent fundamental-rights jurisprudence, O'Connor suggests that strict scrutiny should be applied to such abortion regulations.[42]

Finally, the trial court must balance the competing private and public claims. If a statute totally destroys the right or imposes substantial risks and costs that tend to destroy the right to decide in favor of abortion, the trial court should determine whether the regulation serves a public interest that is compelling enough to restrict performing an abortion. As Justice Brennan conceded in *Carey* v. *Population Services International*, "even a burdensome regulation may be validated by a sufficiently compelling state interest"[43] in safeguarding maternal health, medical standards, and potential life. Even though a majority found the Akron ordinance unduly burdensome, as Justice O'Connor noted, the Court acknowledged that "even a 'significant obstacle' can be justified by a 'reasonable' regulation."[44] If *Roe* protects women against absolute obstacles, official interference, or coercive restraint, O'Connor concluded, it is unnecessary to find that every state regulation inhibiting abortions to some degree is invalid.[45]

While Justice O'Connor does not abdicate to legislative judgment in abortion cases, her approach clearly is more deferential to legislative authority than Justice Blackmun's. She recommends that judges approach abortion policies cautiously before entering this political thicket. When the Court faces complex problems "'with many hard questions and few easy answers'," writes O'Connor, it would "'do well to pay careful attention to how the other branches of Government have addressed the same problem'."[46] As the plurality's opinion in *Casey* suggests, Justice O'Connor's approach encourages trial judges to exercise self-restraint vis-à vis legislative decisions on abortion policy.

## Casey, the Promise of Liberty, and the Public Welfare

Adhering to Justice Blackmun's compelling-interest standard, in *Casey* District Court Judge Daniel Huyett found six sections of the Pennsylvania Abortion Control Act unconstitutional.[47] Huyett concluded that the informed-consent, parental-consent, spousal-notification, reporting, and public-disclosure sections were coercive, substantially increased the risks and costs of abortion, imposed significant burdens, or erected serious obstacles to women seeking an abortion. The Commonwealth, he observed, had not stated a sufficiently compelling reason to justify burdening women's decisions. Applying a minimum-rationality standard, however, Judge Huyett sustained a provision requiring physicians to determine the gestational age of the fetus. Since all of the plaintiffs perform such tests to determine whether the fetus is viable as well as the risks and most appropriate method of performing an abortion, the court concluded that the requirement conforms to accepted medical practice.[48]

Speaking for the court of appeals, Judge Walter Stapleton largely reversed the lower court's decision, sustaining all but the Act's spousal-notification provision.[49] Since *Roe* involved the outright prohibition of abortion, Stapleton distinguished *Casey* from the Supreme Court's 1973 decision. Unless a regulation impinges directly on a woman's fundamental right to decide in favor of abortion, Stapleton reasoned, courts should employ less than a strict-scrutiny, compelling-interest standard of judicial review. Denying that most of the Pennsylvania regulations unduly burdened women's right to decide, Stapleton applied the deferential minimum-rationality standard of recent economic-liberty decisions. Apparently, he believed that O'Connor had articulated a consensus in earlier cases that a Supreme Court plurality would accept.[50]

In attempting to determine whether the Pennsylvania regulations unduly burdened women's decisions, Judge Stapleton turned to the empirical evidence. He articulated seven specific, quantifiable criteria for determining whether a statute imposes an undue burden on a woman's liberty by

> (1) causing a delay before the abortion is performed; (2) raising the monetary cost of an abortion; (3) reducing the availability of an abortion by directly or indirectly causing a decrease in the number of legal abortion providers; (4) causing or forcing the woman to receive information she has not sought; (5) causing the woman to find the person or persons whom the state has required that she notify or obtain consent from; (6) causing the woman to endure any negative or hostile response from a person whom the state has required the woman to notify or obtain consent from; and (7) taking away the power to decide whether to have an abortion by giving another person, usually a parent or spouse, a veto power on the abortion decision.[51]

How many women does a specific regulation affect? Are the additional costs caused by delays, reporting requirements, and medical procedures significant? By increasing the exposure of abortion facilities to public hostility, do disclosure requirements inhibit a substantial number of women from obtaining abortions? Do the regulations significantly reduce the number of legal abortion providers? In answering these questions, Judge Stapleton focused on the overwhelming majority of Pennsylvania women for whom the state's regulations are not unduly burdensome. With the exception of the spousal notification provision, he minimized the statute's foreseeable impact on the small number of women who may find the other provisions destructive to their liberty.

The court of appeals found that the spousal-notification section unduly burdened married women who chose not to consult their husbands because they feared physical violence or economic and psychological coercion to continue their pregnancies. The spousal-notification provision penalized women who sought to exercise a constitutionally protected right, without the state's intrusion on their liberty to decide to have an abortion. Despite a waiver provision, the court of appeals concluded that the section could not survive strict scrutiny because it was not narrowly tailored to serve the Commonwealth's interests in safeguarding the marital relationship or the putative father's interest in having children. The notification provision imposed an undue burden on women's liberty without expressing a sufficiently compelling state interest.[52]

The district court's and the court of appeals' conflicting opinions posed several important questions for the Supreme Court. Was *Roe* still the law of the land? Is the right to decide in favor of abortion a fundamental right or merely a liberty interest? How should judges measure the burdens that various state regulations impose on pregnant women seeking an abortion? Could the Court develop a principled way to reconcile the competing individual rights and public interests at stake in the abortion controversy?

In a five-to-four decision, the Supreme Court sustained the court of appeals' holding in *Casey*. A majority concluded that "the essential holding of *Roe* v. *Wade* should be retained and once again reaffirmed."[53] Nevertheless, a plurality consisting of Justices O'Connor, Kennedy, and Souter sustained Pennsylvania's regulations of abortion, with the exception of the spousal notification requirement. In balancing the competing private and public claims, the plurality employed a diluted version of Sandra Day O'Connor's unduly-burdensome standard. The plurality also abandoned Justice Blackmun's trimester analysis and compelling-interest standard.

Searching for a middle course, the Court articulated three important principles in *Casey*. First, before viability a woman has a right to decide whether to have an abortion and "to obtain it without undue interference from the State."[54] Prior to viability the state's interests in maternal health and potential life are not sufficient to prohibit abortions or impose substantial obstacles on a "woman's effective right to elect the procedure."[55] Second, the Court affirmed the state's authority to restrict abortions after viability, except when necessary to protect a woman's life or health. Third, a majority acknowledged the state's legitimate interest in safeguarding maternal health and potential life from the onset of pregnancy.

The Court used *Casey* to affirm its understanding of the Fourteenth Amendment's due process clause as a limitation on state legislative power. At the same time, the plurality affirmed the states' authority, under the police power, to promote the public welfare. A majority explicitly recognized that due process has a substantive as well as a procedural component. Since *Mugler* v. *Kansas*, wrote O'Connor, Kennedy, and Souter, "the Clause has been understood to contain a substantive component as well, one 'barring certain government actions regardless of the fairness of the procedures used to implement them'."[56] Specifically referring to the term 'liberty' as the controlling element in *Casey*, the majority confirmed Justice Harlan's view that in the United States due process has become a bulwark "'against arbitrary legislation'."[57]

Although the majority acknowledged that 'liberty' includes the specific protections of the Bill of Rights, it asserted that the due process clause protects all fundamental rights (both enumerated and unenumerated) from the states' invasion. Due process is a constitutional promise "that there is a realm of personal liberty which the government may not enter."[58] The Court denied that the framers' understanding of the Bill of Rights and the states' practices at the time of the Fourteenth Amendment's ratification established "the outer limits of the substantive sphere of liberty which the Fourteenth Amendment protects."[59] According to the majority, the Supreme Court must exercise its "reasoned judgment" in determining the specific interests that the due process clause encompasses. The Court admitted the importance of tradition in defining these interests, but rejected the view that due process is a static concept, frozen "'at some fixed stage of time or thought'."[60]

In defining the "liberty of all," the Court appealed to a long line of precedents relating to marriage, the family, and reproductive freedom. As O'Connor, Kennedy, and Souter observed in their joint opinion:

> These matters, involving the most intimate and personal choices a person may make in a lifetime, choices central to personal dignity and autonomy, are central to the liberty protected by the Fourteenth Amendment. At the heart of liberty is the right to define one's own concept of existence, of meaning, of the universe, and of the mystery of human life.[61]

However, the plurality rested its opinion on the right of women as autonomous individuals to make intimate decisions affecting their future as well as their equal status and dignity in society.

After affirming its commitment to substantive due process, the Court attempted to buttress its argument by appealing to *Roe's* precedential value.[62] However, the majority's appeal to precedent seems fatuous. As Harry Blackmun conceded, the Court abandoned his trimester analysis and compelling-interest standard. The plurality chose viability as a pragmatic dividing line concerning the scope of the state's regulatory power. Before viability the state can express its legitimate interests in maternal health and potential life as long as its regulations do not unduly burden the woman's decisional liberty. After viability the state can restrict or even prohibit abortion, except when necessary to safeguard the woman's life or health.[63] While the Supreme Court affirmed that the due process clause contains a substantive component encompassing reproductive liberty, it abandoned the analytical core of Justice Blackmun's *Roe* opinion.[64] Thus the majority's appeal to precedent reads like an apologia to *Roe's* advocates.

Sandra Day O'Connor's approach fared only somewhat better than Harry Blackmun's because the plurality diluted her standard of judicial review.[65] Thus the state can enact legislation that is designed to inform, even persuade, but not coerce a woman into childbirth as a means of promoting potential life.[66] The state can adopt regulations that are reasonably related to safeguarding women's health, as long as these requirements "do not constitute an undue burden."[67] Regulations that are coercive or significantly increase the costs and risks or reduce the availability of abortions would constitute an undue burden. The plurality's definition gives the states significantly greater regulatory discretion than Blackmun's *Thornburgh* opinion, O'Connor's earlier dissents, or Judge Stapleton's opinion in *Casey*. With the exception of the spousal-notification requirement, either a plurality or a majority concluded that the other provisions do not impose undue burdens on women.

Both Chief Justice Rehnquist and Justice Scalia aimed broadsides at the Court's decision and the plurality's opinion. Rehnquist denied that abortion is a fundamental right under the due process clause. "Unlike marriage, procreation and contraception," he noted, "abortion 'involves the purposeful termination of potential life'."[68] The abortion decision is *sui generis*; it is different from the other rights of "'personal or family privacy and autonomy"' that the Court has accorded constitutional protection.[69] Rehnquist characterized abortion as a liberty interest rather than a fundamental right. Therefore, the states can regulate the performance of abortion "in ways rationally related to a legitimate state interest."[70] Employing the minimum-rationality standard of *Williamson* v. *Lee Optical Co.* (1955) and other economic-liberty cases, he concluded that all of the regulations rationally furthered Pennsylvania's legitimate interests in safeguarding maternal health and potential life.

In contrast to Rehnquist, Scalia denied categorically that the Fourteenth Amendment affords any protection for abortion.[71] Scalia rejected the fundamental rights argument "because of two simple facts: (1) the Constitution says absolutely nothing about it [the right to an abortion], and (2) the longstanding traditions of American society have permitted it to be legally proscribed."[72] Beginning with *Roe*, Scalia argued, the Supreme Court had imposed its will on the American people, displacing the political choices and value judgments of their elected representatives with the justices' personal preferences. In the absence of a constitutional mandate, he observed, the Pennsylvania law should be upheld as a rational exercise of the state's authority.[73]

Attacking the plurality's version of the undue-burden standard as "inherently manipulable" and "hopelessly unworkable in practice," Justice Scalia dismissed it as "unprincipled in origin."[74] The plurality's opinion was a "verbal shell game" that concealed "raw judicial policy choices concerning what is 'appropriate' abortion legislation."[75] In Scalia's judgment, the undue-burden standard is a meaningless extra-constitutional invention that "invites the district judge to give effect to his personal preferences about abortion."[76] Since *Roe* had been wrongly decided, it should be buried rather than resuscitated. After delivering the coup de grâce, Justice Scalia denied that *Casey* had resolved the conflict over abortion or unenumerated fundamental rights. By foreclosing the democratic resolution of the abortion controversy, the decision would merely prolong the conflict between judicial conceptions of liberty and legislative determinations of the public welfare.[77]

## Conclusion

Although *Casey* has not resolved the abortion controversy, the Supreme Court explicitly affirmed its commitment to the fundamental-rights, substantive due-process jurisprudence that it has developed since the late 1880s. Beginning with the *Minnesota Rates Case*, the Court employed the Fourteenth Amendment's due process clause to limit the exercise of state legislative power vis-à-vis the individual's economic liberty. Since *Meyer* v. *Nebraska* the justices have expanded this realm of personal autonomy to include decisions concerning marriage, the family, and procreation. In *Griswold* and *Roe* the Supreme Court enlarged the outer limits of personal liberty to encompass contraception and abortion. Justice Black's funeral oration to the contrary, substantive due-process survives as a source of unenumerated rights and a limitation on legislative power.

Despite dire predictions that the Court would abandon *Roe's* basic principle, the *Casey* majority stated explicitly that the due process clause protects women's decisions to terminate pregnancy by abortion. As Justices O'Connor, Kennedy, and Souter noted in their joint opinion, women have an effective right to elect abortion "without undue interference from the State."[78] However, the *Casey* plurality also acknowledged that women's reproductive liberty is conditional rather than absolute. Therefore, at some time during pregnancy the state can express its legitimate interest in protecting the potential life of the fetus.

The joint opinion leaves the states considerably greater discretion to regulate abortion than the Court's opinions from *Roe* to *Thornburgh.* By abandoning Harry Blackmun's trimester analysis and limiting the use of his compelling-interest standard, Justices O'Connor, Kennedy, and Souter have returned to state legislatures the difficult political task of protecting women's reproductive liberty and the fetus's right to live. Prior to viability, the plurality leaves the states room to adopt laws that are rationally related to such valid public interests as protecting maternal health, regulating the medical profession, or assuring that women's decisions are voluntary and informed. However, the joint opinion prohibits the states from using their regulatory power to destroy or seriously impair women's right to decide to have an abortion. From the time of fetal viability, the states can enact laws that restrict or even prohibit the performance of abortion in order to protect potential life unless these statutes burden women significantly by increasing the risks to their health and life.

Since *Casey* was a facial challenge to Pennsylvania's Abortion Control Act, the lower courts must determine the degree to which specific regulations burden women's abortion decisions. As subsequent litigation indicates, trial judges now must begin the arduous task of deciding whether abortion regulations impose minimal, substantial, or severe burdens on women seeking to exercise their liberty.[79] Trial judges also must decide whether the states' alleged interests in regulating abortion outweigh women's interests in terminating pregnancy. Ultimately, the Supreme Court must determine whether the unduly-burdensome standard leads to principled judicial decisions or, as Justice Scalia claims, is "inherently manipulable" and "hopelessly unworkable in practice."

*Casey* is a course correction rather than a sea change in the Supreme Court's substantive due-process jurisprudence. Despite Scalia's criticism that the plurality's opinion interferes with the democratic process, *Casey* invites the states to explore the limits of their regulatory power. In deciding whether the states have exceeded their police powers, the plurality cautions the lower courts to exercise self-restraint. When entering this political thicket, the plurality reminds trial courts to pay careful attention to legislative factfinding and judgment. In a representative democracy, the plurality implies, legislative policies are entitled to great respect unless they unduly burden fundamental rights.

Despite its Herculean effort, the *Casey* Court has failed to fashion a principled resolution to the basic conflict between liberty, conceived in terms of individual autonomy, and republican definitions of the public welfare. The Supreme Court's failure stems from its understanding of both individual rights and the public welfare. Implicitly, a majority of justices defines individual liberty in dignitary terms. While dignitary rights are indivisible, they are transitive, i.e., they can be arrayed on an ordinal scale. Thus it is possible to develop a hierarchy of rights and, on that basis, to decide conflicts of rights among individuals. At the same time, the majority views the public welfare in utilitarian terms. In a republican society the legislature's function is to weigh competing interests, strike a balance, and allocate scarce values or resources, i.e., to determine the public good in cost/benefit terms. In other words, public goods are divisible and transitive.

Although dignitary rights and public goods are both ordinal and transitive, they can not be arrayed on the same scale because the former are indivisible, while the latter are divisible values. Therefore, it is impossible to balance individual liberties (conceived as dignitary rights) and the public welfare (viewed in utilitarian terms) on the same scale. As long as the Supreme Court treats privacy as a dignitary right, it must restrain public intrusions unless they advance a right that has a greater value in the transitive hierarchy, e.g., a person's right to life.

Alternatively, the Court could adopt a utilitarian theory of rights, which would leave legislatures free to weigh "rights" as public goods in cost/benefit terms. This would undermine the Supreme Court's substantive due-process jurisprudence, since the legislature is responsible for making calculations of the public welfare in a republican society. The justices' role would be reduced to determining whether the legislature had followed constitutionally prescribed rules in distributing public goods. While this work should not be interpreted as an appeal for a utilitarian theory of rights, it does point to the Court's dilemma in attempting to balance individual liberty and the public welfare. The justices' current methodology simply does not permit a principled resolution of the controversy.

*Professor of Political Science, The Pennsylvania State University, University Park Campus.*

# Notes

1. 262 U.S. 390 (1923). See also *Pierce* v. *Society of Sisters*, 268 U.S. 510 (1925); *Skinner* v. *Oklahoma*, 316 U.S. 535 (1942); *Loving* v. *Virginia*, 388 U.S. 1 (1967); *Moore* v. *East Cleveland*, 431 U.S. 494 (1977); *Zablocki* v. *Redhail*, 434 U.S. 374 (1978); *Cleveland Board of Education* v. *LaFleur*, 414 U.S. 632 (1979), and; *Turner* v. *Safley*, 482 U.S. 78 (1987). But see *Bowers* v. *Hardwick*, 478 U.S. 186 (1986).

2. 405 U.S. 438 (1972).

3. 410 U.S. 113 (1973).

4. See their joint opinion in *Planned Parenthood of Southeastern Pennsylvania* v. *Casey*, 112 S.Ct. 2791 (1992).

5. 83 U.S. (16 Wall.) 36 (1873).

6. *Id.*, Field (dissenting), at 87–89, 90–93, 96–97; Bradley (dissenting), at 116, 120.

7. See Charles W. McCurdy, "Justice Field and the Jurisprudence of Government-Business Relations: Some Parameters of Laissez-Faire Constitutionalism, 1863-1897," 61 *J. of Amer. Hist.* 970-1005 (1975), at 980-81, 982-83, 985, 994-95. See also William E. Nelson, *The Fourteenth Amendment: From Political Principle to Judicial Doctrine* (Cambridge, Mass.: Harvard Univ. Press, 1988), at viii, 10, 156-58, 166-69; hereinafter Nelson, *The Fourteenth Amendment*.

8. See *Chicago, Milwaukee and St. Paul Ry. Co.* v. *Minnesota*, 134 U.S. 418 (1890). See also Nelson, *The Fourteenth Amendment*, at 168-73. See also Richard C. Cortner, *The Iron Horse and the Constitution: The Railroads and the Transformation of the Fourteenth Amendment* (Westport, Conn.: Greenwood Press, 1993), at xii-xiii, 126-28.

9. Frank R. Strong, *Substantive Due Process of Law: A Dichotomy of Sense and Nonsense* (Durham, N.C.: Carolina Academic Press, 1986), at 92, 95-98; hereinafter, Strong, *Substantive Due Process of Law*. See also Nelson, *The Fourteenth Amendment*, at 198, 199.

10. 165 U.S. 578 (1897).

11. 262 U.S. 527 (1923). See also *Coppage* v. *Kansas*, 236 U.S. 1 (1915).

12. See, for example, Raoul Berger, *Government by Judiciary: The Transformation of the Fourteenth Amendment* (Cambridge, Mass.: Harvard Univ. Press, 1977), at 197-200.

13. See Herbert Hovenkamp, *Enterprise and American Law, 1836–1937* (Cambridge, Mass.: Harvard Univ. Press, 1991), at 93–94, 269. See also McCurdy, 61 *J. of Amer. Hist.*, at 974; Strong, *Substantive Due Process of Law*, at 3–40, and; David M. Gold, *The Shaping of the Nineteenth Century Legal Mind: John Appleton and Responsible Individualism* (NY: Greenwood Press, 1990), at 139–46. See generally Alan R. Jones, *The Constitutional Conservatism of Thomas McIntyre Cooley* (NY: Garland Publishing, Inc., 1987).

14. 165 U.S., at 589.

15. 198 U.S. 45 (1905).

16. See, for example, Strong, *Substantive Due Process of Law:*, at 91–97.

17. See Note, "Resurrecting Economic Rights: The Doctrine of Economic Due Process Reconsidered," 103 *Harv. L. Rev.* 1363–83 (1990), at 1370–71, 1373.

18. For an overview of the origins and evolution of noneconomic substantive due-process rights see Ira C. Lupu, "Untangling the Strands of the Fourteenth Amendment," 77 *Mich L. Rev.* 981–1077 (1979); hereinafter, Lupu, 77 *Mich. L. Rev.* See also Jeffrey S. Koehlinger, "Substantive Due Process Analysis and the Lockian Liberal Tradition: Rethinking the Modern Privacy Cases," 65 *Ind. L.J.* 723–76 (1990); Daniel O. Conkle, "The Second Death of Substantive Due Process," 62 *Ind. L.J.* 215–42 (1987); Harry H. Wellington, "Common Law Rules and Constitutional Double Standards: Some Notes on Adjudication," 83 *Yale L. J.* 221–311 (1973), hereinafter Wellington, 83 *Yale L.J.*; Thomas L. Emerson, "Nine Justices in Search of a Doctrine," 64 *Mich. L. Rev.* 219–34 (1965); Robert B. McKay, "The Right of Privacy: Emanations and Intimations," 64 *Mich. L. Rev.* 259–82 (1965); Arthur E. Sutherland, "Privacy in Connecticut," 64 *Mich. L. Rev.* 283–88 (1965), and; John R. Green, "Liberty under the Fourteenth Amendment," 27 *Wash. U.L.Q.* 497–562 (1942).

19. See James E. Bond, *I Dissent: The Legacy of Chief Justice James Clark McReynolds* (Fairfax, Va.: George Mason Univ. Press, 1992), at 130. Although McReynolds was not a systematic jurist who clearly articulated the reasons for his opinions, the "implicit rationale" of *Meyer* and *Pierce* v. *Society of Sisters*, 268 U.S. 510 (1925), has influenced the evolution of personal liberty and privacy jurisprudence. "In the last two decades the Court, expanding the category of fundamental rights even further to include privacy rights, has revived the doctrine of substantive due process whose use by McReynolds subjected him to the bitterest criticism." *Id.*

20. 262 U.S., at 390.

21. 372 U.S. 726 (1963).

22. See, for example, Goldberg (concurring), quoting from *Meyer* in *Griswold* v. *Connecticut*, 381 U.S. 479 (1965), at 488, and White (concurring), at 502. See also Brennan (opinion of the Court), citing *Meyer* as authority for a right to privacy in *Roe* v. *Wade*, 410 U.S. 113 (1973), at 152.

23. 381 U.S.

24. *Id.*, at 502–07. John Marshall Harlan concurred in a brief opinion, but relied on his extensive dissent in *Poe* v. *Ullman*, 367 U.S. 497 (1961), at 522–55, in which he anchors the right in the Fourteenth Amendment's concept of liberty.

25. 405 U.S., (opinion of the Court), at 453.

26. 410 U.S. (opinion of the Court), at 153–54.

27. *Id.*, at 154, 163–64.

28. According to Dr. John Botti, Associate Professor of Obstetrics and Gynecology and Director of the Division of Maternal-Fetal Medicine at the Hershey Medical School, the point of viability may vary according to the gestational age and weight of the fetus at the time of delivery. At twenty-two weeks and a weight of 500 grams a fetus has approximately a twenty-percent probability of surviving. At twenty-six weeks the probability increases to approximately fifty percent. However, there is a statistically significant probability that fetuses delivered in this gray zone will have serious long-term health problems. Even using ultrasonography to determine the gestational age of the fetus, the probability of a two-to-three week error in calculating gestational age is high. Similarly, the safety of an abortion during the second trimester may vary according to the technique employed. Until about the middle of the second trimester (the twelfth through the sixteenth week) dilation and evacuation is the most commonly used technique. After this time, prostaglandin inducement of labor is the most commonly used method.

29. 410 U.S., at 163–65.

30. 112 S.Ct., at 2816–18.

31. See Douglas (opinion of the Court), *Griswold*, 381 U.S., at 486.

32. On the origins of the Supreme Court's dual standard for evaluating intrusions on economic versus other personal liberties, see Justice Stone (opinion of the Court), *U.S.* v. *Carolene Products Co.*, 304 U.S. 144 (1938), at 152–53, citations omitted. As James Ely notes, Stone's opinion depreciated the framers' respect for property rights and the important linkage between property rights and other personal liberties. See James W. Ely, Jr., *The Guardian of Every Other Right: A Constitutional History of Property Rights* (N.Y.: Oxford Univ. Press, 1992), at 132–33, 134. See also Craig R. Ducat and Harold W. Chase, *Constitutional Interpretation*, 4th Ed. (St. Paul, Minn.: West Publishing Co., 1988), at 67; Wellington, 83 *Yale L.J.*, especially at 277–79, and; Geoffrey P. Miller, "The True Story of Carolene Products," 1987 *S.Ct. Rev.* 397–428 (1987), at 399. Stone's hands-off, minimum-rationality test, as Miller argues, freed interest groups to lobby legislatures without judicial scrutiny.

33. See Edward Keynes, *The Promise of Liberty: The Substance of Due Process* (forthcoming).

34. 198 U.S., at 64. See also Note, 103 *Harvard L. Rev.*, at 1370–71, 1373. The author of the note argues that the unions and large bakeries promoted the regulation to eliminate competition from nonunion shops. See also Geoffrey P. Miller, "Public Choice at the Dawn of the Special Interest State: The Story of Butter and Margarine," 77 *Calif. L. Rev.* 83–131 (1989), at 103–04, 122–25. As Miller suggests, during this era much legislative factfinding was a farce, a masquerade for interest groups that used the regulatory process to prevent economic competition.

35. 410 U.S., at 117–19 n. 1.

36. 410 U.S. 179 (1973).

37. See Edward Keynes, with Randall K. Miller, *The Court vs. Congress: Prayer, Busing, and Abortion* (Durham, N.C.: Duke Univ. Press, 1989), at 257.

38. 462 U.S. 416 (1983).

39. 476 U.S. 747 (1986).

40. 109 S.Ct. 3040 (1989).

41. For a detailed discussion see Judge Walter Stapleton's opinion in *Planned Parenthood of Southeastern Pennsylvania* v. *Casey*, 947 F.2d 682 (3rd Cir. 1991), at 689, quoted below.

42. 462 U.S., at 462–63. Or, as Justice Brennan observed in *Carey* v. *Population Services International*, the Court should apply strict scrutiny to "state regulations that burden an individual's right to decide to prevent

conception or terminate pregnancy by substantially limiting access to the means of effectuating that decision" as well as "to state statutes that prohibit the decision entirely." According to Brennan, a law that prohibits abortions entirely or substantially limits access to abortions should trigger strict scrutiny and a compelling-interest standard of judicial review. 431 U.S. 678 (1977), at 688.

43. *Id.*, at 686.

44. 462 U.S., at 463. As she noted, Powell had followed this approach. *Id.*, at 434, 435, 438. For further analysis and criticism of O'Connor's argument, see Susan R. Estrich & Katherine M. Sullivan, "Abortion Politics: Writing for an Audience of One," 138 *U. Pa. L. Rev.* 119–55 (1989), at 132–33, and David J. Zampa, "The Supreme Court's Abortion Jurisprudence: Will the Supreme Court Pass the 'Albatross' Back to the States," 65 *Notre Dame L. Rev.* 731–80 (1990), at 748–55. See also Ann E. Fulks, "*Thornburgh*: The Last American Right-To-Abortion Case?" 26 *J. Fam. L.* 771–92 (1987–88), and Nancy K. Rhoden, "Trimesters and Technology: Revamping *Roe* v. *Wade*," 95 *Yale L.J.* 639–97 (1986).

45. 462 U.S., at 464.

46. *Id.*, at 465, quoting *Columbia Broadcasting System, Inc.* v. *Democratic National Committee*, 412 U.S. 94 (1973), at 103. If O'Connor is deferential to legislative judgment it is "because of the limited *nature* of the fundamental right that has been recognized in the abortion cases." 462 U.S., at 465 n. 10.

47. *Planned Parenthood of Southeastern Pennsylvania* v. *Casey*, 744 F.Supp. 1323 (E.D. Pa. 1990). The 1988 and 1988 amendments to the Act provided that in a medical emergency a physician could waive the consent and notification requirement only if there was "a serious risk of substantial and irreversible impairment of [a] major bodily function or death." In all other cases, physicians were required to wait at least twenty-four hours before performing an abortion. Physicians, rather than trained counselors, were required to provide women with information on the nature, risks, and alternatives to abortion, the probable gestational age of the fetus, and the medical risks of continuing pregnancy. Although the statute contained a parental-consent provision, it also provided for a judicial bypass procedure.The spousal notification section required women to inform the spouse unless (1) he was not the father, (2) he could not be found after a diligent effort, (3) the pregnancy resulted from sexual abuse, or (4) there was a danger of bodily injury. The public-disclosure provision required abortion providers to release statistical information on the performance of abortions in cases involving the use of public funds.

48. *Id.*, at 1388–90.

49. *Planned Parenthood of Southeastern Pennsylvania* v. *Casey*, 947 F.2d 682 (3rd Cir. 1991).

50. *Id.*, at 693–94.

51. *Id.*, at 698.

52. 947 F.2d, at 709–15.

53. 112 S.Ct., (majority), at 2804. The majority included Justices Blackmun, Stevens, O'Connor, Kennedy, and Souter. The opinion was authored jointly by O'Connor, Kennedy, and Souter, with Blackmun and Stevens concurring in part and dissenting in part with the judgment and decision of the Court. Chief Justice Rehnquist, joined by Justices White, Scalia, and Thomas, authored a separate opinion dissenting and concurring in part with the Court's judgment.

54. *Id.*

55. *Id.*

56. *Id.*

57. *Id.*, quoting from Harlan (dissenting), *Poe*, 367 U.S., at 541 (quoting *Hurtado* v. *California*, 110 U.S. 516 (1884), at 532.

58. 112 S.Ct. (majority), at 2805.

59. *Id.*

60. *Id.*, at 2806.

61. *Id.*, at 2807.

62. *Id.*, at 2810–16.

63. *Id.*, at 2816–17.

64. Despite his partial concurrence, Justice Blackmun criticized the plurality for abandoning *Roe's* analytical core, i.e., the trimester approach and the compelling-interest standard. Only by abandoning this analytical tool could the plurality sustain regulations virtually identical to statutes that the Court previously had declared unconstitutional. *Id.*, Blackmun (concurring and dissenting in part), at 2844–47.

65. *Id.*, at 2820. As Justice Scalia argued (concurring in the judgment in part and dissenting in part), the plurality eliminated "the more narrow formulations used in Justice **O'Connor's** earlier opinions. Those opinions stated that a statute imposes an 'undue burden' if it imposes '*absolute obstacles* or *severe* limitations on the abortion decision'." *Id.*, at 2878. See also O'Connor (dissenting), *Thornburgh*, 476 U.S., at 828.

66. Admittedly, it is difficult to distinguish between persuasion and coercion. But the Court has not even ventured a distinction in *Casey* or other abortion decisions.

67. 112 S.Ct. (plurality), at 2821.

68. *Id.*, Rehnquist (concurring and dissenting in part), at 2859.

69. *Id.* Since a majority of states regulated abortion at the time of the Fourteenth Amendment's ratification, the Chief noted, there is little support for the argument that the right is deeply rooted in the traditions or conscience of the American people.

70. *Id.*, at 2867. The term "rationality" is employed in an instrument al sense. That is, there must be some relationship between the means that state has chosen to regulate abortion and one of three permissible objectives, namely, protecting maternal health, promoting potential life, or regulating the medical profession.

71. Given the basic conflict between Scalia's and Rehnquist's arguments, it is remarkable that both justices signed one another's opinions. It is also rather surprising that Justices White and Thomas concurred in the two opinions.

72. *Id.*, Scalia (concurring in the judgment in part and dissenting in part), at 2874.

73. If the state's exercise of power is beyond the Court's judicial competence, one wonders why it is necessary to proceed any further. As Scalia's view implies, the Court should merely dismiss such cases for want of jurisdiction.

74. *Id.*, at 2877.

75. *Id.*, at 2878.

76. *Id.*, at 2880.

77. *Id.*, at 2884, 2882.

78. *Id.*, opinion of the Court, at 2804.

79. See, for example, *Ada* v. *Guam Society of Obstetricians & Gynecologists*, cert. denied, 113 S.Ct. 633 (1992); *Barnes* v. *Mississippi*, 992 F.2d (5th Cir. 1993); *Sojourner* v. *Edwards*, 974 F.2d 27 (5th Cir. 1992); *Barnes* v. *Moore*, 970 F.2d 12 (5th Cir. 1992); *Herbst* v. *O'Malley*, 1993 U.S. Dist. Lexis 2479 (D. N.D. Ill.); *Fargo Women's Health Organization* v. *Sinner*, 819 F.Supp. 862 (D. N.D. 1993); *Benton* v. *Kessler*, 1992 U.S. Dist. Lexis 14747; *Jane L.* v. *Bangerter*, 809 F. Supp. 865 (D. Utah 1992); *Planned Parenthood of Southeastern Arizona* v. *Neely*, 804 F.Supp. 1210 (D. Ariz. 1992); *Preterm Cleveland* v. *Voinovich*, 1993 Ohio App. Lexis 3770 (Ohio C. App. 1993), and; *In re Petition No. 349*, 838 P.2d 1 (Okl. 1992).

# Chapter 5:
# The Illusions of Justice

**Jay Knaack***

This essay in Law and Semiotic is about contesting justice: why justice goes wrong when formalized standards become frozen and rules irrelevant. This requires looking at the ways in which claims for justice are constructed, or the way in which the norms, standards and rules of what is to be considered just are authorized, phrased and certified. An examination of these linguistic constructions enable us to look at justice as consisting in various sorts of illusions, (many of which are well known), and to also see justice as a matter of social discourse, that is, as part of social process, rather than as any sort of fixed state of social relations, end state of society, or single group of principles. Here various states or principles which are often viewed as basic for justice are considered to be part of the process of dialogue and dispute, construction and reconstruction.

Whether our interest turns to justice in theory, in principle or in practice, we find that all forms of justice reduce to local justice,[1] and the criteria used today are not much different from those used at other times, although some have fallen into disuse and others are given new clothing. Justice from our point of view (the view of social institutions and of language as social interchange) is about whether and to what extent individuals have their place in the sun: "a place in the sun" is generally defined in terms of one's social, economic and legal status compared to, (or in relation to), some social standard or some ideal construction of a political, historical, or rhetorical norm. The criteria for status, and norms of status, are linguistic categories. They are systems of classification. Similarly, a rule of justice is also a system of classification: identifying a good or state of individual being, criteria or qualification for it, and implicit criteria for its justification. Justification may be forthcoming for the procedures used in making the norm or for the results of enforcing the norm. Because these statements are systems of classification, they are often phrased in categorical form. They therefore appear impersonal and impartial. They are also impersonal and impartial commands. They also tend to require justifiable sacrifices and rewards, benefits and burdens. These we shall see are the principle illusions created by the categorical form and its practical employment in social direction and command. These illusions give rise to an assumption that justice consists (or ought to consist in) either a state of social relations of some definite sort, or of a balance between competing and equally worthy claims for status. Such ideally constructed or imagined states can also provide the illusion of national and global authenticity and applicability. However, in our case we are also looking at conflicts and competition between differing conceptions of justice, not just different claims to justice from within one set framework.

What occasions this sort of view is that in the United States today we have what we call various "justice policies" which are more general than political policies, but which serve to orient or limit the scope or intent of a political (legal, or institutional) policy. Such policies and their theoretical application is discussed and contested almost daily in the media and in social conversation. While we may all pay lip service to the conception of liberty and equality for all, and justice under law, etc., in practice we are all too well acquainted with and uneasy about the endless mire of rules and regulations we confront daily: standards and criteria, expectations, qualifications, proper procedures, loopholes, provisos, disqualifications, exceptions, and winning and losing combinations of the above. Getting justice may often be a matter of luck as well as design (or determination), while constructing just rules is often a continual headache. Enforcing justice, unfortunately, is becoming more problematic, requiring more and more resorting to committees and expert interpreters. From an administrative point of view, problems of justice often become problems of appointing the proper persons to sit on authoritative committees and boards. In law and many of our other institutions, qualifications and criteria intended to be impartially administered are continually contested. The lawyer's dream of a mechanical jurisprudence, or judicial deduction made without the interference of social and moral factors seems to be even more distant. Issues of remedial and corrective or compensatory justice do in fact demand the protection of the young and elderly, the empowerment of the socially disenfranchised, and economic efficiency as well as economic maximization. Many people do wonder whether ways in which we are stretching our traditional forms of justice are themselves just. However, we should, I think, look at justice from the most broad and historical perspective possible, in order to get some grasp of justice in theory and practice.

In the broad, and often ethereal and celestial world of western justice theory, we find that speaking of justice turns out to be also speaking about a number of different things which appear to be related: virtue, education, citizenship, the distribution of property and office, the limits of personal action, the proper structure of political and legal institutions, etc. Now in a republic, such as the United States, we expect collisions between regional and popular differences to result in compromise, or balances, sometimes called the common "good." Our Constitution provides for no positive state of social relations, but basically for procedures for extending or limiting the sphere and extent of activities allowed. Hence, if one's personal status is conceived of as any positive state, it will always be precarious, since the political jockeying for status, criteria and standards are bound to change and favor now one sort of group or activity, and now another. Now from the more traditional point of view, a theory of justice is also inseparable from a theory of virtue (or citizenship). Therefore a person educated to participate in our republic (which is popularly called a "Democracy" to everyone's mutual confusion), must think in terms of and be willing to compromise on regional and popular issues. But this in effect means that citizens must be able to accept trade offs between conceptions of justice, or balances between different claims to justice, or, in tough cases even sacrificing one sort of justice for another, including what they perceive to be just for themselves. And indeed, this seems to be pretty much what we have come to whether we accept it graciously or not. For example the justice of fair trial and protecting the accused from the power of the state can indeed conflict with justice for the plaintiff to gain a swift and sure remedy. In order to redress that, one has to add another series of provisos. (procedures, criteria, qualifications) to each side of the equation, and so on. This has to be done to avoid unacceptable invasions of privacy on one hand (searches and seizures) and to ensure protection for those who are endangered by threats and so forth. One of my chief concerns in general (and not especially with trial law) is that because justice is not only a messy business, but also a demanding one, that we only too often leave its construction in the hands of experts, who may be deaf, or to politicians and loud mouths who may be blind, so that the deaf and the blind lead themselves down the proverbial path to bathe each other in the wash tub of certainty and rectitude.

I now wish to turn to the more spectacular subject of politics and justice, before I turn to the somewhat dismal and academic subject or linguistics, and lastly to the well worn subject known of as the illusions or mythologies of justice.

Politics and Justice can be for convenience divided into two topics: politics within a system of justice (in this case our own), and political competition between conceptions of justice (in this case, party platforms, policy strategies, action committee agendas). Speaking of politics within the system of justice, I refer to the reader to William Louthan's study published in 1979,[2] which still has a great deal of validity, especially in his treatment of the selection of judges and the administration of legal education and the criminal justice system. The most spectacular feature of that day, and ours, is the appointment of Supreme Court Judges, whose personal life and political opinions come under heavy, well publicized scrutiny. Obviously there would not be much concern over their appointment if everyone agreed that simply being a good judge was a proper qualification. But points of constitutional interpretation do in fact effect people's liberty and rights, their tax dollars and opportunities, and they rightly believe and suspect that judges ought to have the sort of judicial policies they themselves consider to be judicially correct. But the questions of justice within the system are many: there are the questions of just taxation, ruling or legislating on campaign spending and contribution, jury selection, committee membership, voting procedures, police training, triage in prison hospitals, granting tax breaks, or deciding on who will benefit from foreign trade policies. On the local level, issues of justice include levying sales taxes, school taxes, spending for traffic lights, sewer repair, allowing mall expansions, and the granting of licenses to vendors at local festivals, and to builders, contractors, manufacturers, etc. Usually somebody pays, somebody wins, somebody is stopped, somebody gets the go ahead. Internal politics can center around competing policies, appointments, qualifications for administrators, and favored public projects, among other things.

On the local, state and national political scene, on the other hand, claims between competing concepts of justice are often indistinguishable from political process, party programs and the agendas of political action committees. These are contested every day by actors in the media and in the meeting of clubs, boards and committees covered by the media for political news. Such policies may, of course, contain a core of special interests being advanced under the guise of what is supposed to be just for all (which is what we often and rightfully suspect is the case).

One such policy, for example, may be one which favors the family and embraces laws and policies designed to strengthen and benefit the family. (Both pro and anti-abortion advocates advance their cause under this policy name). Another policy is one that favors liberty, and maintains that justice is subordinate to and defined by the demands of liberty (as defined by the advocate to suit his or herself). (The liberty policy can be espoused by Civil rights advocates, as well as by those opposed to expanded liberties as interferences with their liberties). Yet another policy advanced in the political arena may favor maximizing economic equality, and another favor reducing economic inequality. Another policy may derive the demands of justice from the imperative to maximize wealth or to maximize the social goods and services available for exchange, and yet another from the imperative of economic efficiency or the maximization of resource utilization and labor (or other things). Another, politically popular policy is one that favors law and order or reforming the judicial and penal system or procedures, or properly enforcing what is already supposed to be the law. Law and Order policies usually aim to correct perceived ills in the system and restore justice to what it is presumed it is supposed to be. Yet another policy may favor eliminating government involvement in society, which is perceived to be the cause of other forms of injustice. Some of these policies have gained sophisticated articulation, such as in the works of Profs. Ronald Dworkin, Richard Posner and John Rawls. Among other writers in the United States, it is important to mention Henry George, Friedrich Hayek, Russell Kirk, Norman Thomas, and followers of Ayn Rand, among others.[3]

Now when authors, academics, rhetoricians and vote seekers espouse these sorts of principles, they are apparently meant to be taken as demands for justice for all of society, or as means for correcting justice in some areas of life so as to correct justice (or obtain justice) in all areas of life. It may certainly be comforting to think that any one of these policies (or regional theories) could constitute the "whole" of justice, or the just society. Today, however, people have become uneasy with these global intentions, and particularize the theories as the justice policy of this or that party, or president, economic advisor or author. Nevertheless, these implicit appeals to correcting justice and achieving sweeping social consequences is worth while pondering. At one time we might have debated justice between a Democracy or a Republic, Monarchy and Aristocracy, Technocracy and Anarcho-Socialism: but now we debate the justice of supply side or demand side economics, family protection or liberty. Indeed, it seems to be the concept of the just society itself which is at stake, an issue which has become an integral part of our on going national political debate. Quite obviously people do disagree about justice and many people do not perceive our society to be a just one, no matter what claims may be made to the contrary, and people find it unjust in differing ways and for differing reasons. Justice policies, however, are usually defended in such a way as to suggest that they can serve to correct a "bundle" of injustices at once, and therefore gain wider credibility and support. For example, policies to strengthen the family, might, it can be argued, contribute to cutting down on crime and property loss, strengthen work values and social ethics, and contribute to civic responsibility. However, it is sometimes difficult to disengage the demands for justice from the results of political compromise or the more persuasive political interests, or from bureaucratic or administrative convenience (that is, necessity or inertia). Sometimes making policies amounts to ordering agencies and administrators to tighten qualifications or to loosen them (for example, qualifications to receive unemployment benefits, business tax breaks, prison parole, etc.). Some justice policies are readily identified with the interests of specifiable economic groups, as in the case of policies devised to increase investment and production by granting larger tax breaks to investors and on business profits. This can be justified in terms of its potential to create employment, more taxes, and therefore better schools and crime control. On the other hand, a policy may favor tax breaks for consumers or labor, which will supposedly increase spending and therefore profits, investment, taxes and funds available for schools and crime control. One of the most important justice policies in the United States concerns the Federally set prime lending rate. Another concerns the government's amount of expenditures and investment and manipulation of the budget in terms of future income and future indebtedness. I think it is conventional for both citizens and administrators to view these policies as means for correcting imbalances in economic and social life between various segments, or within various segments of the population. Nevertheless, anyone who perceives an imbalance (or shortage) on one side of any equation, can plausibly turn it into a national issue with wider implications. Hence, the cause of justice can become immensely potent tool in procuring votes and political power and in discrediting other actors and justice policies. Public debate often borders on vicious slander and hate mongering on one hand, and visions of love, light, caring and utopia on the other.

It might seem platitudinous to suggest that justice issues are important because they effect our lives and the direction of our society and legal system, (and that is perhaps why people would prefer that no action be taken at times and places suitable to their own interests in the justice of the status quo). However, it is also worth while looking at the doctrine of signs to discover what we can about the significance and operation of claims for justice. Sometimes, claims for justice may simply be illusions that promise the impossible in order to advance some interest extraneous to justice; at others, genuine claims for justice may be silenced and ignored by washing them away in illusions about how things really are just, or about how things cannot be chnaged or improved. And this introduces my own observation that people do sometimes expect much more from justice than they can ever possibly hope for, and yet are all too willing to accept much less than they can and should have. (One of the best overviews of reasons why people accept economic inequalities, in terms of class analysis, in my mind, is still W. G. Runciman's study of Relative Deprivation).[4]

Semiotic or the study of signs was presumably invented, or envisioned, independently by Charles Sanders Peirce and Ferdinand de Saussure (although Semioticians have found other forerunners in the History of Philosophy).[5] Similarly, there are many studies of the nature of language and rhetoric before the modern era, too numerous to mention. de Saussure, as I understand him, suggested that there could be a "science" of signs which would be some sort of Sociology, or, as I see it, a Sociology of ritual forms. In my mind, de Saussure emphasized the purely conventional nature of language (rather than supposing there is anything necessary or "natural" in the sounds, or meanings of words). Words are simply conventional marks for social concepts which constitute the semantics of language. He called language a "system of classification." Secondly, one supposes that he meant to show that linguistic forms and verbal behavior are often ritualistic, or matters of social form or formality. I also suppose he meant for us to understand that our use of language is more mechanical than we think, since we employ shared syntactical forms and when speaking or writing fit suitable antonyms and synonyms into those forms. One of the many people influenced by him, Claude Levi-Strauss, goes so far as to claim that systems of social classification think through the actor: the power of language to enshrine and perpetuate social calssifications is such that the actor perceives the world and speaks of it (Understands and defines it) in terms of the social classification used in traditional linguistic forms.[6] From this perspective, language is a highly conservative affair (since it constitutes the primary way in which human experience and wisdom are preserved and transmitted) which also explains why, in formal intercourse and structured settings, (law, school, religious worship, training in the skills, for example), formula are repeated over and over and great emphasis is put upon proper use and order.

Peirce, as I have always interpreted him, emphasized the practical side of discourse, particularly its use in directing action and discovery. Practical problems of survival give rise to inductions and deductions about our expectations, and to conventional explanations and predictions, and conventional directions and commands. The way some followers of Peirce, (at least this one), summarize this, is to say that language in use is always context dependent for its meaning and those meanings involve purposeful interaction with the environment and other actors. I think both Peirce and de Saussure were overly optimistic in their talk of a "science" of signs. Even if syntactical forms were rigidly fixed, the opportunity for semantical combinations seems endless. Far from there being a definitive number of types of signs, it seems that new classes of signs can be created for new purposes or new domains. To artificially limit language to a series of explanatory or model building categories seems to me and to others to simply go against the entire spirit of Peirce and de Saussure by taking them too literally, and pulling down a veil where some illumination was supposed to have occurred, (that is, by imposing another structure between actors and the structures they use). Similarly, I now suppose, there is no such thing as a universal grammar based in natural language, or any such thing as universal motivation. Having said that, however, does not bar us from attempting to apply some of their insights to the language of justice or claims for justice, especially if upon deep analysis it supports the view that there can be no definitive science of justice either. Just as "meaning" is an open ended question liable to new directions and interpretations, so justice itself should, if it does not: close worlds once considered just can become dogmatic and injust.

Let us now turn to the first and most popular illusion of justice. For example, I will use the phrase "only United States Citizens, with a diploma from an accredited High School, and a test score of at least (x) on test (a) and at least a median score of (y) on test (b) can apply for type (T) scholarship at this college." This statement contains four criteria, which can be manipulated by administrators: tightened or loosened. Administrators will indeed require some latitude for marginal cases. If the criteria are too strict, it may appear injust to some applicants and some administrators. Now from a Semiotic point of view, these strings of criteria are like schema, descriptions and directions which facilitate decision making and institutional effectiveness. They are dependent for their meaning upon High School and College courses of study and expectation and would be meaningless without them.

From the Pragmatic point of view, such schema become habits of action and decision making for administrators. For the student, they represent the real world. For both, they appear fixed, necessary and scarcely questionable. They become guidelines for achieving success, and for predicting failure.

Next let us compare our hypothetical scholarship qualification with the statement that "all suspects must be properly arraigned, tried and acquitted or found guilty." To set forth the various definitions and criteria involved in this process would require many pages, and to administer them a good deal of education and experience. Nevertheless, this remains one of the most popular models for the belief in mechanical and automatic decision making. All the judge has to do, it is sometimes claimed, is see if the law fits the case. In the interest of justice, it is commonly believed, judges should only apply the publicly sanctioned law. Either the case fits or it does not as Lawyers would want us to believe. Yet lawyers themselves get paid to argue that either the case does not fit (for the accused) and that it does fit (for the plaintiff). According to White,[7] the dilemma of justice is that judicial discretion is necessary: if one makes the criteria too strict and narrow, one can err injustly: if one then makes the criteria too loose and wide, one can err injustly on the other side. But more than that, Louthan comments that the area of criminal justice contains the most, not the least, latitude and opportunity for discretion.[8] If both Professors White and Louthan are anywhere near correct, what has gone wrong? Is our belief that the criminal courtroom case is the paradigm of justice based on wishful thinking, or propaganda broadcast by the professionals in order to justify themselves? The thing usually claimed is that justice is not perfect, or that it works often enough, or that it is the best alternative to whatever else might happen,etc. Yet, lawyers and many citizens become perturbed by judges being forced to interpret the law, enforce laws, and make awards because justice is not perfect, laws are badly made, and the criteria of reasonable action comes under fire. I suppose that at least shows that we can and sometimes do entertain conflicting beliefs about our expectations for the justice system.

Next let us compare our statements with a third: "Only those who have attained their twenty first birthday may vote." I choose this because, for the moment at least, this appears fairly neutral. The rule is presumably justified by assuming that only citizens of twenty one have achieved the maturity to vote and the responsibility for making laws. The rule of justice is impartial: it applies to all citizens, and it is impersonal, it makes no reference to age, sex, economic status, or mental or academic competence. It is also considered to be above persons or personal decision making, that is, of a higher authority than any individual. Furthermore, it is a directive and a permission and a right, and implicity suggests that citizens of twenty one should vote or have a duty to vote in order to fulfill the purpose of justice in voting, i.e., the preservation of justice itself. Furthermore, the statement implies that anyone who disobeys or interferes with the twenty one rule will be penalized, or should be penalized. It can therefore suggest to each person that all others ought to obey that rule and ought to be penalized if they do not. Hence, the rule implies expectations about how people ought to behave in general (allow rights to vote) and not infringe this (by voting under age, stuffing ballot boxes, tampering with balloting machines, buying votes). There are many provisos and rules and procedures that accompany the rule and without which the rule tends to become mere sham or wishful thinking. The point I want to make is that the impersonal, categorical nature of such a rule (like many other claims to justice) tend to become self-explanatory, customary, socially binding and definitive: disallowing any alternative. Therefore, it can appear universally valid (due to universal usage) and necessary. It may be necessary insofar as voting qualifications are socially and politically justifiable, and necessary insofar as they set a definite standard or test of qualificaion, but the actual details may not be necessary. Perhaps this is all common place, but it needs to be spelled out, because these connotations are not imaginary, they are often implicit, and they also can be used to explain why the rules of justice are considered to constitute the internal order of social relations. Hence, the rules of membership in our institutions and clubs, the qualifications for advancement, membership, rights, and so forth, may be arbitrary from some point of view or other, but because of their form they appear just: impartial, above persons, impersonal, necessary, self explanatory, and implicitly justified. They furthermore, it may be presumed, hold for everyone of the right description (universally) and anyone (universally) who violates them may be liable to censure or punishment.

Next, let us examine the following example: "Workers at the age of sixty five may be let go of their jobs since they are expected to retire." In the United States, this implicit and popular social rule has been given a good number of explanations and justifications. This has forced people to save for their old age, though many cannot, and has allowed employers to dismiss people who wished to continue working and who were productive. In some cases, employers have dismissed employees against their better judgment because of the rule, not because of any of the justifications for the rule. Now, one can say that the elderly deserve retirement since they have made their contribution. One can also say that the young should have a chance to make their contribution. So the elderly sacrifice their desire to work for the young. Yet, the elderly presumably have the rewards (of savings, of life fulfillment) which the young will some day gain. Now the implicit idea here is that rules of justice distribute the benefits and burdens of society in just ways.

Just why there is this traditional attachment of justice to the just distribution of social benefits and burdens is not easy to see, since it more often then not appears to be little more than an empty rationalization. Now in a criminal or civil proceeding involving compensation and punishment, we might think that the person fined and punished is getting a just reward (burden) for failure to shoulder the other burden (responsibility) for upholding the law, therefore the guilty are rightfully burdened for not assuming their proper burden. This sense of reciprocity is also implicit in the idea that everyone should have their fair chance, taxes should match the income, contributions should match the talents, rewards should match the effort, and so forth. The idea is that standards of justice require "sacrifices" by some (those excluded from some category) in order for there to be benefits for others (who fall in the categories) or vice versa. Hence, all of society can be imagined to be a realm in which all sacrifice for everyone else (legitimately under legitimate rules) and everyone benefits from everyone else's sacrifices, although in different ways, at different times, and for different reasons.

Now if we grant that claims for justice also tend to make this sort of implicit appeal or are presumed to, then I am in a position to suggest that the demands of justice for impartiality and impersonality and necessity, also allow actors to view themselves as but one among many: as impersonal actors comparable to others, and as legitimately liable to making the sacrifices, or assuming the liabilities, demanded by justice. Obviously, if the reader has followed me this far, he or she may be ready to start balking and thinking that all of this sounds like an exercise in explaining unthinking conformity to social formality. And indeed it is. The idea that justice is rewarded is so deeply ingrained in childhood and our education that it seems unexceptional. This conviction however, may actually serve us well when people desire fuller justifications for justice and laws and regulations that are not apparently useful or warranted. But it may also contribute to the sort of utopian or blind wishful thinking that envisions a perfectly just society in which virtue is its own reward when some particular favored principle or policy is carried out. These illusions, important for any analysis of reciprocity, can also be related to the sense of the scared and the profane. Standards of Justice (whether really just or not) can serve as a prophylactic mental and social barrier against doubt and uncertainty about the decisions of others. They can also serve as a comforting barrier against doubts about obedience and acquiesence. They can also serve to enforce ethnic, racial, sexual, and economic prejudices. This also allows actors to imagine that they can avoid censorship by conformity, that conformity is self justifying, and blame for injustices belongs to those victims of the rules who are excluded and claim compensation.

The primary illusions generated by Justice are due to linguistice form and its function as social imperative and schema of internal order. The oldest such illusion is the illusion of natural desert: the actor who disobeys the law will be punished by nature or something they do will turn against them. Who ever tries to escape their burdens and duty today will have them doubled tomorrow. There can be no justice without suffering. Suffering under justice is its own reward.

Another illusion, mentioned above, is the belief that a particular justice policy once enacted will enable justice to flow in other related areas. This can be related to our tradition in which politics, law, education, virtue, and economic distribution are all considered to be related and relevant to the well being of each and to the well being of all. Perhaps the most comprehensive, and earliest treatment of this belief is to be found in Plato's outline for utopia in *The Laws*. There, the just state must be self sufficient in food and productive and defensive power. Property is equally distributed to eliminate envy among the citizens, who are also forbidden to participate in commerce or accumulate wealth. Population is kept at a steady state and is also strictly controlled along with labor, monetary standards, imports and exports, immigration and emigration, art, literature and religion and education. However, even Plato's Thousand Year Utopia could not have withstood the ravages of soil depletion, labor shortages, illegal immigrations, and pressures on wages and prices, the very same sorts of pressures threatening the achievement of modern forms of justice in the third world. The illusion of a completely tranquil and just society is, of course, a vision of a society no longer in need of discussing or debating justice; a society that may become injust due to inertia.

Another illusion is that of Global justice, or justice between all nations of the earth. The idea is to farily distribute reproductive rights (to bear children), the allocation of resources for survival and production, and the fair distribution of trade opportunities and opportunities for profit taking. But what standards could be used to favor the reproduction of one nation's children over another? If that may turn out to be the ultimate question of global justice, then it becomes a matter of reaching an agreement of what constitutes a fair distribution of the sacrifice of not having children, merely to maintain current imbalances of injustice.[9]

In conclusion I wish to briefly mention the topic of people's perception of justice, and how important their perception is. Perhaps, in some case, it is more important than actual just results. The well known problem is, that injustice may be perceived as justice, while justice may be perceived as injustice. Elster,[10] (following Kahneman and Tversky) shows that what people consider to be just may depend upon "framing effects" or the various ways in which just procedures or justice policies are verbally presented, argued for (and one might add, contrasted with other alternatives). This idea is akin to talking about rhetoric and favorable and unfavorable and effective and ineffective labeling. So, for example, the funding for some program of social justice (e.g., school reform) may be perceived of as just because it purports to meet some important or urgent public need, (violence in High Schools, lowered test scores), not because the funds allocated would be effective in solving those needs. These sorts of policies may be of genuine intent, but have only symbolic significance. However, even if those who are supposed to benefit from the policy do not, they too may feel that justice has been somehow done, thus substituting moral satisfaction for actual justice.

**Professor of Philosoply, the University of West Florida*

# Notes

1. The phrase "local" justice refers to Jon Elster, 1992, *Local Justice.* New York: Russell Sage Foundation. This is a good summary of distributive procedures and goals. This also contains an interesting overview and treatment of many of the latest arguments over differing justice policies.

2. William C. Louthan, 1979, *The Politics of Justice*. Port Washington: Kennikat Press Corp.

3. Richard A. Posner, 1972, *Economic Analysis of Law.* Boston: Little, Brown and Company; Ronald Dworkin, 1977, *Taking Rights Seriously.* Cambridge: Harvard University Press; John Rawls, 1971, *A Theory of Justice.* Cambridge: Harvard University Press; Norman Thomas, 1931, *America's way out: a program for Democracy.* New York: The MacMillan Company; Henry George, 1886, *Progress and Poverty: an Inquiry into the Causes of Industrial Depressions, and of Increase of Want with Increase of Wealth; the Remedy*. New York: Henry George; Russell Kirk, 1953, *The Conservative Mind, from Burke to Santayana.* Chicago: H. Regnery Company; Friedrich A. Hayek, 1948, *Individualism and Economic Order*, Chicago: University of Chicago Press; Ayn Rand, 1964, *The Virtue of Selfishnes: a New Concept of Egoism.* New York: New American Library.

4. W. G. Runciman, 1966, *Relative Deprivation and Social Justice: a Study of Attitudes to Social Inequality in Twentieth-Century England.* Berkeley: University of California Press.

5. Charles Sanders Peirce, 1955, *Philosophical Writings of Peirce.* New York: Dover Publications; Ferdinand de Saussure, 1966, *Course in General Linguistics.* New York: McGraw Hill Book Co.

6. Claude Levi-Strauss, 1969, *The Raw and The Cooked.* New York: Harper & Row; 1966, *The Savage Mind.* London: Weidenfeld & Nicolson.

7. James Boyd White, 1985, *Heracles' Bow Essays on the Rhetoric and Poetics of the Law.* Madison: The University of Wisconsin Press.

8. William C. Louthan, *The Politics of Justice.* see note 2.

9. See for example Dennis L. Soden, 1988, *The Tragedy of the Commons: Twenty Years of Policy Literature 1968–1988.* Monticello: Vance Bibliographies; and Barry Commoner, 1976, *the Poverty of Power: Energy and the Economic Crisis*. New York: Alfred Knopf.

10. Jon Elster, *Local Justice.* see note 1.

# Chapter 6: Implications of the Multicultural Turn for the Practice of Morality

J. Ralph Lindgren*

Multiculturalism is being usefully addressed in a variety of ways. Some discuss it as a state of affairs (Gutmann, 171), others as a philosophical doctrine (Wolf, 785), and still others as a political agenda (Geyer, 513). The approach taken here is akin to all of these, but more narrowly focused on multiculturalism as the object of a decision, viz., the decision to recognize the existence of a plurality of cultures. "Culture" is used here to mean groups organized by a distinctive set of values. "Recognize" is used here in a diplomatic sense of acknowledging the status of other cultures. Thus, for example, the Palestine Liberation Organization recently recognized that state of Israel. The acknowledgement involved here is also similar to acknowledging a deed, which amounts to accepting or certifying that it is legally binding. The idea here is that once acknowledgment is made that another population lives by a distinctive set of values, a certain status is accorded that group, a status that carries with it an obligation of impartiality at some appropriate level. Thus, once the Quakers of colonial Pennsylvania recognized the Lenni Lenape as another culture, they were arguably under obligation to avoid such exploitative practices as "the Walking Purchase."

The decision of whether or not to recognize, acknowledge or grant status to a population that lives by lights that are not altogether compatible with one's own has implications not only for the future dealings of the respective groups, but also for the way each can carry on it own moral thinking. This paper draws out some of the latter implications and suggests the minimal adjustments needed for coping with them.

## Moral Monism

To the extent that one elects not to recognize a plurality of cultures, morality consists in a range of exercises that perform basically two functions — cultural grooming and adjudication of conflict. Thus, morality in its dimension as education helps members to straighten out the tangles that creep into their moral lives, to extend an already shared way of life into new or novel areas, and to prepare for fulfilling key roles in the cultural. Doing so both affords needed psychic comfort and provides guidance as well. Hence, the metaphor of cultural "grooming."

The second function of morality is the more directly affected by the multicultural turn and so will be the main focus here. Morality in its adjudicative function is a particular form of conflict settlement. It treats all conflicts as disputes and presumes that all disputes are resolvable by adjudication. In support of that process, the values supported by the culture are ordered hierarchically in order to assure that moral values override aesthetic values as well as individual preferences, and that the more important moral values override less important ones when these conflict. This approach to conflict settlement is often called ethical monism. "Monists think that the conflicts [among incompatible values] can be resolved because it is possible to establish an authoritative system of values in which there is a highest value that will justifiably override lower ranked values and in which the standing of all values will be determined by their contribution to the highest ranked value."(Kekes, 19)

To the extent that one does not recognize a plurality of cultures, one is at liberty to view non-conforming individuals and populations as beyond the pale — as wicked, heathen, barbarian. Since the way of life held to be distinctive of one's own culture is regarded as the standard for right thinking and right living, those who deviate from its norms necessarily diverge from all justified form of life, and so are eligible for extermination, enslavement, exploitation, ostracization, manipulation, etc.

The classic objection to morality in this form is that, in a diverse environment, it tends to encourage too dangerous a course of action. The practice of morality in the absence of a recognition of a plurality of cultures is predicated on the conviction that there is one right answer to all conflicts, both within and among groups, an answer that permits, even demands, enforcement against recalcitrants. This posture is too reminiscent of the bloody religious wars of the past and present to retain credibility. Isaiah Berlin, for example, saw ethical monism as an encouraging final solutions.

> The possibility of a final solution — even if we forget the terrible sense that these words acquired in Hitler's day — turns out to be an illusion; and a very dangerous one. For if one really believes that such a solution is possible, then surely no cost would be too high to obtain it: to make mankind just and happy and creative and harmonious for ever what could be too high a price to pay for that? To make such an omelette, there is surely no limit to the number of eggs that should be broken - that was the faith of Lenin, of Trotsky, of Mao, for all I know of Pol Pot. (Berlin, 15)

## Failed Attempts to Salvage Moral Monism in Diverse Environments

There appears to be no logical requirement that a culture accord overriding importance to the peaceful settlement of conflicts with non-conforming individuals and populations. After all, capital punishment and holy war are time honored approaches to diversity. However, to the extent that peoples draw lessons of pacific settlement from the experience of long and bloody conflict, they may elect to according some status to non-conforming populations. The most popular way of envisioning how to harmonize dangerously conflicting cultures and doing so in a way that does not seriously disrupt the existing practice of morality is by regarding all recognized cultures, including one's own, as part of a mega-culture, the moral values of which are satisfied by all peoples, except in their own unique ways. We find that suggestion in expressions such as "we are all children of God" and "we all belong to the human family." Another familiar appeal along these same lines bids contending factions to focus on "the common good." Larry May, for example, urged that:

> Communal harmony is best sustained when all of the members of a community are striving to advance the common good. Many of the most serious harms perpetrated within a group are the result of internal conflicts in which one faction is pitted against another. ... When the members of a community see themselves as sharing responsibility for the harms that are perpetrated within, and by, their communities, they will come to share a sense of respect for one another that will diminish harm and advance the common good. (May, 171)

The fatal difficulty that attends the mega-culture approach is that the values supported by diverse cultures are often incompatible, not simply alternative expressions of the basically the same form of life. Rawls acknowledged this when accepting "the fact of diversity." (Rawls 1993, 36–7) He went on to attempt to salvage not all of morality, but the more limited "domain of the political." (Rawls 1993, 38)

Based on his longstanding conviction that "justice is the first virtue of social institutions," (Rawls 1971, 3) Rawls insists that stable, democratic institutions cannot be sustained unless they are regarded as just by the great bulk of participants, i.e., as warranted by overriding moral values honored in their various cultures. (Rawls 1993, 35) The challenge, as Rawls sees it, is to show how this can be accomplished, given that no comprehensive set of moral values enjoys universal support in modern democracies. Stable cultures require a consensus among members at least on the values in terms of which the justice of their social arrangements are to be assessed. However, these values need not be the architectonic feature of a master set of values to which alternative conceptions are subordinate. They may be, Rawls now thinks, only a component that is compatible with the principal value systems supported within the population. This approach to satisfying the requirements of justice is what Rawls calls a political conception. "The political conception is a module, an essential constituent part, that in different ways fits into and can be supported by various reasonable comprehensive doctrines that endure in the society regulated by it." (Rawls 1993, 12, 144–5) The potential of the political conception of justice lies in that, were the principles it proposes found acceptable by contending cultures, they could serve as the basis for adjudicating conflicts among them. In this way "political liberalism looks for a political conception of justice that we hope can gain the support of an overlapping consensus of reasonable religious, philosophical, and moral doctrines in a society regulated by it." (Rawls 1993, 10)

The universal module approach to conflict settlement, as I will call it, relies on two assumptions. First, otherwise incompatible value systems would be rendered harmonious in their operation if only all would incorporate the same principles by which to resolve intercultural disputes. If there were a consensus among competing cultures on these pivotal substantive standards, the most disruptive challenges to the stability of democratic institutions could be resolved. Second, the principles proposed for inclusion in the universal module — the familiar equal liberty and difference principles, often referred to jointly as "justice as fairness" (Rawls 1993, 5–6) — are not partisan. The idea here is that justice as fairness is impartial as between cultures and so is worthy of incorporation into each of them. Critiques of the impartiality assumption are reviewed here, those of the consensus assumption are deferred until the next this section.

One criticism of the universal module approach is that it fails to avoid partisanship. Indeed, it fails even to avoid the most obvious forms of favoritism. Rawls is quite overt about rejecting those cultures that cannot approve justice as fairness. For him, these fail the test of reasonableness and so must be ruled out in principle. There can be no toleration of political views that are rooted in 'unreasonable' doctrines. "[T]he practical task [occasioned by such unreasonable views is that] of containing them — like war and disease — so that they do not overturn political justice." (Rawls 1993, 64n19. Also see: 152) Another way that the claim of impartiality fails is that under justice as fairness people loyal to cultures that do not give pride of place to tolerance and pacific resolution of conflict tend to lose out under the ordinary workings of social institutions. "[W]ays of life that depend upon close and exclusive bonds of language and culture — The French in Canada or the Bretons in France — may lose, within a liberal society also tolerating quite different and more open ways of life, some of the authority and cohesion that they would have if they formed complete societies unto themselves." (Larmore 43)

## Cooperation without Consensus

Even assuming that partisanship could be avoided in formulating the principles of justice that are to make up the universal module, the consensus assumption exposes the universal module approach to a fatal objection. When considered abstractly, the prospect that competing convictions can be reconciled if common ground could be found in a process of adjudication according to agreed principles seems workable. However, when considered in concrete terms, a consensus on procedure and even on substance turns out to be both insufficient to generate agreement on results among divergent cultures and unnecessary for the maintenance of cooperative associations.

The universal module approach relies on the sufficiency of a consensus on the principles of justice. That seems plausible in the abstract. However, considered more closely the module neglect to consider that both procedural and substantive considerations must be interpreted when applied to the resolution of disputes. Such interpretations inevitably are projected in terms of the background values of the cultures that develop them. So, even if there is a consensus over the procedures that are to be followed in resolving disputes of a given type, there is always, among diverse cultures, the likelihood of divergence over how that procedure is to be applied.

> For one thing, even where there is a consensus about process, there may nevertheless be sharp disagreement regarding matters of implementation. Even where people agree on, say maintenance of law and order, civility of interaction, an equitable distribution of resources—and many other such 'procedural' principles of human action in the public domain—such procedural agreements are much too abstract to define particular public policies. (We can agree on the need for 'law and order' and yet (quite plausibly) disagree sharply on questions of civil disobedience and the limits of appropriate protest.) Process consensus is a lot to ask for—but , still is not sufficient for a benign social order. (Rescher 171)

Nor does a consensus on substantive principles fair any better. Rawls' reading of modern history finds that western peoples who are committed to widely diverse belief systems nevertheless assent to a modest list of common substantive principles. In spite of our differences we assent, e.g., to religious toleration and to the prohibition of slavery. Rawls hopes to build on that overlapping consensus on substantive principles. (Rawls 1993, 8) But this move neglects to take seriously the differing reasons within each culture for assenting to these principles and so neglects to anticipate that peoples in different cultures are likely to place very different interpretations upon even those principles which, when stated abstractly, appear to announce deep common ground. A variety of incommensurable interpretations even of such settled convictions as religious toleration is supported by significant numbers of citizens. For example, some interpret the Establishment Clause as requiring government neutrality as between theist and non-theists convictions, while others interpret it as requiring only non-alignment of government with respect to various forms of theism. (Lindgren 113–16)

Whereas the universal module approach relied on the assumption that a consensus across cultures on principles of justice can be sufficient to found a stable and diverse culture, Rawls' rejection of the more pragmatic approach to culture-building that he styles a "mere modus vivendi" is based on the assumption that such a consensus is a necessary condition for a stable culture amid circumstances of diversity. (Rawls 1993, 144–50) In this conviction, Rawls has a great deal of company. James Hunter, for example, questions the viability of public institutions in a democracy in the absence of a public philosophy. "... [W]ithout a common agreement about what is good or what is right (or at least about the rules for determining the good and the right), all that remain are the particularistic claims about what is good and what is right articulated by varying and opposing factions." (Hunter 313)

Amos, the Hebrew prophet, posed the following question long ago: "Can two walk together unless they be agreed?" (Amos 3:3) Replying in the negative, both Rawls and Hunter are convinced that stable cooperative arrangements cannot be sustained in a democratic society in the absence of a consensus on at least a short list of basic moral principles. Were that position defensible, the burden of the decision to recognize a plurality of cultures would be enormous. Fortunately, it is not defensible.

Margaret Gilbert recently presented an explicit case in favor of the view that consensus is necessary for the maintenance of cooperative arrangements. Relying on an analysis of our concept of 'shared action,' she pointed out that the physical proximity of two walkers is not sufficient to establish that they are walking together. One of them might be distressed by the presence of the other, in which case they clearly are not "walking together." Were both agreed on the goal of walking side by side for a time, the matter would be more promising. Under those conditions, each would be "entitled to rebuke" the other, should he draw ahead or fall behind, an entitlement which is paired with obligations on the part of both walkers to avoid falling subject to such criticisms. On Gilbert's analysis "walking together" requires that "each party has made it clear to the other that he is willing to *join forces* with the other in accepting the goal that they walk in one another's company." (Gilbert 7) On Gilbert's analysis, unless the parties to a cooperative arrangement are entitled to criticize one another whenever one diverges from the agreed upon goal or process, there is no way to distinguish their arrangement from a temporary confluences of particularistic behaviors.

The case against the thesis that consensus is a necessary condition of cooperation rests on three sets of counter-examples. First, animals other than human beings exhibit in a vast array of stable cooperative rituals. Geese fly in formation. Prairie dogs signal approaching danger to others in their communities. Pilot fish clean the teeth of sharks hundreds of times their size. No credible evidence exists that any of the cooperative arrangements that abound in the rest of nature rely on entitlements to criticize non-compliance or on agreements at to goals or principles.

Second, in a powerful recent critique of the consensus thesis, Nicholas Rescher listed an impressive array of human cooperative schemes that are not predicated on jointly accepted goals, but are also of considerable antiquity.

> *Few-Party Electoral Systems.* Electoral systems of the few-party, winner-take-all type familiar in the English-speaking democracies involve an adversarial process that is very remote from any sort of consensus-tropism. In such systems, issues are resolved by majority vote (or some close cousin thereof), rather than by mechanisms that militate towards the formation of a communal consensus of the sort at issue (for example) in the business meetings of the Quaker sect. ...
>
> *Anglo-American Legal Procedures.* In the Anglo-American tradition, legal proceedings, be they civil or criminal, are strictly adversarial procedures. The system does not endeavor to bring the conflicting parties into the consensus of a voluntary or constrained agreement: its very heart and soul is conflict and adversarial antagonism. ...
>
> *Binding Arbitration* Binding arbitration is now widely used in developed societies as a process for settling conflicts in labour relations and for resolving contractual disputes. In such situations, the arbitrator is not, however, a 'marriage counsellor'—a negotiation facilitator who tries to bring the parties to a consensual meeting of minds, leading them towards a commonly agreeable solution that they will mutually regard as just and proper. On the contrary, so far as those two conflicting parties are concerned, the process is a fundamentally adversarial one. ...
>
> *Intellectual Conflicts.* Throughout science, scholarship, and the professions, there is a pervasive conflict among rival ideologies, methodologies, or theories. In virtually every setting of intellectual endeavor (any profession, discipline, or specialty), the phenomenon of rival 'schools of thought' is commonplace. Such schools of thought are in a condition of conflict and rivalry, competing for the adherence of 'the larger community' and—perhaps most importantly—for that of posterity. ... (Rescher 159–63)

The third and perhaps most compelling set of counter-examples come from market-centered economies. Adam Smith observed long ago that although goods and services are exchanged in markets "according to an agreed valuation" (Smith 1976a, 86), that value is not decided "by any accurate measure, but by the higgling and bargaining of the market, according to that sort of rough equity which, though not exact, is sufficient for carrying on the business of common life." (Smith 1976b, I:49) Furthermore, although the greater part of our needs are satisfied through the cooperation of others, that cooperation is typically not secured by appeal to a consensus on moral principles.

> Whoever offers to another a bargain of any kind, proposes to do this. Give me that which I want and you shall have this which you want, is the meaning of every such offer; and it is in this manner that we obtain from one another the far greater part of those good offices which we stand in need of. It is not from the benevolence of the butcher, the brewer, or the baker, that we expect our dinner, but from their regard to their own interest. We address ourselves, not to their humanity but to their self-love, and never talk to them of our own necessities but of their advantages. Nobody but a beggar chuses to depend chiefly upon the benevolence of his fellow citizens. (Smith 1976b I:26–7)

Since the eighteenth century, market-centered economies have gained widespread acceptance among liberals and progressives. Jules Coleman recently pointed out that one of the great attractions of markets "is the fact that they allow interaction among individuals without first requiring or presuming the existence of broad agreement about fundamental values, goods, or ends among exchange partners. ... In some ways, this may be a shortcoming of markets, but it is an important virtue as well." (Coleman 62–3)

## Legitimacy without Obligation

Jettisoning the ancient hope of universal community based on consensus is not the only implication of the multicultural turn. The legitimacy of institutional authority has traditionally turned on claims of moral obligation, and in particular on claims of justice. These are made good by showing that key moral values are supported by the institutions in question. To the extent that such claims are made good, the authority is deemed legitimate and members of that culture are held to be under moral obligation to support the institution. In a diverse modern society this linkage between moral values and institutional legitimacy can be accomplished only by privileging the values of a restricted sub-set of affected cultures. Doing so, however, is inconsistent with the decision to recognize other groups as cultures. By taking the multicultural turn one forgoes the prerogative of privileging the values of one's own culture as regards mutual dealings. Thus, those who claim both to recognize the right of mentally challenged citizens to live where they please and then oppose a zoning ordinance which would permit group housing for them in their own neighborhood on the grounds of "not in by back yard" are acting inconsistently.

Another of the implications of the multicultural turn, then, is that the legitimacy of social institutions cannot rest on their consistency with contested moral requirements. Moral obligation is too strong a basis for establishing institutional legitimacy in a culturally diverse setting. In such environments, only those who undertake special duties, e.g., by way of an oaths of office, are morally obligated to obey the law or support other institutions. (Raz 233–49)

The uncoupling of legitimacy from moral obligation is not as disastrous as might be feared. The legitimacy of institutional power does not requires that we collectively morally approve of either of the various configurations it takes or of uses to which it is put. Its legitimacy requires only that the vast majority of those affected by those powers find their way clear to going along with them. As Rescher recently argued, acquiescence is sufficient for legitimacy. "What matters for social harmony is not that we agree with one another, but that each of us acquiesces in what the other is doing, that we 'live and let live', so that we avoid letting our differences become a *casus belli* between us." (Rescher 164) On this view, the legitimacy of an institution or a regime is established if the great majority of those affected by it are not so dissatisfied that they are prepared to risk the consequences of an alternative arrangement, such as actual armed conflict. Rescher offered a particularly telling historical example in support of this analysis.

> Shortly after the end of the Civil War, in early 1866, Robert E. Lee, generalissimo of the just-defeated Confederacy, was asked to testify before a hostile Joint Committee on Reconstruction of the US Congress. Interrogated about the stance of the former secessionists towards Washington's plans and programmes for them, Lee was pressed on whether (as Senator Jacob M. Howard put it) 'they are friendly towards the government of the United States'? Choosing his words carefully, Lee replied, 'I

> believe they entirely *acquiesce* in the government'. The difference between *acquiescence* and *agreement* cannot be shown much more clearly. (Rescher 164–5)

This approach to legitimacy takes the same approach as that adopted to businesses which operate in a free market economies. The ones that deserve to survive, the ones that are owed our support, are those that better serve their clientele. As such, the move to base legitimacy on acquiescence is apt to strike us as at once exciting and risky. Exciting in that it provides another incentive for institutions to strive for increased productivity. Risky in that it portends instability unless present institutions are perceived by the great bulk of the people who are affected by them as preferable to available alternatives. Rawls rejects this approach out of concern for the risk it poses to stability. Acquiescence cannot found a stable association, according to Rawls, because the arrangements that are tolerable fluctuate with the changing interests and relative power positions of the parties. (Rawls 1993, 147) William Galston, on the other hand, is less averse to relying on acquiescence. He points out that while some may well go along with the institutions of a society because they are not presently so dissatisfied at to mount armed struggle, others are likely to go along with them for more positive reasons. Some go along because they agree with some of the outcomes that the institutions generate. Still others deeply believe in the function they perform in society. When the mix of motives for "going along" is favorable relative to available alternatives, an institution has quite a stable outlook.

> A society can be legitimate if the preponderance of its members conscientiously subscribe to it while the rest stand in what Rawls would call a modus vivendi relationship to it. Those in the latter category will seek in the long run to alter the basic structure of society as their relative bargaining position improves, and in the short run they may feel compelled to engage in selective nonobedience. These sorts of reservations are tolerable (within limits); in any event, they are inevitable. (Galston 298)

## Morality without Pretense

A decision to recognize other cultures requires that one relinquish the prerogative of assessing everyone's conduct and all institutions by the values that inform one's own way of life. Once the multicultural turn is taken, morality must become less pretentious. One must then resist the impulse to proclaim moral truth for all times and all peoples. The alternative is continued pressure toward final solutions and holy wars. How might the reach of moral claims be restrained? One constraint that would suffice would be a commitment to relativism — the view that the merit of normative judgments is limited to the cultures in which they occur. Were cultural relativism adopted the authority of moral values would have to be abandoned not only with respect to cross-cultural dealings, but also as regards dealings that occur entirely within one's own cultural.

Relativism, however, is an unnecessarily strong constraint upon the practice of morality. People who are proud members of cultures with strong traditions of moral education may be expected to find that too high a price to pay for multiculturalism. Fortunately, it a price that is not required by the multicultural turn. Relativism is not implicated by the decision to recognize a plurality of cultures. That decision does not commit one only to the view that, in a culturally diverse environment, there are a multiplicity of truths of the matter, each valid only within a distinct culture. It does not require that one take a position on whether there is a truth of the matter in moral disputes, and if so, which truth claim should be endorsed.

Susan Wolf argued that the answers to such questions are indeterminate. (Wolf 789) Such ontological claims, however, are also unnecessarily strong. The multicultural decision does not commit one to any particular moral ontology. What it does commit one to is the weaker epistemological claim that in a culturally diverse context we are often not in a position to decide such questions. The answers to questions of moral truth, when posed in a culturally diverse settings, are underdetermined.

The weaker epistemological constraint upon the practice of morality in a diverse cultural environment is analogous to one reason that the U.S. Supreme Court occasionally gives for avoidance of judgment. The Court regards some types of disputes as inappropriate for decision by a court. These are said to be non-justiciable. Of these, one in particular is in point here, viz., those that turn on "political questions." These are disputes that are deemed inappropriate for judicial resolution because, among other things, of "a lack of judicially discoverable and manageable standards for resolving them." (*Baker v. Carr*, 369 U.S. 186, 217 (1962))

In culturally diverse contexts, we often come across much the same type of situation as regards the issuance of moral judgments. Disputes abound over how to evaluate behavior prohibited by one culture recognized within a society, but enjoined by another. The criminalization of polygamy in the Utah Territory during the last Nineteenth Century turned on just such an issue. No standards were available then for its resolution by principled adjudication. When the Court decided to uphold those statutes (*U.S. v. Reynolds*, 98 U.S. 145 (1879), it either violated the status that had been accorded the Mormons or, as is more likely, showed that it did not recognize Mormonism as a culture. Where the Court to have resisted the impulse to reach beyond scope of discoverable and manageable standards in that situation, it would have required the government to adopt a live and let live policy and overturned the statutes for Free Exercise reasons. So also would moralists of the day who spoke for traditions that regarded monogamous marriage as sacred.

As Berlin observed, it is the pretentiousness of moral conviction that sends chills up the spines of all who are deeply apprehensive about the prospect of continued holy wars. This paper might be seen as a proposal about how moral conscientiousness might be retained the while we recognize one another's differences. The contention here is that peaceful coexistence is attainable, even in the midst of acknowledged incompatibilities, if only we carefully avoid pressing our ways of life upon one another, whether out of missionary zeal or from righteous indignation. With the exception of including this lesson of the multicultural turn, the practice of morality in its dimension as cultural grooming, can remain as vibrant as ever. We can all go on encouraging one another to adhere faithfully to the authoritative moral values of our own cultures, the while showing respect for the cultures of others by steadfastly resisting the impulse to issue authoritative moral evaluations of conduct and institutions in those areas of public life in which we lack discoverable and manageable standards for resolving cross-cultural disputes.

By way of illustration, the approach urged here for multicultural moralists would not only support constitutional protections against discrimination based on sexual preference, but would also oppose linking "most favored nation status" and improvement in a nation's "human rights" record. In this way, a less pretentious practice of morality is likely to offend against political correctness on both the right and the left. This may be the most credible way to showing that it is onto something!

Since classical Greece the term "justice" has been used to denote those properties that distinguish practices and institutions that deserve the support and loyalty of peoples they affect from those in which that support is optional. It is in this sense that John Rawls proclaims that "justice is the first virtue of institutions." (Rawls 1971 p. 3) For example, if a government is found to be just, subjects are held to be under obligation to obey its commands or laws. The clear implication of these conclusions reached in this paper is that the recognition of a plurality of incompatible cultures requires that justice relinquish the position as the first virtue of institutions to the more pragmatic quality of workability. In a context of value pluralism, justice cannot be the primary concern.

**Clara H. Stewardson Professor of Philosophy at Lehigh University.*

# References


Berlin, Isaiah. 1991. *The Crooked Timber of Humanity*. New York: Alfred A. Knopf.

Coleman, Jules. 1992. *Risks and Wrongs*. Cambridge: Cambridge University Press.

Galston, William A. 1991. *Liberal Purposes: Goods, Virtues, and Diversity in the Liberal State*. Cambridge: Cambridge University Press.

Geyer, Michael. 1993. "Multiculturalism and the Politics of General Education," 19 *Critical Inquiry* 499–533.

Gilbert, Margaret. 1990. "Walking Together: A Paradigmatic Social Phenomenon," in Peter French, et al. (eds.) *The Philosophy of Human Sciences*. Midwest Studies in Philosophy XV. Notre Dame, IN: Notre Dame University Press, 1–14.

Gutmann, Amy. 1993. "The Challenge of Multiculturalism in Political Ethics," 22 *Philosophy and Public Policy* 171–206.

Hunter, James D. 1991. *Culture Wars: The Struggle to Define America*. New York: Basic Books.

Kekes, John. 1993. *The Morality of Pluralism*. Princeton, NJ: Princeton University Press.

Larmore, Charles E. 1987. *Patterns of Moral Complexity*. Cambridge: Cambridge University Press.

Lindgren, J. Ralph. 1991. "Making the Transition to a Pragmatic Liberalism: Diversity, Contingency and Social Solidarity," 58 *The Modern Schoolman* 111–22.

May, Larry. 1992. *Sharing Responsibility*. Chicago: University of Chicago Press.

Rawls, John. 1971. *A Theory of Justice.* Cambridge, MA: Harvard University Press.

__________. 1993. *Political Liberalism.* New York: Columbia University Press.

Raz, Joseph. 1979. *The Authority of Law: Essays on Law and Morality.* Oxford: Clarendon Press.

Rescher, Nicholas. 1993. *Pluralism: Against the Demand for Consensus.* Oxford: Clarendon Press.

Smith, Adam. *1976 [1759]. The Theory of Moral Sentiments.* Oxford: Oxford University Press.

__________. 1976 [1776]. *An Inquiry into the Nature and Causes of the Wealth of Nations.* 2 vols. Oxford: University Press.

Wolf , Susan. 1992. "Two Levels of Pluralism," 102 *Ethics* 785–798.

# Chapter 7: Rawls on Justice—Once Again

Joseph Margolis*

For the scrupulous, moral theory is difficult at best: for the scrupulous cannot quite convince themselves that they are not merely promoting their utopian dreams or their distopian fears or catering to their own deep appetites all the while they try to be "neutral," "fair," "objective," "disinterested." I cannot see how to reassure them completely: I cannot see how objectivity in moral questions can be freed from whatever profound convictions we find ourselves harboring about the meaning of life and how it should be lived; and, about such convictions, I cannot see that there is any simple right or wrong to proclaim.

The history of moral philosophy is largely the history of ingenious minds that have not worried too strenuously about such questions. They see complexity all right; but, by and large, they get on with the business of working out what they suppose to be the best calculus. If, for instance, it were true that, as the animals they (we) are, humans manifested intractable cannibal proclivities, some philosophers would announce (perhaps on Aristotelian grounds) that these had their suitable place in a reasoned eudaimonism; and others (possibly on Kantian grounds) would regard their repudiation as prima facie evidence of the play of pure practical reason. If cannibal appetite were a fact, then, I say, it would not be likely that there would be *any* plainly true moral instruction that we could be sure of that would favor either policy—or any other, for that matter, that could come to terms with it—except for the vacuous instruction that we should, somewhere, come to terms with it pertinently. I am inclined to believe both responses could be counted on to generate a "reasonable" first case for an exemplary life. I am prepared in advance to honor each—without yielding to either—and I should not be the least troubled by the certainty that they would be incompatible with one another.

In a bookish way, I have always been impressed by Sophocles's immense humanity (and conceptual aplomb) in composing the *Antigone*, and even more by Aeschylus's sense, in the *Oresteia*, of the historicized conditions under which one great vision of justice supplants another without eliminating it. I see no reason to think my little parable could possibly put to rest these grander confessions of the inherent, probably unresolvable, conflicts of serious moral judgment. (The resolution of the *Oresteia*, I remind you, is the work of a very human *deus ex machina*.) The assurance that such conflicts can be resolved I regard as hopelessly utopian. The conviction that moral theory is therefore pointless I regard as extravagantly distopian. And the blithe pursuit of one or another theorizing response, to the exclusion of others incompatible with its own presumption, I regard as a kind of cannibal appetite.

## I

I have just read with interest John Rawls' citation, in his recent book *Political Liberalism*,[1] of a delicious remark of Bossuet's: "I have the right to persecute you [Bossuet declares] because I am right and you are wrong."[2] Of course! The only trouble is that contemporary moral philosophy is—at least secretly—unsure of any such grounds. I am inclined to think moral philosophy *is* scrupulous in its heart but not in its printed word. But I may be wrong. In any case, to worry the point is suddenly to call into doubt my own grounds for believing that I could ever simply recognize a *morally reasonable* treatment of the supposed *fait* of our cannibalism. Could it be that the presumption that we know what such a treatment would be like is already the hostage of our philosophical scruple? I think so. More to the point, Rawls himself, surely one of the most thoughtful American discussants of what a *reasonable* moral and political vision involves, falls foul of Bossuet's pronouncement in his own fine labor to eschew it.

Rawls is worth quoting on the matter:

> Since many doctrines are seen to be reasonable, those who insist, when fundamental political questions are at stake, on what they take as true but others do not, seem to others simply to insist on their own beliefs when they have the political power to do so, Of course, those who do insist on their beliefs also insist that their beliefs alone are true: they impose their beliefs because, they say, their beliefs are true and not because they are their beliefs. But this is a claim that all equally could made; it is also a claim that cannot be made good by anyone to citizens generally . . . . reasonable

> persons see that the burdens of judgment set limits on what can be reasonably justified to others, so they endorse some form of liberty of conscience and freedom of thought. It is unreasonable for us to use political power, should we possess it, or share it with others, *to repress comprehensive views that are not unreasonable*.[3]

Rawls has put his finger on the strategic question. I don't mean the question of moral liberalism extended to political behavior. There is that, of course; and, in that regard, *Political Liberalism* is the clear sequel of *A Theory of Justice*,[4] which it (that is, the new book) builds upon (and corrects).[5] I mean that Rawls implies a principled distinction between the *truth* of divergent, possibly opposed, substantive moral doctrines or morally informed doctrines of practical political justice (those, for instance, that could claim to subscribe to liberal political democracy) and their being morally and politically *reasonable* (or its being "liberally" reasonable to make room for their political play *as* merely "reasonable"). Frankly, I cannot see how, if there is no assured ground on which to vote in Bossuet's favor, it is possible to vote (*still* in Bossuet's favor) by sorting out what *is* "reasonable" and "unreasonable" in the way of moral or morally informed political doctrine.

That is, I cannot see how to show that a sincere moral agent, convinced that Bossuet has gone too far (as a moral realist) but also convinced that he (that is, the agent) *can* spot, among competing "comprehensive" doctrines (without pretending to assess their truth), those that are politically "reasonable" and those that are not, would not be able to do Bossuet's dirty work for him with an entirely clean conscience—arguing all the while that he (the agent) never supposed he had the moral truth in his back pocket. I don't see the difference between the *objective truth* of realist moral claims and the *objective reasonableness* of moral claims (as such, in the political liberal's space), except that the second is bound to be more generous than the first and except that the explanation of the entailed policy might possibly involve setting aside a bivalent logic. Furthermore, on Rawls' argument, the force of political dispute—as distinct from moral dispute—can never *be* more compelling than the other, since it presupposes a fair resolution of the problem of defining moral justice.

The matter is complicated, as you see: I can afford only a few words in summarizing Rawls' very large thesis. The most important point is this: "political liberalism," in Rawls' hands, uses the (liberal) moral theory of "justice as fairness" as a "module" influencing only the "basic structure" of a political constitution. By this Rawls means that "the political conception of justice . . . is, of course, a moral conception," but it applies only to a particular constitutional structure (Rawls prefers "a modern constitutional democracy")—that is, it applies, largely, only procedurally.[6] The "political conception of justice" that results is "a freestanding view"; that is, "it offers no specific metaphysical or epistemological doctrine beyond what is implied by the political conception itself."[7] Hence, it is not a form of moral realism. The individual persons who participate politically certainly possess their own "metaphysical or epistemological doctrine[s]" that color *their* political roles. But the *liberal* judgment of what is "reasonable," or "unreasonable" to allow as politically fair interventions is *not* informed (as it would be for Bossuet) by any metaphysical or epistemological privilege. Fine. My charge, then, is that, as a matter of principle, Rawls cannot draw a demarcation line between questions of reasonableness that are either merely procedural or accord, procedurally, with whatever is substantive in "the political conception itself"; and that, as a consequence, Rawls cannot draw a demarcation between the moral realist's claim and his own. To fail to do so, however, is to confirm the futility of "justice as fairness" in the political space for which it was originally proposed.

## II

Consider, for instance, that I believe abortion to be morally wrong. More than that, though I recognize that there are many in my society who believe abortion to be morally acceptable (on certain grounds at least) and, believing that, scrupulously try to formulate a moral doctrine to back the claim up and place it in a suitable "metaphysical and epistemological" space. *I* believe, from the vantage of my own "comprehensive" moral view, that *their view is both morally and politically unreasonable.* How so? you ask. Well, I say, the matter of taking "an innocent life" is too deeply entrenched in my vision to permit me to concede that *any* doctrine that opposed it, while not demonstrably false, was not unreasonable. How could you *show* that I was *wrong*, or politically (even "liberally") *unreasonable*, so as to rule it out legitimately? I think it's plain there cannot be a principled ground for such a claim; and, lacking such a ground, *you* cannot show, in good conscience, that *anyone*, however agnostic about moral realism, could not effectively gain the same *political* end (the realist claims) by retreating to sweet reasonableness. I don't say Rawls is that kind of man, but how would he or could he rule such a move out? I can't see that he can, and I can't see how anyone can. (Rawls obviously thinks he can.)

I think this means: *if we can't know what is morally true, we can't know what is morally reasonable either.* If so, then, certainly, moral and political liberalism collapses on its own terms. More than that, we may suspect that even this most decent of moral theories must be deluding itself beyond the scruple of the original caveat with which I began.

I think there is something very deep in this that moral philosophy would rather not acknowledge. Don't misunderstand me. I am *not* saying that, if we give up something like Bossuet's sense of the confident discovery of what's "objectively" right and wrong, we must also give up a policy of debating what it is "reasonable" to allow to compete in the moral marketplace. I am not recommending moral skepticism. I say only that we cannot *know* what is morally reasonable and unreasonable if we cannot *know* what is true or false in moral matters. To shift from the true to the reasonable is not merely to replace one alethic policy by another, but to replace an epistemic (and ontic) policy as well. Rawls resists the admission, shifting from "theoretical realism" to "practical realism." Indeed, it is the key to his entire theory—and, of course, the key to liberalism itself. I am bound to expose the untenability of the thesis regarding justice. The collapse of liberalism is a mere by-product. Furthermore, if the argument holds for strict moral disputes, it cannot fail to hold for morally informed political disputes as well.

Consider that Rawls makes a brief reference to the abortion issue. He speaks in terms of respecting "three important political values: the due respect for human life, the ordered reproduction of political society over time . . ., and finally the equality of women as equal citizens. . . . Now I believe [he says] *any* reasonable balance of these three values will give a woman a duly qualified right to decide whether or not to end her pregnancy during the first trimester."[8] I don't find the argument anywhere, I must say. I happen to share Rawls' "prejudice" about what is "reasonable," but, at this point in the argument, that's all it is. I cannot see how it can be suitably universalized. And I cannot see how Rawls' argument works either in terms of the original moral notion of justice and rights or in terms of practical political liberalism (constitutional democracy, say).

In support of this provisional challenge, I offer three intuitions about theorizing on moral and political matters that I judge nearly all the best-known theories conflict with, which, once acknowledged, make them suspect in the deepest possible way: first, conjectures in the empirical sciences noticeably converge over time, without necessarily coming to a universally affirmed judgment or explanatory theory, whereas the reverse is true in moral and political matters; second, not only is there no general agreement about the validity of moral and political judgments on important and unavoidable matters (even if there often is an important measure of agreement about other such matters), there is also no general agreement about how to decide whether such agreement is or is not *reasonable* where deep disputes arise; and third, there is no principled distinction between what it means to say that someone knows or reasonably believes this or that in moral and political matters *in general* and how to *show* that someone *does* actually know or reasonably believe this or that *in particular*.

These are disarming intuitions. They do not appear to prejudice any substantive moral or political questions. Let me explain what I mean. If I say abortion is wrong, you may suppose that I mean that, if it is wrong, then: (i) it is wrong for all in *similar* circumstances, and (ii) it is wrong for *all* in these and those particular circumstances. Reasoning along line (i) simply ensures consistency of usage, and is not morally or politically serious in the abstract, although inconsistency certainly can have repercussions. Reasoning alone line (ii) captures what is sometimes called moral universality, which says that whatever is right or wrong for each *is* right or wrong only if it is right or wrong for all (relevantly). (Richard Hare had confused the two notions in his early discussions of universalizability.[9]) I say only that line (i) is morally trivial and line (ii), morally and politically doubtful.

Here, I have no pointed quarrel with either of these options. What I want to insist on, rather, is that there *is no way* to decide, empirically (or rationally, or reasonably, if that is supposed to make a difference), whether arguments in accord with (ii) *ever* obtain: there is no way to tell, for instance, whether *everyone*—or everyone acting "rationally" or "reasonably"—would agree (or would be found to agree) with any would-be moral or political pronouncement. One cannot help but idealize here. Fair enough. The only trouble then is that *every* such idealization presumes to discern either what is true or what is reasonable *in the moral or political way*, and that returns us to the difficulty mentioned earlier in connection with Rawls' reading of Bossuet. I think the abortion case makes this quite clear. Also, if we allow universalizability along line (ii) to be mere presumption, then it would be very hard to show that Rawls' strategy *was not* a cryptic version of the moral realist's view.

## III

The conundrum that lies at the base of Rawls' entire theory is the essential conundrum of the entire tradition of Western moral (and political) philosophy. I certainly don't think that all moral and political theorists are committed to liberalism. But they do sort themselves out in the following way: either they argue as moral realists, even if they don't share Bossuet's values; or if they give up the pretense of objective moral knowledge alleged to be on a par with objective science, they fall back to what is (objectively) rational or reasonable to believe morally (or politically); or if they give that up as well, they present themselves as moral skeptics. The important point to bear in mind is that these are *not* the only, or even the most viable or most interesting options. In fact, what I have just claimed is that Rawls *is* a kind of mild Bossuetian (or moral realist) who unwittingly obscures (by his own concessiveness) options that he never considers. Kant, I think, is the exemplary champion of the second option. So it is quite right that, as a Kantian himself, Rawls should be its most important liberal advocate—against the utilitarians, for instance, who are usually full-blown Bosseutians themselves.

The dialectical thrust of the argument goes very deep. I can't imagine tracing it effectively in any more reliable way than in Rawls' company. Start then with his picture of a liberal political society that (as he sees matters) precludes anything like Bossuet's own pronouncement:

> In a reasonable society, most simply illustrated in a society of equals in basic matters, all have their own rational ends they hope to advance, and all stand ready to propose fair terms that others may reasonably be expected to accept, so that all may benefit and improve on what every one can do on their own.[10]

If one really knew the answer to what was morally true and false about the "ends" of human life, there would be no need for political liberalism: it would be more than redundant, it would be irrelevant. Not knowing that, we fall back (Rawls believes) to "fair terms" that tolerate the idiosyncracy of the "ends" of others *within our political order*. "Political liberalism," Rawls says, "takes for granted not simply pluralism but the fact of reasonable pluralism." He asks us to consider the question: "How is it possible that deeply opposed though reasonable comprehensive doctrines may live together and all affirm the political conception of a constitutional regime?"[11]

To the counterquestion: "What is the 'reasonable'?" Rawls answers:

> The first basic aspect of the reasonable . . . is the willingness to propose fair terms of cooperation and to abide by them provided others do. The second basic aspect . . . is the willingness to recognize the burdens of judgment and to accept their consequences for the use of public reason in directing the legitimate exercise of political power in a constitutional regime.[12]

Rawls means of course that: (i) the liberal is justified in using force, politically, to disallow *unreasonable* "comprehensive doctrines" (or judgments or commitments that they subtend), but (ii) the liberal is not justified in doing so with regard to *reasonable* "comprehensive doctrines." Now, however diminished, isn't that the realist's outlook all over again?

I need to put one more piece of evidence in place before presenting my own objections. I say again that these objections are not directed merely against Rawls but against the entire drift of Western moral philosophy. I hold that the fatal weakness of the entire tradition, which gives up (politically) the pretense of any objective discovery of ultimate moral values, ultimate moral norms, ultimate moral "ends," but then insists on a more temperate objective judgment of what is "reasonable" and "unreasonable" (in spite of that), *cannot legitimate its claims*; and yet, that double failing *need not be judged to entail moral skepticism or moral or political anarchy*. I say that the essential mistake is the thesis of Rawls' own theory and that it is not merely local to liberalism. As you may now guess, its acknowledgement has the effect of placing the usual *three* categories of "moral philosopher" (mentioned above) in a larger space then the Western tradition is in the habit of admitting; in that sense (I say), we see that there are other possibilities for a "reasonable" morality (and politics). My argument up to this point has been to the effect that Rawls cannot show that *he* is not a moral realist, though he is certainly a liberal. But that can't be the whole of the story. One wants to know why Rawls should have slid back into the realist's camp, why he cannot escape doing so, why *no* analytic moral philosopher who is not a skeptic can escape.

That is a more interesting prize.

I shall risk one further clue before I supply the evidence I have in mind. (The clue will help explain the force of the evidence intended.) The clue is this: *thinking has (or is) inherently a history*; what is *rational* or *reasonable* is an artifact of human history. *There is no reason common to the human species that is timelessly such*—completely ahistorical in structure. Rawls is wrong to think that *if* Bossuet cannot in principle legitimate *his* extraordinary claim, it is still open to us to legitimate, as being objective in the universal sense (ii), claims about what it *is* "reasonable" to believe and act on. There's the mistake. The finding *I* offer is simply this: *justice, like the "reasonable" itself, which it is supposed to embody, is inherently historicized.*

Now for the last bit of evidence. Rawls anticipates the challenge I have just put to him, but he answers in an unacceptable way. Hear him out:

> why should free institutions lead to reasonable pluralism, and why should state power be required to repress it? Why does not our conscientious attempts to reason with another lead to reasonable agreement? It seems to do so in natural science, at least in the long run . . . . We might suppose, say, that most people hold views that advance their own more narrow interests, and since their interests are different, so are their views. Or perhaps people are often irrational and not very bright, and this mixed with logical errors leads to conflicting opinions. But while such explanations explain much, they are too easy and not the kind we want. We want to know how reasonable disagreement is possible, for we always start at first within ideal theory. Thus we ask: how might reasonable disagreements come about?

One explanation is this. Let's say that reasonable disagreement is disagreement between reasonable persons: that is, between persons who have realized their . . . moral powers to a degree sufficient to be free and equal citizens in a constitutional regime, and who have an enduring desire to honor fair terms of cooperation and to be fully cooperating members of society. Given their moral powers, they share a common human reason, similar powers of thought and judgment: they can draw inferences, weigh evidence, and balance compelling considerations.[13]

Of course, *this* doesn't quite explain "reasonable" disagreements. Rawls means to constrain such disagreements *within the uniformities of ideal reason.* The sources of disagreement that *are* reasonable, for Rawls, are then produced by what he calls "the burdens of judgment." Most of these have to do with such relatively neutral matters as "hard cases." They are not ultimately troubling. But not all the "burdens" are like that. Rawls finally comes to the essential "burden"—which Isaiah Berlin had (Rawls thinks) correctly marked in the following way: "Some among the Great Goods cannot live together. That is a conceptual truth. We are doomed to choose, and every choice may entail an irreparable loss."[14] Rawls straightforwardly accepts Berlin's instruction: "any system of institution," he says, "has, at it were, a limited social space."[15]

Of course Rawls is right to support Berlin. That's not the point. The point is: *if* he's right then: (i) liberalism cannot claim to be *reasonable* in the universalizing sense—*ever*; (ii) if (i) is true, then no moral or political philosophy that is not already committed to something like Bossuet's strong thesis can be *reasonable* in the universalizing sense—*ever*; and (iii) if (ii) is true, then no moral or political philosophy can—*ever*—be legitimated, if legitimation must accord with the second of the two senses of universality given. In the analytic tradition, the upshot of admitting (i)–(iii) is simply moral skepticism.[16] I claim, however, that we *can* avoid the conclusion, if we but historicize reason—*a fortiori*, if we historicize justice (and our other moral and political notions). But if we act thus, we cannot be liberals in Rawls' sense.

The nerve of the argument, then, is this. Either we claim to know what is morally right and wrong (Bossuet, metonymically); or, failing that or not invoking such a claim in the political context, we fall back to what is morally reasonable (the "original position") or what it is reasonable to allow in a certain constitutional space (liberal democracy, say). *We claim "objectivity" in both cases*. In the first, we fall back to metaphysical and epistemological realism; in the second, we do so in an attenuated way when we fall back to "justice as fairness" under "the veil of ignorance." It seems that we do not quite do that under the "modular" terms of political dispute: there we appeal "only" to universalizability (ii) among "reasonable" agents and with regard to whatever we import, "modularly," of the principles of justice that define our political space. On the argument I've mounted, however, neither the second nor this third strategy can be distinguished in practice or principle from a temperate version of the full-blown realist's assurance. The abortion dispute is the evidence of that: that is, the absence of any operative sense of "universalizability" (ii).

## IV

We must retreat a little to see what is at stake. I suggest an argument by analogy. Rawls himself provides the clue. "Reasonable disagreement is disagreement among reasonable persons," he says, in the longish citation I gave a moment ago. That means that the criteria of reasonableness are already in place *before* disagreement sets in. At least that is so if we "always start" (as Rawls says) "within ideal theory." What he means is that, first, reasonable disagreement presupposes ("within ideal theory") the theory of justice developed in *A Theory of Justice* (or something akin to it). He says as much: "the guidelines and procedures of public reason are seen as selected in the original position and belong to the political conception of justice."[17] (Now, *that is* realist in some sense.) Secondly, as I have just argued, the "reasonable" is *politically* or *practically* obliged to compromise with *whatever* we may suppose is essential to its application in the universalizing sense. (That was the "burden" of Berlin's "conceptual truth.") *Berlin's dictum doesn't really have to do with being "reasonable." It has to do with the fundamental values we presume to favor.* Rawls scants the point. Thirdly, and finally, Rawls supposes—the claim is the familiar one—that, at least as moral agents, we "share a common human reason, similar powers of thought and judgment: [we] can draw inferences, weigh evidence, and balance compelling considerations." (This also comes from the longish citation.) It is this third constraint I now wish to challenge.

I say Rawls is wrong in this; most of moral philosophy—most of philosophy, in fact—is similarly wrong. Here I draw your attention to the fact that Rawls has an opposite number in current European philosophy: namely, Jürgen Habermas (and, less neatly, Karl-Otto Apel). Habermas actually perceives that Rawls is a natural ally—and a natural opponent. Habermas (mistakenly) believes that the difference between them is merely that Rawls' argument is "monological" whereas his own is "dialogical" (that is, inherently social in its reclamation of what is morally reasonable: "rational," as Habermas prefers to say).[18] Habermas means by this that the mark of what is morally reasonable (not *a priori* in Apel's sense—or in Kant's, for that matter) cannot be worked out "objectively" in the monologic way. (*That*, he thinks, is the fatal weakness of Rawls' "original position," which, it is true, is methodologically solipsistic.) Habermas insists, however, that what is morally reasonable (or "rational") *can* be discerned, empirically, in the conditions of social communication—in its universalized form. He worries a bit, in passing, about the (same) difficulty Rawls fails to master in embracing Berlin's conceptual truth.[19] Like Rawls, however, and equally in the liberal spirit, Habermas fails to come to terms with the implications of idealizing the "reasonable." (In fact, it is not certain that Habermas is *not* a solipsist masquerading as a dialogist.) But if that were all there were to say, both Rawls and Habermas might suppose that a little tinkering might restore the doctrine to philosophical health. Here I invoke an argument by analogy.

One says, casually enough: it is against reason to offer as a genuine argument one that is known to violate the principle of noncontradiction. It is not "rational" to argue by way of violating the principle; and it is "unreasonable" to advance such an argument, where the interests of practical life require a valid argument. There is every reason to believe that both Rawls and Habermas support the claim. I do not oppose it, but it is completely vacuous. I go further: I say that, for any *interpreted* use of the principle of noncontradiction, it is always possible to relieve the charge by reinterpreted the terms of the argument. That is: if the principle of noncontradiction is a necessary truth, no sentence interpreted as a contradiction is *necessarily* so interpreted. Thus, if you say, with Aristotle,[20] that noncontradiction *is* a necessary truth, then it is important to insist as well on the further truth—which Aristotle would deny—that there is no necessary way to interpret the world or our thinking about the world. Aristotle holds *that* to be a false doctrine (arguing against Protagoras), because he believes that there *are* necessities *de re* that have universal scope. Quine rejects such claims, of course.[21]

The point of arguing in this way is quite straightforward. There *is* no way of formulating any *prior* rule of reason (like noncontradiction) in purely formal, uninterpreted terms that *then* may be said to apply, criterially, universally, necessarily, uniformly, to all interpreted sentences and arguments. The formal rules of reason are no more than abstracted (perhaps idealized) *from* natural-language usage—*for* at least the exemplars *of* such usage. A geometric argument interpreted as contradictory for Euclidean space might not be contradictory if interpreted for some non-Euclidean space. The paradoxes (the contradictions) generated by Bell's theorems for classical mechanics are not paradoxes (or contradictions) if we give up classical mechanics for quantum physics. It is a mistake, some have persuasively argued, to suppose that formal logic and mathematics are merely *applied* to the actual world, after having (somehow) first secured their necessary truths in their own abstract world. No, the argument goes, those "formal" disciplines are really part (even if they are a peculiar part) of the empirical sciences themselves.[22] If so, then there cannot be an ordered hierarchy of what is relevantly "reasonable" or "rational" that proceeds *from* uninterpreted sentential formulas and argument forms *to* interpreted sentences and interpreted arguments. The syntax and semantics of a language are inseparable.

The bearing of this seeming aside is this: just as there is no prior rule of reason that actual discourse must conform to in order to be reasonable or rational, so there is no *prior* sense of "reasonable person" in terms of which Rawls could relevantly claim that "reasonable disagreement is disagreement among reasonable persons." *That's all*! The argument fails—massively—and for a reason analogous to the one that affects Aristotle's argument.

In fact, there are two distinct lines of argument that Rawls pursues that parallel in an uncanny way those that Aristotle favors. One holds that there *are* prior rules of reason that cannot be violated, on pain of violating reason. The other holds that the rules of reason, though entirely formal, somehow *entail*—when applied in an interpreted domain—interpreted (necessary) truths apt for that domain. In Rawls' hands, this now means that the "lexicographical" account of justice offered in *A Theory of Justice* is already the work of "reasonable persons" in the "original position," behind "the veil of ignorance"[23]: hence, that, within the further space of a "constitutional regime," the acceptance of the principles of justice lead to the adoption of political liberalism—and *hence* to a "reasonable" policy on substantive matters like abortion. Nothing could be prettier. The only trouble is; it won't work. Where's the argument? Liberals are said to be able to recognize a "reasonable" disagreement because they are already "reasonable persons," having committed themselves to the substantive principles of justice mentioned. In *Political Liberalism*, Rawls "corrects" the failure to distinguish, in *A Theory of Justice*, between questions of "moral philosophy" and questions of "political philosophy."[24] He does not, however, give up or alter in essentials the theory of justice of the earlier book. He (now) admits that the questions a "reasonable person" might raise in the two contexts are not quite the same. In fact, it may happen that, *in* the political world, one may have cause to wonder whether the putatively "reasonable" theory of justice of Rawls' own (or another's) moral philosophy is actually viable in, or reconcilable with, the realities of political life. It was in this spirit that I drew attention to the implications of Berlin's dictum.

Furthermore, Rawls' philosophical strategy—"reflective equilibrium"-—by which he claims to arrive at the doctrine of "justice as fairness" is itself a most curious notion. It apparently proceeds by dialectically reviewing, first, "the conceptions of justice known to us through the tradition of moral philosophy and any further ones that occur to us," which are themselves fitted to our considered judgments on moral matters; what we there discern is then reflectively matched with what, independently and in the widest sense, "would be [the principle of justice] chosen in the original position in preference to other traditional conceptions of justice"; finally, "to be acceptable," "a political conception of justice" [that is, a constitution structured for producing justice] "must accord" with the outcome of the exercise of "reflective equilibrium." By this process, Rawls maintains, "justice as fairness moves us closer to the philosophical ideal; it does not of course achieve it."[25] What could Rawls possibly mean if he does not intend a diminished moral realism?

## V

What this shows very plainly is that Rawls must have ruled out at the very start the possibility that justice is a historically changing idealization of the actual evolving possibilities of human practice viewed against the accumulating tradition of moral and political philosophy. Certainly, Marx's best vision of an evolving moral and political ideal pursues such a possibility.[26]

Closer to Rawls' own sense of how to proceed (but opposed to his model) is the radically historicized conception developed at considerable length by Roberto Mangabeira Unger, which counters both the supposed historical "necessitarianism" of Marx and the static moral and political visions of liberals and libertarians.[27]

I am not recommending either Marx's or Unger's thesis. But *both* adopt what may be called "constructivist" conceptions of moral and political justice—of a sort that Rawls nowhere considers in sketching the "original position." Unlike Rawls, who also claims to be a "constructivist," both Marx and Unger hold—to my mind, convincingly—that: (i) *no* reflection at any single moment of time or at any series of discrete moments could possibly capture what is "rational" or "reasonable" in the way of conceiving justice; (ii) our moral and political beliefs and ideals are formed by the institutional circumstances of our actual and contingent social life; (iii) we are nevertheless thereby empowered to transform the "artifact" that is our society (the one in which we were formed) in ways that could not have been historically imagined before; and (iv) the imaginative prospects of justice depend on a critical review of, and projection from, continually radicalizing the evolving possibilities of social life against the ahistorical disposition of institutional inflexibilities and the thinking that goes with that disposition.

When Rawls introduces his own "constructivism," he contrasts it with "moral realism" (hence the pertinence of my returning to Bossuet). He lays out very cleanly the difference between his own view of "political constructivism" and the vision of "rational intuitionism" viewed as an exemplar of moral realism. The key distinctions (for my present purpose) are these. Moral intuitionism holds that "moral first principles and judgments, when correct, are true statements about an independent order of moral values . . . that are known by theoretical reason." "Political constructivism," on the other hand, holds that "the principles of political justice (content) may be presented as the outcome of a procedure of construction (structure) . . . based essentially on practical reason and not on theoretical reason." There are other considerations but these are the decisive ones. The moral realist adheres to the standard conception of truth, and the constructivist applies only "an idea of the reasonable" to the matters that arise in the political sphere.[28]

The entire issue may be seen to depend, therefore, on whether the manifestations of reason itself—the "rational" and/or the "reasonable"—*are* or *are not* artifacts of our historical life. For if they are, then the method of "reflective equilibrium" and the presumption of "political constructivism" simply misperceive the enabling condition under which the theory of justice *can* be made out to be "reasonable." On the argument, it cannot be reasonable except in historicized terms. I claim that the evidence that shows that Rawls has failed to make his own case for the native invariance of the "reasonable" is betrayed by his inability to keep himself from falling back to some attenuated form of moral realism (Bossuet's challenge), by his inability to accommodate Berlin's dictum (which is not a matter that can be settled by separating the "reasonable" from the "unreasonable"), and by his inability to make a principled (universalized) distinction between the reasonable and the unreasonable.

I draw two decisive conclusions from the foregoing: first, that, if we give up the presumption that there is an independently real moral order which we can discern, then the "objectivity" of the moral and political world can only be consensual, that is, a function of the convictions of those who reflexively judge their own judgments and behavior and actual prospects; second, that if we adopt the consensual view, then, on the argument given, universalizability (ii) cannot serve criterially. Now, I say: Rawls is unwilling to subscribe to the first, and the second goes contrary to his own conviction. That means not only that liberalism fails, but the entire family of views fails that makes universal consensus decisive without presuming cognitive resources in the "realist" sense (Kant, for instance, Habermas, Apel, Hare, Gewirth, Gauthier at least). *Reasonableness and rationality exhibit no determinate universal form in an interpreted and historical world.* Reasonableness is a "construction" as is moral and political justice—and for the same reason. It cannot function criterially, except as a historically provisional posit of consensual practice that is expressly not universalized. There is only one option by which to save the "consensual objectivity" of moral and political judgment—that is, if we are not to yield to the opportunistic and the merely arbitrary: *we must historicize justice and reasonableness.*

My sense, frankly, is that that *is* what Rawls trades on but is unwilling to admit. The liberal tradition *can* be recovered—in some way along Rawls' own lines—by giving up the fiction of the "original position," which already presumes a universally valid strategy, and by giving up the fiction of universal consent, which is both profoundly inaccessible and incapable, as we have seen, of excluding the realist's presumption, or of meeting Berlin's dictum, or of distinguishing between "reasonable" and "unreasonable" options.

What is distinctive about these findings may not strike the eye at once. Of course, I give up the presumption of the moral realist; but Rawls is willing to do so as well. I also give up the criterial function of universalizability (ii), which Rawls pretends to be able to invoke—at least by approximation. I also historicize reason and the norms of justice. On both counts, Rawls is ambiguous; for, although justice is a construction, Rawls holds that, *by* construction, it is also an approximation to the "philosophical ideal"—which is not (apparently) constrained or skewed by a changing history. History, it seems, makes *our* approximation to the ideal more likely! But there is no sense in Rawls that the ideal might itself be a moving historical projection from what is possible here and now. If the *constructive* role of history were conceded, then of course the admission of the "original position" and of reasoning "under the veil of ignorance" would be worse that useless.

What is most telling in all this is that, as a moral constructivist, Rawls betrays the insoluble *aporia* of every constructivism that makes justice (or other moral and political norms) constructions of a rational or reasonable process but does not make reason (or the "reasonable") a historical construction as well. It is open to us, of course, to fall back to the moral realist's view, but there is no satisfactory defense of moral realism.[29]

What we see then is that there is no defense of the moral constructivist's view, *if it fails to treat reason as an artifact of social history.* That single adjustment is the only way in which to avoid the *aporiai* of Rawls' position (which are not merely local to Rawls) or the triumph of the moral skeptic. What it signifies is that we are bound to acknowledge the following constraints on moral and political theorizing: first, universalizing (ii) cannot be criterial; second, a bivalent logic cannot be suitable to moral and political theories of justice; and, perhaps most important, third, what is reasonable and unreasonable are *faute-de-mieux* claims relativized to what are institutionally or traditionally entrenched as reasonable. I mean that moral theory proceeds dialectically: *if* these or those doctrines are admitted to be "reasonable," *then* what you and I *now* offer may be shown (by current lights) to be *not less reasonable* than they.

I offer one final consideration against Rawls' thesis. Grant that, at some time $t$, some consensus is reached on a hotly contested political issue; now, grant further that *that* consensus begins to have a definite causal effect on the ongoing life of the society in which consensus has been reached. If so, then what will be regarded as a "reasonable" consensus at time $t+k$, later than $t$, will be a function of the causal history of the first decision and likely to conform to an altered conception of the "reasonable." This obvious argument shows: (a) that it is unreasonable to regard "reasonableness" as ahistorical, ideal, or relatively invariant; (b) findings about what is "reasonable" at any time $t_k$ are bound to depart from any would-be ideal, and are bound to vary from one society to another, from one subsociety to another, from one stage of any person's judgment to another; and (c) canny politicians, realizing this, might well plan a series of gradual policy changes, so that a congruent consensus could actually be built up by changing the tolerance of important sectors of a given society bit by bit. I don't insist that a policy of the (c)-sort can always be relied on; but it makes for a rational policy, on grounds that Rawls cannot allow and cannot discount. Principles of reasonableness, I should say, are inseparable from the actual historical experience of a viable society. That alone exposes the utter indefensibility of Rawls' doctrine.

Needless to say (once again with Sophocles and Aeschylus), conflicting values are not a sign of failure either at the level of moral judgment or at the level of moral theory. I claim that, once we give up realism, there is: (i) no way to avoid admitting, as judgments of what is morally and politically "reasonable," judgments that cannot be confined within a bivalent logic; and that there is: (ii) no way to avoid admitting that reason itself is a historical construction. Liberals cannot admit either concession but they cannot offset them either. Hence, liberalism fails. But that failure is not a local affair. Nearly all contemporary moral philosophies resist these concessions even if they eschew moral realism. That's why I say: either Rawls' theory leads to moral skepticism, or it leads to the two concessions I have just set down. *Tertium non datur.*

* *Professor of Philosophy, Temple University*

# Notes

1. John Rawls, *Political Liberalism.* New York: Columbia University Press, 1993, p. 61n.

2. This was cited in Susan Mendus, *Toleration and the Limits of Liberalism.* Atlantic Highlands: Humanities, 1989, p. 7, which Rawls mentions.

3. Rawls, *Political Liberalism*, p. 61; italics added.

4. John Rawls, *A Theory of Justice.* Cambridge: Harvard University Press, 1971.

5. Rawls, *Political Liberalism,* pp. xv–xvi.

6. Rawls, *Political Liberalism,* p. 11.

7. Rawls, *Political Liberalism,* p. 10.

8. Rawls, *Political Liberalism,* p. 243n32; italics added.

9. See Richard Hare, *Freedom and Reason.* Oxford: Clarendon, 1963, Ch. 2, for instance at pp. 12–13.

10. Rawls, *Political Liberalism*, p. 54.

11. Rawls, *Political Liberalism*, p. xviii.

12. Rawls, *Political Liberalism*, p. 54.

13. Rawls, *Political Liberalism,* p. 55.

14. Isaiah Berlin, "The Pursuit of the Ideal," *The Crooked Timber of Humanity.* New York: Knopf, 1991; cited in Rawls, *Political Liberalism,* p. 197n.32.

15. Rawls, *Political Liberalism,* p. 57.

16. See J.L. Mackie, *Ethics: Inventing Right and Wrong*. Harmondsworth: Penguin, 1977.

17. Rawls, *Political Liberalism*, p. 62.

18. See Jürgen Habermas, *Moral Consciousness and Communicative Action,* Trans. Christian Lenhardt and Shierry Weber Nicholsen. Cambridge: MIT Press, 1991, p. 198—in the context of "*Discourse Ethics*: Notes on a Program of Philosophical Justification," and "More Consciousness and Communicative Action."

19. See Habermas, "Discourse Ethics," §ii.

20. Aristotle, *Metaphysics,* Book Gamma.

21. See W.V. Quine, "Two Dogmas of Empiricism," *From a Logical Point of View*. Cambridge: Harvard University Press, 1953.

22. See John Stachel, "Comments on 'Some Logical Problems Suggested by Some Empirical Theories' by Professor Della Chara," in Robert S. Cohen and Marx W. Wartofsky (eds.) . Dordrecht: D. Reidel, 1983; and Hilary Putnam, "What Is Mathematical Truth?" and "The Logic of Quantum Mechanics," *Philosophical Papers,* Vol. 1 Cambridge: Cambridge University Press, 1975.

23. Rawls, *A Theory of Justice*, pp. 42–43; §26.

24. Rawls, *Political Liberalism,* pp. xv, xxx.

25. Rawls, *A Theory of Justice,* pp. 49–50; *Political Liberalism,* pp. 9–10.

26. For a general overview of this aspect of Marx's conception, see Joseph Margolis, "Praxis and Meaning: Marx's Species Being and Aristotle's Political Animal" in George E. McCarthy (ed.) . Savage, Md.: Rowman and Littlefield, 1992.

27. See, for instance, *False Necessity—Anti-Necessaritarian Social Theory in the Service of Radical Democracy* (Part I of *Politics, A work in Constructive Social Theory*) Cambridge: Cambridge University Press, 1987, Ch. 1.

28. Rawls, *Political Liberalism,* pp. 90–94.

29. See Joseph Margolis, "Moral Realism and the Meaning of Life," *Philosophical Forum,* XXII (1990).

# Chapter 8:
# Natural Law or Social Contract? The Foundation of Rights in Hobbes and Locke

William E. Murnion*

A comparative analysis of the foundation of rights in the political theories of Thomas Hobbes and John Locke is warranted as much by recent international debate about the universality of human rights[1] as by renewed scholarly interest in the revolutionary origins of American democracy.[2] The basic issue today is the same as it was when Hobbes and Locke first wrote about it three hundred years ago: Is the foundation of rights natural or conventional? Are rights an endowment of nature, more particularly an attribute of human nature, and therefore inalienable from any person and ineradicable by any political institution? Or are they simply a political construct, the product of contract and constitution, corresponding to specific duties and enforceable at law? These two positions derive from diametrically opposed theoretical perspectives and lead to radically different practical consequences. Therefore it is worth reexamining the arguments Hobbes and Locke gave for their contrasting conceptions of the foundations of rights at the inception of the controversy: not only did they largely define the terms of the debate over social justice for the entire modern era; their classical statements of the relation between natural law and social contract have lost none of their trenchancy in the intervening centuries.

## The American Context

Before launching into the study of Hobbes and Locke, though, it must be recognized that contemporary debate about the foundation of rights on the international level should come as no surprise to Americans accustomed to the bicentennial dialectic within our own political tradition between naturalism and conventionalism. While the Declaration of Independence presumes a natural foundation for rights, the Constitution of the United States grants them a conventional foundation. The tension between these two poles of interpretation reverberates at every major turning point in our history, not to mention in every Supreme Court decision.

If the poles must be regarded as mutually exclusive, the tension can be interpreted, in Ackerman's terms, as a conflict between "monists" and "foundationalists."Monists suppose "democracy requires the grant of plenary lawmaking authority to the winners of the last general election" and, consequently, reduce rights to whatever interests are currently in the majority. Foundationalists, by contrast, contend that rights must be incorporated into a constitution simply because they are right and, consequently, demand judicial review of legislation to prevent a tyranny of the majority.[3] But if Ackerman is correct, and these poles need not be interpreted as mutually exclusive, the tension should rather be placed within a dualist perspective in which the dichotomy between monism and foundationalism is transformed into a complementarity between "normal politics" and "constitutional politics." That is, it means a periodic suspension of the ordinary procedures by which duly constituted representatives of the people make and administer statutory law to allow the People itself to rise up and invoke a higher law to guarantee fundamental rights.[4] No matter whether the foundation of rights is monolithic or dialectical, however, the basic question remains whether it is ultimately conventional or natural.

The contrast in perspective between the Declaration of Independence and the Constitution points up the issue. To legitimate revolution and the consequent independence of the "United States of America" from the "State of Great Britain," the Second Continental Congress invoked in the Declaration of Independence "the Laws of Nature and of Nature's God." It cited what it regarded as the "self-evident" truths "that all men are created equal, that they are endowed by their Creator with certain unalienable Rights, that among these are Life, Liberty and the pursuit of Happiness," to frame its indictment of what it believed was the crown's tyranny over the American states. This rationalist stance represents an alternative both to the strictly religious framework of the Congress' earlier "Declaration of the Causes and Necessity of Taking Up Arms" (July 6, 1775), the exordium of which was to "the Divine Author of our existence," and also to the pure constitutionalism of the First Continental Congress' "Declaration and Resolves" (October 14, 1775), in which the members appealed to their rights and liberties "in the first place, as Englishmen, [as] their ancestors in like cases have usually done."[5] Evidently, the signers of the Declaration of Independence thought the self-evidence of natural law provided the strongest foundation for rights violated by the crown's "long train of abuses and usurpations."[6]

By contrast, the Constitution of the United States is a social contract, exemplifying a conventional foundation for rights. The foundation it contains is the American people's act of adoption enunciated in the preamble: "We the people of the United States, in order to form a more perfect Union, establish justice, insure domestic tranquillity, provide for the common defense, promote the general welfare, and secure the blessings of liberty to ourselves and our posterity, do ordain and establish this Constitution for the United States of America." This "Federalist" version of the Constitution was created by the Congress without any mandate (June 21, 1788) and became official simply by ratification in constitutional conventions of all thirteen states (May 29, 1790). It had no charter of rights comparable either to the prototypical Declaration of Rights by the British Parliament in 1688 or to the bills of rights commonly incorporated into the more recently enacted constitutions of the various states. Even the "Anti-Federalist" complement of the Bill of Rights, passed by Congress on September 25, 1789, and ratified by three-quarters of the states on December 15., 1791, seems at first glance to remain within the framework of convention. It spells out, article by article, the rights guaranteed before the law by the Constitution to each citizen of the United States as such.[7]

The radical democracy of this popular institution of rights both reflected and inspired a political culture of popular sovereignty.[8] It has resulted not just in subsequent amendments to the Constitution, ordinarily expanding though occasionally contracting the number and nature of rights to which Americans are deemed to be entitled, but perhaps even in virtual reconstitution of the American polity in certain "constitutional moments" like Reconstruction and the New Deal.[9] In any case, the Supreme Court has never accorded to Americans, citizens or aliens, any rights but those guaranteed by the Constitution—even if, as in the case of the right to privacy, it has had to resort to the stratagem of finding this right implicit in a conjunction of several other explicitly granted rights.

Yet even within the conventionalist framework of the Constitution there are echoes of the naturalist perspective of the Declaration of Independence.

In the preamble, although the form is conventionalist, the content reinforces the Declaration's naturalist supposition of the inalienable rights of life, liberty, and the pursuit of happiness with the people's proclamation that among the reasons for constituting the United States are the establishment of justice, the securance of liberty, and the promotion of the general welfare. That the Bill of Rights did not pretend to be a taxative or indeed an exclusive certification of the rights of the American people is evident from the admission in the Ninth Amendment that "the enumeration in the constitution of certain rights shall not be construed to deny or disparage others retained by the people." That it acknowledges, in addition, an indeterminate penumbra of rights—some perhaps conventional, but certainly those retained by the people being natural—is patent from the recognition in the Tenth Amendment that "the powers not delegated to the United States by the constitution, nor prohibited by it to the states, are reserved to the states respectively, or to the people." Perhaps more important than these generic commitments to substantive rights is the explicit guarantee by the Fifth Amendment of procedural rights in the prohibition against depriving anyone of "life, liberty, or property, without due process of law," a guarantee extended by the Fourteenth Amendment from federal to state jurisdictions. Thus the Constitution, more particularly the Bill of Rights, supposes a foundation for rights other than the Constitution itself and beyond legitimation by convention alone.[10]

This ambivalence in our inaugural documents about the foundation of rights—about whether they belong to Americans as human beings or as citizens, about whether they are fundamentally moral or legal empowerments—has been reflected in the opposition between the major schools of Constitutional interpretation: natural law vs. legal realism, judicial activism vs. strict constructionism. But my interest here is not in the subsequent judicial interpretation, but in the prior theoretical background, of the contrasting perspectives on rights exemplified in the Declaration of Independence and in the Constitution. And in exploring this issue, I want to focus not upon the immediate context—the ideological cleavages among the Founders between federalism and anti-federalism, between republicanism and liberalism—but upon the wider horizon—the universe of political discourse prevailing within the Anglo-American world at the time. More precisely, I want to concentrate upon the contrasting political philosophies of Thomas Hobbes and John Locke.

True, it is a matter of historical controversy, not just whether Hobbes and Locke were the intellectual progenitors of the American political establishment, but whether ideology was the primary factor in the formation of that establishment, as opposed to economic and social forces. Charles A. Beard is, of course, notorious for his thesis that the instigation for the Constitution (and, by implication, the Revolution as well) was the desire of American propertied classes—"merchants, money lenders, security holders, manufacturers, shippers, capitalists, and financiers and their professional associates"—for additional advantages over "the non-slaveholding farmers and the debtors" in their midst.[11] Louis Hartz also attributed the formation of the ideology of Revolution and Constitution to social forces, but he thought a common egalitarianism, unique to the American colonies, was responsible for the genesis of a liberalism shared by the entire citizenry, despite economic differences and political divisions.[12] More recently, Gordon Wood has followed Hartz's lead in portraying the combination of Revolution and Constitution as a radical transformation, socially as well as politically. But Wood has argued that an egalitarian democracy emerged in the United States only in the early nineteenth century, the final stage in a spontaneous grass-roots progression from the monarchical hierarchies of colonial society through the aristocratic republicanism of the Constitutional era.[13] Despite their factual and interpretative disagreements, therefore, these authors emphasize the salience of functional over ideological factors in the creation of the American political establishment, and thus would disparage the importance of Hobbes and Locke for understanding the formation of liberal democracy in the United States.

Other authors would join in this depreciation of Hobbes and Locke, although they would contend for the preeminence of ideology over sociality in the genesis of both independence and democracy in the United States. Clinton Rossiter acknowledges a role for Hobbes and Locke, but sees them primarily as transmitters of the "great tradition" of natural law rather than as innovators in an essentially modern theory of statecraft.[14] John Diggins, too, argues for Locke's influence on both the justification for the Revolution and the conception of the Constitution, but he depicts Locke as the mediator of an essentially Calvinist view of political virtue rather than as the originator of an essentially secular political philosophy.[15] More radical are those who reject altogether the importance of Hobbes or Locke for the foundation of the

American political tradition. Bailyn, Pocock, and Wood have collaborated to locate this tradition within the larger context of "classical republicanism" or "civic humanism," leading from Machiavelli, through Sidney and Harrington, to the Country opposition to Walpole and the Court, without any significant contribution from Hobbes or Locke.[16] Garry Wills, on the other hand, has just as vigorously, if single-handedly, tried to trace the thought form of both the Declaration of Independence and the Constitution back to roots in the Scottish Enlightenment, a programmatic reaction to the empiricism and individualism of the English Enlightenment.[17] And J.C.D. Clark, while he agrees with Rossiter in arguing for the basic influence of natural law upon the American advocates of revolution, ascribes the transmission of this tradition to various denominations of Protestant dissenters to the Anglican ascendancy, whose interests both Hobbes and Locke represented.[18]

Common to all of these genealogies is the supposition that the Founders of the country did not really mean what they said, in either the Declaration of Independence or the Constitution. Supposedly, they were merely dressing their interests in a cloud of rhetoric when they drew upon the language of liberal democratic political theory, of which Hobbes and Locke were the primary authorities, to cite the violation of rights as their justification for rebellion and to claim the protection of rights as their motivation for founding a new nation based upon representative democracy and a separation of powers. Yet there remain historians, call them Whiggish if you want, who continue to support the original and still common view that the Founders consciously and honestly employed the theories of Hobbes (perhaps covertly) and Locke (perhaps tacitly) to create the dynamic balance of natural law and constitutionalism evident in the formative documents of the American polity.[19] Within this school, Thomas Pangle is perhaps the one who has criticized most effectively the alternative etiologies of American political culture and argued most cogently for the predominant influence of Locke (and, by implication, Hobbes) upon the formation of the American political establishment.[20]

Whatever may be the eventual resolution of these historical controversies, Hobbes and Locke nevertheless formulated classic theoretical statements on the alternative foundations of rights. They both preserved a place in their theories for natural law and social contract, but their contrasting interpretations of the dialectic between these two kinds of foundation resulted in contrary conceptions of rights: Hobbes' being conventionalist, Locke's naturalist. Hobbes was concerned with legitimating the absolute power of a sovereign in a commonwealth to protect the subjects' natural right to life, and so he postulated a compact in which the subjects mutually agreed to a sovereign exempt from the covenant itself but authorized to delimit the exercise of even their right to life. Locke was resolved, however, to prevent the government from interfering with what he regarded as the people's natural rights to life, liberty, and property, and so he required the constitution of a commonwealth to leave the people with the authority to prohibit the government from exceeding its constitutional powers. Irrespective of whether the origins of a commonwealth are ideological or functional, and regardless of whether a concern about rights is retrospective or prospective, the theories of Hobbes and Locke are of interest, therefore, because they pose in the starkest terms the contrast between a conventionalist and a naturalist conception of rights, in both their foundations and their consequences.

## Hobbes' Conventionalist Theory of Rights

Hobbes' political theory, at least in *Leviathan*, must be seen as a legitimation of the acquisition of sovereignty through conquest, with the consequence that, as he presents it, the foundation of rights is the will of an absolute sovereign (17:120; 22:155–56).[21] Ostensibly, it is true, Hobbes presents the establishment of sovereignty "by acquisition" as merely a possible alternative to the normal establishment of sovereignty "by institution" (17:21). The first part of *Leviathan* leads, step by step, from an analysis of the "general inclination of all mankind, a perpetuall and restless desire of Power and power, that ceaseth onely in Death" (11:70; see 10:62–69; 13:87–88), to a description of the "naturall condition of mankind" as a war of "every man, against every man" (13:86–90), and thence to the enumeration of the laws of nature that dictate the making and keeping of a mutual covenant establishing a commonwealth to keep the peace (14–15:91111).

At this point, Hobbes says, the institution of a sovereign is a necessary concomitant, for without the terror of a power capable of enforcing the covenant, no one could be counted upon to observe it (17: 117–19). The passions of "Partiality, Pride, Revenge, and the like," which motivate the natural right (*ius naturale*) for everyone to do anything "which in his own Judgment, and Reason, hee shall conceive to be the aptest means" to preserve his life (14:91; 17:117; 27:205–06), would otherwise override the virtues of

"Justice, Equity, Modesty, Mercy, and (in summe) doing to others, as we would be done to," which are mandated by the laws of nature (*leges naturales*) (14:91–92; 15:109; 26:188: 27: 202–08).[22] Hence, the only way for anyone to protect oneself, Hobbes argues, is for all to "conferre all their power and strength upon one Man" in a "Covenant of every man with every man, in such manner, as if every man should say to every man, 'I Authorize and give up my right of Governing my selfe, to this Man, or to this Assembly of men, on this condition, that thou give up thy Right to him, and Authorize all his Actions in like manner.'" This institution of absolute sovereignty by the mutual surrender of the power of self-defense is, Hobbes says, what generates the commonwealth, "that Leviathan, or rather (to speake more reverently) that Mortall God, to which wee owe under the Immortall God, our peace and defense" (17:120).

The mystery is, though, how this sovereign gets the power to enforce the covenant and how his potential subjects recognize the efficacy of his power. True, he is formally constituted as sovereign by the covenant of those who jointly make themselves his subjects by founding a commonwealth and authorizing him to act in their person (18:121; see 122–29; 16:111–15; 21:150). Yet, as Hobbes describes him, he is the one who confers validity upon this covenant by making it enforceable (17:118–19, 121; 21:147–48; 27:202). Though his authority may come from the covenant made with him by the members of the multitude, he makes no covenant with them in return, the power he has to enforce the covenant does not come from the covenant itself, and the covenant does not make him accountable to his subjects (17:120; 18:122–24).[23] He has his authority immediately from and is accountable only to God himself (23:167; 42:372). Such power is necessary because neither the rationality of the laws of nature nor the size of the covenanting multitude can insure compliance to the covenant: "For if we could suppose a great Multitude of men to consent in the observation of Justice, and other Laws of Nature, without a common Power to keep them all in awe; we might as well suppose all Man-kind to do the same; and then there neither would be, nor need to be any Civill Government, or Commonwealth at all; because there would be Peace without subjection" (17:118–19).

Evidently, the sovereign must have succeeded in fulfilling the ambition of everyone in the state of nature to acquire enough power to protect oneself from all others in their competing endeavors to protect their right to life by any means whatsoever (10:62–66, 11:70). For it is the sovereign's unique, autonomous, and unrestricted right to this power within the commonwealth that enables him to punish anyone presumptuous enough to violate anyone else's right to life (28:214; 30:244). Given this description of the powers accorded to the sovereign by the covenant, the covenant must serve simply to ratify a *fait accompli*. It must signify that the power of a sovereign becomes *de iure* what it is already *de facto:* absolute and arbitrary (18:121–29; 30:232; Review: 486), indivisible and inseparable (18:127–28; 19:129–38; 22:155–56; 29:222), in both the civil and the ecclesiastical orders (19:12931; 22:155–56).

Indeed, this just what Hobbes spends the bulk of *Leviathan* demonstrating, his argument from reason in part two complemented by an argument from revelation in part three. In every commonwealth, Hobbes says, the sovereign holds the power of life and death over his subjects, able not only to execute any of them at will without injustice (18:124; 21:148; 26:184; 29:224), but to command all of them to assist him in quelling rebellion at home or repelling attacks from abroad (21:151–52; see 28:214, 219). As supreme legislator, not only has he the authority to promulgate, interpret, and enforce civil law, to which he is not subject himself (18:124; 26:184; 29:224); he also has the authority to interpret and enforce the laws of nature, which only by his command literally become law (26:185, 190–91). Hence, the sovereign may remain, like his subjects, bound in conscience and before God by the law of nature, but he may nevertheless violate this law without becoming liable to reproach, much less to rebellion, from his subjects (24:172; 30:237–38; 43:404, 413–14).

In a Christian commonwealth, the sovereign is, in addition, supreme pastor (42:372, 374), with all the authority Jesus transmitted to the church: to fix the canon and interpret the letter of scripture (33:260, 265–69; 42:359, 361–62); to ordain ministers and administer the sacraments (42:372–74); to prescribe the order of ritual and officiate at worship (31:252–53; 42:37478). This means he can determine divine positive law and impose it upon everyone-—except a prophet inspired by supernatural revelation (26:197–99; 40:323; 42:377–78). Even this exception is mitigated both by the sovereign's authority to distinguish true prophecy from false (36:297–99, 305, 311) and by the impossibility of a true prophet's ever opposing him or inciting his subjects to sedition or warfare (18:125; 32:257–58; 36:299, 305, 311; 40:324, 326). In such a commonwealth, Hobbes concludes, the person of the sovereign represents a perfect union of church and state (29:227–28; 39:321-22; 40:327, 331; 42:341–45, 377–78).

But how does Hobbes believe anyone could actually attain the power to be eligible for absolute sovereignty? This mystery he dispels when he turns from the establishment of sovereignty by institution to the establishment of sovereignty by acquisition, that is, by conquest.[24] "[Sovereign Power] is acquired by force, when men singly, or many together by plurality of voyces, for fear of death, or bonds, do authorize all the actions of that Man, or Assembly, that hath their lives and liberty in his Power" (20:138). Dominion or sovereignty of this kind, Hobbes says, is rightly called despotical, for it is like the dominion of a master over a servant, leaving the life and liberty of the vanquished at the disposal of the victor. It is acquired, not precisely by the victory itself, but by the covenant of the vanquished to submit to the victor as long as his life and liberty are spared. This covenant is neither forcible nor obligatory, for either the vanquished or the victor: the vanquished must choose whether to submit unconditionally to the victor, and the victor has at his discretion whether to accept or reject the offer. Otherwise, the dominion would be like that of a task-master over a slave. As it is, the victor may exact, as he sees fit, the use of all his vanquished foes are and have—themselves, their children, their servants, and their goods—under penalty of death, for this is what the vanquished must authorize the victor to do in return for sparing life and liberty (20:141–42).

Now reason and revelation both teach us, Hobbes argue, that the rights and powers of a sovereign by acquisition are exactly the same as those of a sovereign by institution, "and for the same reasons." "His power cannot, without his consent, be Transferred to another: He cannot Forfeit it: He cannot be Accused by any of his Subjects, of Injury: He cannot be punished by them: He is judge of what is necessary for Peace: and judge of Doctrines: He is Sole Legislator; and Supreme Judge of Controversies; and of the Times, and Occasions of Warre and Peace: to him it belongeth to choose Magistrates, Counsellours, Commanders, and all other officers, and Ministers; and to determine of Rewards, and Punishments, Honour, and Order" (20:139). The reasons in both cases for the sovereign to have this panoply of rights are, Hobbes alleges, that subjects authorize a sovereign to do whatever is necessary to save their lives and liberties, and these are the powers he must have to fulfill his mandate (18:121–29; 19:129–38). Hence, a monarch cannot demand more from a nation where he is sovereign by acquisition (nor, presumably, can he accept less in a nation where he is sovereign by institution): "For the Soveraign is absolute over both alike; or else there is no Soveraignty at all; and so every man may Lawfully protect himself, if he can, with his own sword, which is the condition of war" (20:143).

Hobbes sees no difference, therefore, in the legitimacy of either kind of sovereignty. The origin, the substance, and the outcome of the covenant are in both cases the same. The origin of sovereignty by acquisition in the fear of the vanquished does not nullify the covenant in this case, Hobbes contends, for sovereignty by institution originates from the same fear of death or violence. Only the object of the fear differs: in sovereignty by institution, it is the multitude's fear of one another; in sovereignty by acquisition, it is the members' common fear of a conqueror (20:13839). In fact, fear never voids a covenant, Hobbes believes, in a commonwealth any more than in the state of nature (13:90; 14:9798), for fear never interferes with liberty (21:146). A covenant originates, then, in a happy conjunction of power with terror. The consequence is, as Hobbes sees it, that the substance of a covenant of sovereignty is the same no matter what the form. In sovereignty by institution the form may approximate a *pactum unionis*, the members of a multitude agreeing with one another to authorize a sovereign to act in their person. In sovereignty by acquisition it may resemble a *pactum submissionis*, in which a defeated people directly authorize a conqueror to act in their person. But in both cases the substance of the covenant is the same: an act of authorization by which the prospective members of a commonwealth bind themselves unconditionally to a sovereign while the sovereign himself remains unencumbered by any reciprocal contract. The sovereign is autonomous and unaccountable in either case.[25]

Hence, the outcome of the covenant is, as Hobbes explains it, the same in both cases: the unity of the subjects of a commonwealth in the person of the sovereign. Whether the unity occurs in the instant incorporation of a multitude or from the gradual assimilation of individuals, the participation of subjects in the unity of a commonwealth depends upon a prospective sovereign's response: his acceptance of their authorization, his agreement to become their representative, his commitment to act in their person (16:113–14; 19:130; 22:155; 26:184). The sovereign is, in either case, a tyrant: "[T]he name of

Tyranny, signifieth nothing more, nor less, than the name of Soveraignty, be it in one, or many men, saving that they that use the former word, are understood to bee angry with them they call Tyrants; I think the toleration of a professed hatred of Tyranny, is a Toleration of hatred to Commonwealth in general" (Review: 486). Thus the only difference Hobbes admits between tyranny and sovereignty is nominal: "tyranny" is the term employed by people too ignorant to recognize the incomparable benefits of a commonwealth over the state of nature; "sovereignty" the term adopted by those wise enough to realize the preferability of peace at any price to the cataclysm of war (19:130; 29:226; 46:470–71).

Hence, Hobbes clears up the mystery of how anyone could be powerful enough to be eligible for absolute sovereignty when he complements his analysis of sovereignty by institution with his analysis of sovereignty by acquisition. Who but a conqueror (and, Hobbes insists, his designated heirs) has the power required for the job? Only someone with the power of life and death over a people, Hobbes apparently believes, can terrorize them into respecting one another's rights and uniting them to quash rebellion or repel aggression. Formally speaking, sovereignty may be established by institution; realistically, it is established by acquisition. Even if a people is not actually conquered, Hobbes seems to be saying, it needs a sovereign as absolute as a conqueror to establish a commonwealth powerful enough to protect its rights.[26]

The foundation of rights implicit in this theory of sovereignty is clearly conventional, whether the right in question is life, liberty, or property. The right to life Hobbes analyzes by distinguishing between "*ius naturale*" and "*lex naturalis*"—both of which he admits are ordinarily translated by the single English term "natural law" (14:91)—and then interpreting both of these natural factors as effectively conventional. "*Ius naturale*", which he translates as "the right of nature," he defines as "the Liberty each man hath, to use his own power, as he will himselfe, for the preservation of his own Nature; that is to say, of his own Life; and consequently, of doing any thing, which in his own Judgement, and Reason, hee shall conceive to be the aptest means thereunto" (14:91). In the state of nature, as Hobbes describes it, the vindication of this right is an exercise in futility. The natural equality of ability among men—not least "as to strength of body, [since] the weakest may kill the strongest" (13:87)—leads everyone to anticipate that self-preservation requires him "to master the persons of all men he can, so long, till he see no other power great enough to endanger him." This is a stratagem that instigates the infamous war "of every man, against every man" which makes life in the state of nature "solitary, poore, nasty, brutish, and short" (13:87–89).

"*Lex naturalis*", which Hobbes translates as "law of nature," then comes into play. A law of nature, as he defines it, is "a Precept, or generall Rule found out by Reason, by which a man is forbidden to do, that, which is destructive of his life, or taketh away the means of preserving the same; and to omit, that, by which he thinketh it may be best preserved" (14:91). Laws of this kind (nineteen in chapters fourteen and fifteen, complemented by a crucial twentieth law in the Review) amount to "Articles of Peace" (13:90; 15:110–11), mandating the institution of the coercive power of the commonwealth for the sake of self-preservation (14:93, 96, 99; 15:101). To pursue peace if possible, consequently to be content with as much liberty for oneself as for others, and to keep any covenants made with them: these and the other laws of nature are the "dictates of reason" Hobbes believes enjoin a conversion from the state of nature to the state of the commonwealth (15:111). In the state of nature, however, where they lack a promulgator and enforcer, at least a human one, they are not, properly speaking, laws, just theorems or conclusions, binding only *in foro interno* (15:110–11) and inept to provide justice (13:90; 14:91, 96; 26:18889). Only with the establishment of a commonwealth, by a people's simultaneous commitment to the third law of nature ("That men performe their covenants made") and their authorization of a sovereign, do these prudential norms truly become laws, founding justice and binding in the external forum, precisely because of becoming enforceable (15:100–04). They have the public status of laws, then, only as civil laws, for it is up to the sovereign in a commonwealth to interpret the laws of nature, promulgating and enforcing whatever determinations and applications he may deem necessary for the common preservation of the lives of his subjects (18:125; 26:185–86, 191–93).

Hence, only within a commonwealth, under the dominion of a sovereign, can anyone reasonably expect to exercise the natural right to life. But the price of common self-preservation, Hobbes makes clear, is a curtailment of the individual right to life. "The Right of Nature, that is the naturall Liberty of man, may by the Civill Law be abridged, and restrained," says Hobbes, "nay, the end of making Lawes, is no other, but such Restraint, without the which there cannot possibly be any Peace" (26:185; see 14:92). This abridgement cannot, of course, entail a renunciation of the right of self-defense, individual or collective, against the sovereign or his ministers. Nor does it induce an obligation of self-accusation, when guilty as when innocent, either of crime or of rebellion. For the precise purpose of a constitutional covenant is effective self-defense (14:93, 96, 98–99; 21:151, 152; 28;214).

Whether Hobbes believes the abridgement of the right to life obliges a subject to kill anyone else at the sovereign's command (presumably to punish crime or to suppress rebellion, as well as to defend the commonwealth) is not entirely clear. He does say, "No man is bound by the words themselves [of the covenant], either to kill himselfe, or any other man" (21:151). And he allows for subjects who send substitutes or suffer from "natural timorousness" to refuse, without injustice, to defend the commonwealth—unless indeed "the Defense of the Commonwealth, requireth at once the help of all that are able to bear Arms" (21:151–51). But he also says that in covenanting, everyone not only gives up the right of defending another, but obliges oneself to assist the sovereign in punishing others (28:214). Then, too, in the Review he comes up with a previously unmentioned law of nature: "That every man is bound by Nature, as much as in him lieth, to protect in Warre, the Authority, by which he is himself protected in time of Peace" (484).

In any case, the covenantal abridgement of the subjects' right to life does entail the sovereign's right to take, without injustice, the lives of the innocent as well as the guilty (28:124; see 21:148; 24:172). Admittedly, in punishing an innocent person the sovereign does offend against the natural law, frustrate the purpose of the covenant, and violate a subject's right to equal protection of the law (21:148; 3o:237–38; see 15:105, 108). But the sovereign has this right of arbitrary punishment because he alone retains under the covenant his right of nature—the "right to everything, to do whatsoever he [thinks] necessary to his own preservation; subduing, hurting, or killing any man in order thereunto"—the power of which is only strengthened by his subjects' having laid their own rights down (28:214). In short, the absolute power all desire in the state of nature to assure self-preservation is what kings, and kings alone, actually retain within the commonwealth, "assuring it at home by Lawes, or abroad by Wars" (11:70).

Liberty suffers the same fate as life. Within the state of nature, in fact, liberty is, as Hobbes defines it, virtually identical to the right to life (14:91). After the covenant, however, individuals lose this liberty, contrary to what the ancient Greek and Roman philosophers tried to maintain, as it becomes the exclusive property of the commonwealth, effectively that of the sovereign (21:149–50). It reverts to the subjects, though, as soon as a sovereign freely or forcibly renounces it or dies intestate (21:153–54). Within the commonwealth, therefore, the true liberties of subjects can only be gauged by the words and the intent of the covenant (21:150). They even include, as we have seen, liberties in respect to the sovereign—of self-defense, of non-self-incrimination and non-self-punishment, and (though the sovereign may retaliate with execution) of draft-evasion, except at the threat of defeat for the commonwealth (21:151–52).

At the discretion of the sovereign, subjects may also enjoy whatever liberties the sovereign pretermits by silence of law, "such as is the Liberty to buy, and sell, and otherwise contract with one another; to choose their own aboad, their own diet, their own trade of life, and institute their children as they themselves think fit; & the like" (21:148). What is more, the will of the sovereign must be interpreted, Hobbes alleges, to accord a subject the same liberty to sue him as another subject for a violation of a right "grounded on a precedent Law" (21:152–53). More positively still, the liberty of subjects corresponds, as Hobbes sees it, to the sovereign's office, both under the law of nature and by the intent of the covenant, to procure the safety of his people. How? By keeping the peace, inculcating virtue, administering equal justice, imposing equal taxation, making and enforcing perspicuous laws, and choosing good counsellors and commanders (30:231–44). The entire compass of the right to liberty is surprisingly broad, given Hobbes' restrictive conception of the right to life, but it remains essentially conventional, given its dependence upon the good will of the sovereign.

The same is true of the right to property. As Hobbes sees it, there is no property in the state of nature, but justice in the commonwealth is virtually identical with the distribution and protection of property. The reasons he give for no right to property in the state of nature are both positive and negative: everyone has the right to use everything (thus the war of all against all), but no one has the power to protect anything (thus no mine or thine) (13:90). Without justice—in the natural law sense of a commitment to the keeping and enforcing of covenants—there can be no justice—in the scholastic sense of a constant will to give everyone one's own (15:100–101). But within the commonwealth the power of the sovereign has to enforce the covenant gives him the right both to distribute property to his subjects and to exact from them the taxes he needs to defend it (18:125). By distributive justice he has the right to make the laws governing the division of land, the assignment of export-import licenses, and the conditions of exchange (24:171–74).

Historically, it is evident, Hobbes says, that this power over a people is acquired by conquest: both in ancient Israel and in medieval England the victors distributed the spoils (24:171–72). Equity and the common good mandate that such a distribution be fair, but if it isn't, a subject may not so much as accuse the sovereign of injustice, let alone make war upon him (24:172; 30:237). What is more, though a subject's right to property excludes the use of it by all other subjects, it does not usurp the sovereign's dominion over it in the interest of "the common Peace and Security" (21:172; 29:224–25). More specifically, the sovereign must have the right to raise whatever taxes he deems necessary for protecting subjects from one another and defending them from foreign enemies (29:228–29). Again, the natural law mandates this be done equitably, but a failure to do so, though it will inevitably lead to "the ruine of the Common-wealth," is still not an injustice (30:237–39). Just as life and liberty are, as Hobbes describes them, conventional rather than natural rights, so also is property.

The immediate reason Hobbes gives for this conventionality of right is, as we have seen, the necessity of a commonwealth for securing justice. But the ultimate reason is, I have argued, his reduction of sovereignty by institution to sovereignty by acquisition. Hobbes does believe the institution of a commonwealth by a mutual covenant of authorization is perfectly rational given that the alternative is the state of nature, but he nevertheless believes the covenant to be a formality given that sovereignty is actually acquired by victory. The pragmatism of Hobbes' theory of rights depends, therefore, upon the realism of his supposition about the origin of sovereignty.

This he believed to be justified both historically and theologically (32:255–59; Review: 489–91). On the historical side, Hobbes believed his supposition to be obvious, first of all, from the events of the English Civil War. Although *Leviathan* may have been a decade in gestation, the occasion for its publication in 1651 was "the disorders of the present time" (Review: 491). These arose from the "Engagement Controversy," in which the question was whether magistrates formerly loyal to Charles I should swear an oath of allegiance to Cromwell. For those whom "the Civill warres [had] not yet taught sufficiently . . . in what point of time it is, that a Subject becomes obliged to the Conqueror," Hobbes explained to them that it was when they still had "the liberty to submit" (Review: 484).

But Hobbes showed that he regarded Cromwell's acquisition of sovereignty by victory to be normal, at least for England, by tracing the legitimacy of the monarchy to William the Conqueror's acquisition of sovereignty by conquest (24:172; Review: 486). Any further attempt to justify these origins, he said, would be both unnecessary and pernicious in light of both the usual origin of commonwealths and the perennial threat of sedition. "Therefore I put down for one of the most effectuall seeds of the Death of any State, that the Conquerors require not onely a Submission of mens action to them for the future, but also an Approbation of all their actions past; when there is scarce a Common-wealth in the world, whose beginnings can in conscience be justified" (Review: 486). Hobbes thought the delusion of expecting sovereignty to originate by institution was only compounded by presuming its perpetuation to require consultation: "No great Common-wealth was ever kept up; but either by forraign Enemy that united them; or by the reputation of some one eminent man amongst them; or by the secret Counsell of a few; or by the mutuall feare of equall factions; and not by the open Consultations of the Assembly" (25:182).

Yet Hobbes did not think the origin of sovereignty in power was simply an accidental fact of history; he believed human sovereignty was made to the image and likeness of divine sovereignty. Whichever kingdom of God we consider, he thought, it is a consequence of divine power. The metaphorical kingdom of God over human beings by nature is a function, not of human gratitude for creation, but of helpless submission, "whether men will or not," to God's "irresistible power," more than enough to make any man a sovereign (31:245–47).[27] The civil kingdom of God over Israel, although it was formalized in contract and covenant (20:143–44; 40:322–31), was also a product of divine omnipotence, for God reigned over his people "not by their Consent, but by his own Power" (Review: 487). And the anticipated kingdom of God on earth in glory, when Christ shall come in majesty to judge the living and the dead, will be the supreme manifestation of divine power (35:284; 38:311–20). With these precedents, the genesis of human sovereignty in power becomes not just historically normal but divinely sanctioned.

Clearly, Hobbes thought the function of moral philosophy, and his role as a moral philosopher, was to convince the people of a commonwealth of both the rationality and the providence of what was, in any case, the reality of absolute sovereignty, normally acquired through victory in warfare (13:110–11; 20:145; 31:254; Review: 490–91).

## Locke's Naturalist Theory of Rights

By contrast, John Locke, in his *Second Treatise of Government*, argues that rebellion is the only response to absolute monarchy.[28] Although he agrees with Hobbes that absolute monarchy is indeed identical with tyranny, he rejects Hobbes' contention that "tyranny" is simply an invidious term for the power to be found in any valid form of government. Instead, he argues that absolutism of any kind (whether monarchic, oligarchic, or democratic) is opposed by its very nature to the presuppositions and purposes of civil society. Civil society, Locke believes, is founded upon popular consent and exists to protect the common good. In his opinion a tyrant violates these conditions by his seizure of power and the pursuit of his own interests. The people have, in this case, not only the natural right but a moral duty to resist; and if the tyrant should balk, they have every right to kill him,, restore order, and form a new government. Whereas Hobbes based his legitimation of absolute sovereignty upon the right of conquest, Locke based his justification of revolution upon the right of popular sovereignty.

It is important to recognize, therefore, that Locke's justification of revolution is not just a valid consequence but the primary intent of his theory of natural rights. The purpose of the *Second Treatise* is to legitimate rebellion against absolute monarchy: originally drafted to justify the Rye House plot against Charles II, it was finally published to rationalize the Glorious Revolution against James II.[29] This *Sitz im Leben* does not invalidate but rather illuminate Locke's naturalist theory of rights.[30] Without a natural basis for rights, Locke would have had no foundation for popular sovereignty, and thus no justification for rebellion against absolute monarchy. The challenge of interpreting the *Second Treatise* is to see how Locke's practical intent invigorates his reappropriation of natural law and social contract to make popular sovereignty the foundation of civil society.[31]

Before analyzing Locke's conceptions of the state of nature and the constitution of civil society, therefore, it will be necessary to appreciate the basis and extent of his opposition to absolute monarchy. Absolute monarchy is, in his mind, contrary to civil society by definition, by historical origin, and by its inevitable consequences. By its very definition, Locke says, absolute monarchy is inconsistent with civil society because it leaves a monarch "as much in the state of Nature, with all [the subjects] under his Dominion, as he is with the rest of Mankind" (91:8–9). Since the absolute monarch is supposed to monopolize both the legislative and the executive powers of the society, he preempts the offices for which people surrender their natural legislative and executive rights in leaving the state of nature and constituting civil society (90–91). This may permit the monarch to be an impartial and effective judge in disputes between his subjects—for much the same reason a farmer keeps his animals from hurting one another—but it still leaves his subjects without appeal to an impartial and effective judge on earth in a dispute with the monarch himself(93).

If people leave the state of nature because of the difficulty of defending themselves against those who abandon reason and attack them like savage beasts, why should they only compound the difficulty by surrendering whatever power they may have to one person? (93). "This is to think," Locke says in his bluntest criticism of absolute monarchy, "that Men are so foolish that they take care to avoid what Mischiefs may be done them by Pole-Cats, or Foxes, but are content, nay think it Safety, to be devoured by Lions" (93:30–32). Whether or not he has Hobbes directly in mind in this by-blow, he thinks history shows the threat of injustice from absolute monarchy to be only too real (92). Whenever a monarchy has originated f rom a tacit consent to the natural authority of "some one good and excellent Man," he alleges, people have soon rejected it for a civil society, in which "the Legislature was placed in collective Bodies of men, call them Senate, Parliament, or what you please." "No Man in Civil Society," Locke declares, "can be exempted from the laws of it" (94).

The second reason Locke opposes absolute monarchy is that it originates from a state of war between the monarch and the people of a society. Whether the war is a conquest or a usurpation doesn't matter, for "as Conquest may be called a Foreign Usurpation, so Usurpation is a kind of Domestick Conquest, with this difference, that a Usurper can never have Right on his side" (197:1–4). In either case, there is a forcible replacement of the persons whom the people have designated to fill the offices in the government. And since the people have the right not just to decide upon the form of government but to choose the officials as well, "whoever gets into the exercise of any part of Power, by other ways, than what the Laws of the Community have prescribed, hath no Right to be obeyed, though the Form of the Commonwealth be still preserved; since he is not the Person the Laws have appointed, and consequently not the Person the People have consented to." The seizure of government office, Locke says, is tantamount to anarchy (198).

Locke's target in the *Second Treatise* is usurpation, and his theory of conquest serves as much to discredit the pretensions of usurpation as to refute the claims of conquest. For he argues that conquest can sometimes be the outcome of a just (external) war, but usurpation is always the product of an unjust (internal) war. A conqueror is always a despot, Locke says, "having Absolute, Arbitrary Power" over the lives and liberties of his defeated foes as if they were his slaves (172; 192). But Locke believes this despotism is justified if a people has first forfeited its rights by aggression against another commonwealth, making itself like a thief in the state of nature, liable to be destroyed "as any savage ravenous Beast" (178; 180–81). So the conqueror has in this case a right to the lives and liberties of those who have "actually assisted, concurr'd, or consented to that unjust force, that is used against him" (179:2–2; 172; 196). But historical practice to the contrary not withstanding, he has no right to their properties, except for the sake of reparations—and even then, not to the disregard of the prior rights of their families to self--preservation (178–84; 192). For under no circumstances does the conqueror's despotical power extend to the rights of the innocent—to life, liberty, and property—even should they be forced to consent to his despoliation. And the innocent, Locke insists, include all those who are not actual aggressors, including the families of aggressors, and certainly the posterity of aggressors and innocents alike. Hence, even just aggressors—like William the Conqueror, Locke remarks—have no right of conquest over subsequent generations, for "they owe subjection to the Laws of God and Nature" prohibiting retaliation against the innocent (177; 193–95).

The despotism of unjust conquerors has no right whatsoever. For "the Aggressor, who puts himself into the state of War with another, and unjustly invades another Man's right, can, by such an unjust War, never come to have a right over the Conquered" (176:14). Whatever power such conquerors may have been able to seize by force of arms can never be legitimate unless it is subsequently ratified by free and popular consent (196). Otherwise, the despot remains a "Great Robber," against whom a conquered people retains the right to appeal to heaven for vengeance, no matter how many generations it may take (176). By the same token, Locke says, a usurper, who is nothing but an unjust conqueror from within, has no right to his office. And "if the Usurper extend his power beyond, what of Right belonged to the lawful Princes, or Governors of the Commonwealth, 'tis Tyranny added to Usurpation" (197:7–9).

Tyranny is Locke's third charge against absolute monarchy. "Tyranny is the exercise of Power beyond Right" (199:2–3), in Locke's definition of the term. It involves three factors: the tyrant makes his will rather than law the rule of action; he therefore uses force without authority; and he prefers his own ambition, interest, passion, or private advantage to the good of the people. Thus he makes war upon the people (19:7–13, 22–25; 138:24; 143:13; 151:2–23; 155; 172:8: 176:1–5; 199–202: 205:6; 207:10–11; 214; 227). Any form of government can turn to tyranny, Locke admits (201). But he clearly assumes monarchy is most prone to the temptation, and he certainly thinks it is tyrannous if it becomes absolute. For assuming absolute power must be understood as a declaration of design upon the lives of subjects, he says, since nobody desires to have it except to enslave people and destroy their lives at pleasure (17). The title of the offender, with its connotation of public trust, only aggravates the offense (176:15; 202:24; 227:25; 231). Power of this kind demolishes rather than builds a government, reducing the commonwealth to anarchy (198:8; 203:5; 219:5).

Hence, the very power Hobbes regarded as necessary to a commonwealth—absolute sovereignty—is what Locke thought was antithetical to it. Yet Locke justified his alternative conception of political power by the same form of argument as Hobbes: he depicted a state of nature in which human beings possessed the rights he believed were inherent in them as rational animals, and then postulated a compact to constitute a civil society designed to safeguard these rights. The grounds for Locke's contradiction of Hobbes lie, then, in his contrasting descriptions of the content of these two constructions. Instead of describing the state of nature as a cauldron of passion, anarchy, and war, Locke presented it as a regime of reason, law, and peace, where human beings enjoyed as well as possessed the rights to life, liberty, and property. Thus, rather than regarding the social contract as a desperate act of a people driven to authorize an absolute sovereign to monopolize power and save them from themselves, he represented it as an exercise of popular sovereignty, as people took it upon themselves to found a government entrusted to protect their rights. This conception of popular sovereignty based upon natural rights was the reason Locke then gave for his belief in the people's right to rebellion against absolute monarchy.

It is important, first, to see then how Locke constructs his state of nature as a utopian paradigm for delimiting political power in a commonwealth, as opposed to Hobbes' dystopian nightmare of it as the horrific alternative to absolute sovereignty. The state of nature, Locke says, is the state "all Men are naturally in," enjoying as they do perfect freedom and equality: perfect freedom, in that they "can order their Actions, and dispose of their Possessions, and Persons as they think fit, within the bounds of the law of Nature, without asking leave, or depending upon the Will of any other Man"; equality, in that "all the Power and Jurisdiction is reciprocal, no one having more than another," since all are "born to all the same advantages of Nature, and the use of the same faculties" (4:1–11; see 5–14). Elsewhere he virtually equates this freedom and equality, describing equality as "that equal Right that every Man hath, to his Natural Freedom without being subjected to the Will or Authority of any other Man" (54:9–12).

This state of nature he takes, in one sense, as a historical condition. It is the status of individuals either before they consent to constitute or to enter a political society or after their society is dissolved by conquest (15:13–15; see 14; 30; 36–37; 41–43; 91; 95; 100–04; 211). It remains the situation of independent commonwealths in the absence of a common superior or judge upon earth (14; see 145; 181; 183–84).[32] More importantly, though, the state of nature is for Locke a moral construct—a template of human nature, in both its individual and social dimensions.

As an individual endowment, human nature is, Locke believes, the embodiment of reason, the matrix of the law of nature guaranteeing human rights—in contrast to Hobbes' depiction of human nature as a hive of passion, threatening the human right to life by its incessant drive to power and glory. In another contrast to Hobbes, Locke give no list of natural *laws*, but rather defines natural *law* as reason itself, in its capacity to identify human rights and authorize their defense: "Reason, which is that Law [of Nature], teaches all Mankind, who will but consult it, that being all equal and independent, no one ought to harm another in his Life, Health, Liberty, or Possession" (6:7–10; see 11:31; 12:8–13; 128).[33] In addition to this "legislative" power, everyone also has the "executive" power of punishing transgressions of the law of nature "so far as calm reason and conscience dictates" (8:5). The punishment should be severe enough to protect the innocent, restrain offenders, deter others, and obtain reparation—even if the transgression is against another, not directly against oneself (8–12; see 74:22; 87:1–9; 187; 207). This power applies to lesser breaches of the law of nature as well as to murder, and the severity of the punishment in the state of nature may be as great as for the violation of a comparable municipal law within a commonwealth (12).

For a criminal, in resorting to force to violate the rights of another, renounces reason, Locke avers, and becomes a "wild savage beast," at war with all humankind, liable therefore to be hunted down and executed as an enemy of the whole species (8:9–24; 11:16–32; see also 16:14; 172:10–19). Locke defends what he admits is this "very strange Doctrine" by pointing out that municipal laws are "only so far right, as they are founded on the Law of nature, by which they are to be regulated and interpreted" (12:16–19), and by recalling that a state would have no right to punish an alien unless it could invoke the right of everyone in the state of nature to punish any criminal (9). He adds that whatever dangers this power may raise of partiality or revenge, they are nothing compared to the perils of an absolute monarchy, in which one person "commanding a multitude, has the Liberty to be Judge in his own Case, and may do to his Subjects whatever he pleases" (13:1–29).

The rights to life, liberty, and property that Locke thought emanated from natural law are., as he depicts them, implicitly rational and mutually reinforcing. The right to life, he says, arises from what he claims is the fundamental law of nature, the right to self-preservation (16:9–11; see also 135:31; 149:24–25; 159:17; 171:12; 183:22–28). Because of this law, as we have seen, everyone is bound to preserve the rest of humankind as well as oneself (6:19–25). Consequently, since the loss of liberty threatens the loss of life, neither no one may gratuitously enslave another or allow oneself to be enslaved (17; 23:1–9). Likewise, since self-preservation requires the use of the goods of nature, both reason and revelation indicate that individuals may appropriate from the commons whatever they need (25:1–4; 26; 28:1126: 32:10–18; 35:12–21). So imperative is the right of self-preservation that anyone who attempts to violate it—not just by threatening a person's life, but by attempting to enslave or steal from another—forfeits one's own right to life (17–18; 19:13–24). For the resort to violence dissolves the human ties of reason and puts a person in a state of war with the rest of humankind, making it lawful for everyone else, in the absence of a common superior on earth, to kill him like a beast of prey (16–19). In effect if not in intent, Locke's depiction of the right to life as a common duty of self-defense directly contradicted Hobbes' characterization of it as a license to kill.

Liberty, as the "Freedom from Absolute, Arbitrary Power" (23:1) is also a discrete and basic natural right, although it is implicated in the rights to life and liberty. As a corollary to the right to life, liberty is so valuable that life without it would be indefensible (hence, self-enslavement is prohibitive) and could be unbearable (so a slave is justified in suicidal resistance) (17; 23–24). Evidently, Locke also regards liberty as a concomitant to the right to property since appropriation is certainly a liberty he accords to everyone but slaves (85:13–16; 174:6).

As a distinct natural right, though, liberty is, Locke insists, not license but law: the right "to be free from any Superior Power on Earth, and not to be under the Will or Legislative Authority of Man, but to have only the Law of Nature for [a] Rule" (22:1–4; 6–8). This "law of reason" implies liberty, "for Law, in its true Notion, is not so much the Limitation as the direction of a free and intelligent Agent to his proper Interest, and prescribes no farther than is for the general Good of those under that Law." This means, Locke says, that "the end of Law is not to abolish or restrain, but to preserve and enlarge Freedom: For in all the states of created beings capable of Laws, where there is no Law, there is no Freedom" (57:10–20; see 57–63; 123; 186–87; 190). Thus one function of liberty in the state of nature is the freedom to judge whether someone else has actually violated the law of nature and to punish the offense, whether against oneself or another: "Of that I my self can only be Judge in my own Conscience, as I will answer it at the great Day, to the Supream Judge of all Men" (21:22–25; see 6–8 and 87:1–9). Whereas Hobbes had construed liberty as the lack of restraint, internal or external, to the right to life, Locke parsed it, on the contrary, as a rational ability to follow the law and punish any violations of it.

Yet, for all the importance Locke accords to life and liberty, property is plainly what he regards as the key natural right. For, in the broad sense, he means by "property" whatever can rightfully said to *be* one's own, including life and liberty, in addition to possessions or estate (87:5; see the parallels in the footnote). As such, it comprises the full panoply of rights inherent in human nature, apparently insofar as they are the personal endowment of each human being (27:1–7; 190). In the narrow sense, though, "property" has for him the more conventional meaning of whatever goods of the earth one rightful *makes* one's own (ch. 5 *Passim).* Even in this sense he argues property is a natural right, despite subscribing to the traditional natural law doctrine that God gave the earth to humankind in common "for the Support and Comfort of their being" (26:1–4; 25; 39). For Locke also believes God and reason command humankind "to subdue the Earth, i.e. improve it for the benefit of life" (32:13–14; 35:12–21), so that property becomes a perfection rather than a violation of the commons (32; 34; 44). Appropriation is necessary, he argues, because it is impossible to use whatever is needed for self-preservation—an apple on a tree, a deer in the forest, or an open field—without taking it and making it one's own (26:9–16; 28; 30; 32). This act of personal appropriation is what Locke calls labor, and labor, by adding personal value to the common bounty of nature, is what he thinks give a person title to a piece of property (27–29; 35:13–21; 37:3035; 44; 45:1–4; 51:1–3).

Yet, given self-preservation is the divinely prescribed purpose of property, Locke believes there are several limitations to the right of appropriation: the goods to be appropriated must be common to all humankind (35); after appropriation there must still be "enough, and as good left in common for others" (27:13; 33; 34:7–15); nothing appropriated can be destroyed or allowed to spoil (31:7–11; 37:35–41; 38:9–19; 46: 14–30). These restrictions he regards as comparatively insignificant, however, because of the incommensurable gap between the paucity of population and the "vast Wilderness of the earth" in "the first Ages of the World" (36; 37:30–41; 38; 45–46; 49) and, even now, because of how labor diminishes the need for property by the enormous value it adds to natural resources ((37:10–29; 40–43). Hence, the right labor originally gave to property "left no room for Controversies about the Title, nor for Encroachment on the Right of others," Locke concludes, "for as a Man had a Right to all he could imploy his Labour upon, so he had no temptation to labour for more than he could make use of" (51:3–12; see 31:16–19; 36:5–10; 39:5–7). The very acquisition of property, therefore, that Hobbes had thought internecine warfare made impossible in the state of nature was what, on the contrary, Locke argued was fostered in that state by the complementarity between human reason and industry, on the one hand, and the virtual inexhaustibility of natural resources, on the other (34:1–7).

No wonder Locke conceives of the social setting in the state of nature as a state of peace, in contrast to Hobbes' conception of it as a state of war (ch. 4). The implicit rationality Locke built into natural rights—self-evident, self-limiting, complementary, and self-enforcing—provided him with the instrumentality for portraying the state of nature as "a State of Peace, Good Will, Mutual Assistance, and Preservation," undisturbed by the "State of Enmity, Malice, Violence, and Mutual Destruction" distinctive of war (19:1–5). This is the kind of state in which human beings can live "together according to reason, without a common Superior on Earth, with Authority to judge between them" (19:6–8). Family life flourishes as a harmonious union that originates in a voluntary compact conferring equal responsibility upon husband and wife for the nourishment and education of any children, until, mature enough to understand the natural law, the children themselves become free to marry and have property of their own, bound to their parents only by duties of love and respect (ch. 6; ch.7, 77–86). An economy burgeons as rational and industrious property-owners not only make "Promises and Bargains for Truck" (14:13), but accumulate property to produce surpluses for market, having tacitly agreed to put a value on gold and silver and make money a medium of exchange (37:1–6; 50). In fact, a primitive polity develops as informal monarchies arise, either as patriarchies, when a father's customary authority and natural tenderness dispose his family to consent to a *de facto* exercise of political power (74–76; 105–07), or as principates, when several families agree to submit to the rule of a successful general because of a common concern for self-defense (108–12). Thus the state of nature appears in Locke's rendition of it to have spawned numerous individual communities bound by "Promises and Compacts" (14:8–12), while it also united humanity into one community, one society, distinct from the rest of nature in its conscious submission to the law of nature (128:3–10).[34]

Why, then, does Locke think anyone would every give up the right to the freedom and equality of the state of nature to submit to the dominion of another in civil society? "To which 'tis obvious to Answer," he replies, "that though in the state of Nature he hath such a right, yet the Enjoyment of it is very uncertain, and constantly exposed to the Invasion of others. For all being Kings as much as he, every Man his Equal, and the greater part no strict Observers of Equity and Justice, the enjoyment of the property he has in this state is very unsafe, very insecure" (123:6–12). Locke seems to think two factors combined to precipitate this situation. The first is that the invention of money eliminated the original limits set by spoilage to the acquisition of property, exposing rational and industrious property-owners to "the Fancy or Covetousnesss of the Quarrelsome and Contentious" (34:5–7; 36:32–40; 48). By enabling the exchange of goods for unspoilable gold and silver, money erased the natural limit that spoilage had set to appropriation, converting it from a means of self-preservation to a mechanism of production (37–38; 46-47; 49). The inevitable result, as Locke sees it, was a progressive scarcity of land and "disproportionate and unequal Possession of the Earth" (45:6–12, 19–25; 48; 50:1–10).

Under the circumstances, property-owners became prey to the second factor: "the corruption and vitiousness of degenerate Men" (128:7–8).[35] War then became so prevalent, Locke supposes, that "to avoid this State of War (wherein there is no appeal but to Heaven, and wherein every the least difference is apt to end, where there is no Authority to decide between the Contenders) is one great reason of Mens putting themselves into Society, and quitting the State of Nature" (21:1–5; see 175:3–4). More positively, he believes "the great and chief end therefore, of Mens uniting into Commonwealths, and putting themselves under Government is the Preservation of their Property"—"property, "to be sure, having in this connection the broader meaning he gives it of "life, liberty, and estate" (123:15–17; 124:1–4; see 85:15–16; 88:7; 94:22; 222:12).[36]

Thus Locke sees the constitution of political society as a matter of convenience not necessity; originating from common consent as opposed to natural authority, military conquest, or divine right; and undertaken to specify and enforce natural rights rather than at the cost of alienating them. In the state of nature, there is indeed the law of nature, "intelligible to all rational Creatures," but "Men being biassed by their Interest, as well as ignorant for want of study of it, are not apt to allow of it as a Law binding to them in the application of it to their particular Cases" (124:8–12). Everyone also has the right to be "both Judge and Executioner" of this law, but given the partiality to which people are prone, "Passion and Revenge" as well as "negligence and unconcernedness" tend to corrupt their judgment (125). The clincher is that the force criminals employ is what also makes "punishment dangerous, and frequently destructive, to those who attempt it" (126:5–6). These are practical problems, Locke indicates, needing pragmatic solutions: "established, settled,, known Law, received and allowed by common consent to be the Standard of Right and Wrong"; "a known and indifferent Judge, with Authority to determine all differences according to the established Law"; "Power to back and support the Sentence when right, and to give it due Execution" (124–26). The "inconveniencies" for which these measures are the remedies are significant enough, Locke believes, to have made the state of nature generally a brief episode in human history, leading quickly to the establishment of political society, even before there could be historical records of the event (127; see 14; 101).

However prudent and welcome the constitution of political society may have been, though, it could not have occurred, Locke insists, except by common consent: "Men being, as has been said, by nature, all free, equal, and independent, no one can be put out of this Estate and subjected to the Political Power of another, without his own Consent" (95:1–4; 87). Monarchies, patriarchal or military, may have been the first form of governance, but Locke postulates that the tacit or spontaneous consent from which they must have originated must have also, sooner rather than later, been superseded by an express consent—at least making them elective, but more often converting them into other forms of government (1–2; ch. 6, esp. 53, 70–71, 74–76; ch. 8, 105–13; ch. 15, 170, 173–74).[37] In any case, the consent to the compact constituting a civil society (or a political community or society, or a commonwealth) must be a unanimous agreement of any number of people "to joyn and unite into a Community, for their comfortable, safe, and peaceable living one amongst another, in a secure enjoyment of their Properties, and a greater Security against any that are not of it" (95:6–9; 211). But he argues this consent must also be to abide by majority rule, in both the formation and the operation of the government, if the commonwealth is to be functional (95–99; 132–33).[38] The majority thereby becomes free, he says, to decide both the form and the term of government: whether it will be democratic, oligarchic, or monarchic (either hereditary or elective), as well as whether a particular form is to be temporary or permanent (132). Supreme power in the society, however, remains with the people themselves—effectively with the majority of the people—who retain the right, Locke emphasizes, to judge whether the government is fulfilling its responsibility of following the law of nature, protecting their rights, and serving the common good. (132; see 149:28; 159:20; 155; 168; 205; 212; 220; 243).

Under these conditions, political power—the power of the government—is, as Locke details it, delegated, divided, subordinative, and, ultimately, revocable. The power of the government is delegated, Locke says, because it is not its own, but held in trust for the people (171; see 22;110; 134; 136; 142; 149; 155; 156; 210). The government does indeed act in the name and with the power of the people, so that the people are responsible for its acts as their own (96–99; 134). Yet it cannot be absolute, or arbitrary, or autonomous, for it arises from the delegation, by the consent, and for the benefit of the people (131; 135–42).

Hence, the powers the government has from the people derive from the people's own natural legislative and executive rights, divided within the government, both for safety and efficiency, into two branches (87–89; 128). To the legislative branch, the people delegate their right to determine the law—that is, to specify the implications of the law of nature for their particular society—but only to the extent necessary to safeguard their natural rights (129). To the executive branch, by contrast, the people delegate their entire right to punish violations of the law within the commonwealth, while amplifying this responsibility, under the title of federative power, to include the protection of the commonwealth from outside aggression (145–48). This delegation implies a commensurate obligation for the people to assist in its performance (130). While the executive must always be available to administer the law, the legislative need and should be in session only periodically or as summoned (143–44; 153).

These two branches are not equal, Locke insists. The executive must be subordinated to the legislative inasmuch as the legislative is "the Soul that gives Form, Life, and Unity to the Commonwealth," for "the Essence and Union of the Society consists in having one Will, the Legislative" (212:9–14). The executive's administration of the law depends upon the legislative's determination of it (150; 152). The supremacy of the legislative branch within the commonwealth is enough even to preclude the people's exercise of their natural power of self-governance as long as the legislative remains a responsible and functional body (149). Hence, the executive can be said to be supreme only insofar as the prince is superior to other magistrates of the realm (151). True, the supreme executive does have the prerogative both of convoking and reapportioning the legislative (154–8; 167), as also of interpreting, mitigating, and even amplifying or countermanding the law, but this prerogative is essentially a functionary power, consequent upon the executive's role of leavening justice with equity and adapting the law to changing circumstances (159–66).

Finally, these powers of the government are revocable—and this can be said to be the point to which the whole *Second Treatise* builds.[39] Supreme power in the commonwealth, Locke repeats over and over, remains in the people themselves (21; 129–32; 134; 138; 149–50; 153; 155; 168; 205; 212; 2220; 240; 243). So if the entire society is dissolved from without, by conquest, the government cannot remain, and everyone in the society returns to the state of nature, "with a liberty to shift for himself, and provide for his own Safety, as he thinks fit in some other Society" (211; 243). If a conqueror, just or unjust, becomes an aggressor by forcibly violating the people's rights, they have, therefore, the right of rebellion, with God's blessings upon them (196:10–30).

If, instead, the dissolution of the government occurs from within, through usurpation or tyranny, the society itself is left intact, and the people have the right, not so much of rebellion, but of retaliating against the rebellion perpetrated against them by the usurper or tyrant (226–29).[40] Usurpation occurs if the prince attempts to alter the legislative—by substituting his will for the rule of law, by hindering or interfering with the assembly, or by abandoning his office or delivering the people to a foreign power (211–19). This is something the people have a right not only to remedy but prevent, "by erecting a new Legislative differing from the other, by the change of Persons, or Form, or both as they shall find it most for their safety and good" (220).

By the same token, the people have the right to resist tyranny, which occurs when the legislative or the prince betrays their trust (221). The legislative does this by attempting "to take away, and destroy the Property of the People, or to reduce them to Slavery under Arbitrary Power"; the prince, by making his own arbitrary will the law or by corrupting, through force or bribery, the operations of the legislature (222). In either case, the people have the right to prevent or remedy the forfeiture of trust, by reforming the institutions or replacing the officials of the government (222).

Locke will allow no objections about how this doctrine might ferment frequent rebellion and reduce the society to ruin to gainsay the fact that usurpation and tyranny, by using force without right, constitute war upon the people (223–39). And he insists the people have the right to judge whether the executive or the legislative has actually started a war of this kind by acting contrary to its trust, for the people are the ones who have deputed them to govern in their name (240). "Upon the Forfeiture of their Rulers, or at the Determination of the Time set," Locke contends, "[Political Power] reverts to the Society, and the People have a Right to act as Supreme, and continue the Legislative in themselves, or erect a new Form, or under the old form place it in new hands as they think good" (243:15–20).

Locke did not hammer out this theory of revolution as an intellectual exercise any more than he did it as an incitement to mob rule. He did it to put teeth into his theory of natural rights. The cash value of his picture of the state of nature as a regime of natural law and natural right is its implication of a theory of popular sovereignty, together with the practical corollary of a people's right to rebellion. The preservation of natural rights in civil society was what Locke wanted to insure; the possibility of rebellion was what he wanted to avert. Yet he believed the people could not be secure in the possession of their rights without the threat of rebellion to keep the government honest.

The theory of rights Locke derives from such an argument makes political rights the articulation of natural rights. The natural right to life, in the form of "the first and fundamental natural law" of self preservation, becomes in civil society the primary function of government: "the preservation of the Society, and (as far as will consist with the publick good) of every person in it" (134:4–8). Political power, in Locke's definition of it, specifically includes the power of life and death over the members of a society, for it is the collective power of the members to recognize and punish violations of the law of nature. But this power must be used for the end for which it is intended: "to preserve the Members of the Society in their Lives, Liberties, and Possessions" (171).

Likewise, the right to liberty, as the freedom from absolute and arbitrary authority, becomes in civil society the prohibition against the legislative becoming absolute or arbitrary in making the law (135–37). The legislative does indeed assume supreme power in the society while it functions and acts for the common good (149–50). But the law of nature remains operative in civil society, so that the function of the legislative is to adapt the provisions of this law to the needs of the society and annex penalties to enforce their observation (135).

Lastly, it would be absurd to think the right to property could be lost, being that the preservation of property is the purpose of civil society and the end of government. "Hence it is a mistake to think," Locke says, "that the Supream or Legislative Power of any Commonwealth, can do what it will, and dispose of the Estates of the Subject arbitrarily, or take any part of them at pleasure." The members of the society must, therefore, have a right to the goods to which they are entitled by the laws of the society and to be secure from anyone taking them without their consent (138). What insures the natural rights underlying this and other political rights, Locke has argued, is the threat of rebellion against the government's abuse of its trust.

## Review and Conclusions

What is the import of the manifest contrast between Hobbes' and Locke's political theories for the foundation of rights? Three issues are of prime importance: the correlation between the state of nature and the constitution of the commonwealth; the function of power or force in either setting; and the consequent nature of the rights themselves. Much more could be said about the respective historical origins of the two theories and about their specific implications for our own and other societies. But for now it will be enough to emphasize the middle ground between origins and implications—the place of rights within the theories themselves.

For both Hobbes and Locke, the state of nature and the constitution of civil society are correlatives: the state of nature is supposed to provide the alternative to and the reason for civil society. No doubt the hypothetical condition of the state of nature seemed to be apparent to each of these philosophers in the actual conditions of his own society. But they each articulated their conception of the state of nature to provide a standard for judging their own society. For Hobbes, civil society in his time seemed to be on the verge of anarchy without the benefit of an absolute sovereign. Thus he depicted the state of nature as a state of war, for which the only remedy was a commonwealth centered upon an absolute sovereign with a monopoly of power. For Locke, on the other hand, the civil society of his time seemed to give promise of becoming a stable democracy if only it could be rescued from the machinations of an absolute monarch. Thus he portrayed the state of nature as a state of peace that civil society was supposed to preserve through a limited and divided government based upon popular sovereignty. Contrasting political conditions generated contrary speculative anthropologies and in turn contradictory political visions.

The role of power and force is crucial to both theories. For Hobbes, rationality is a hostage to force in both the state of nature and the commonwealth. In the state of nature, the rationality of the natural law is nullified by the irrationality of the natural right to life. The insatiable drive to power and glory fueled by this right makes everyone an enemy of everyone else, a condition in which it becomes impossible to heed the counsel of peace implicit in the laws of nature. Correspondingly, the covenant that provides the formal condition for the establishment of the commonwealth merely serves to ratify a right of conquest. For the enforcement of the mutual covenant to surrender power to the sovereign depends upon the prospective sovereign having the power to merit such an authorization.

But for Locke, rationality is in control of force in the state of nature just as in the commonwealth. In the state of nature, reason functions as a law insofar as it informs human conduct and authorizes the swift and certain punishment of violence. The law of nature is the matrix of human rights and the armature of the human community. Correlatively, reason incorporates popular sovereignty into the establishment of civil society even as it develops a government to remove the inconveniences of the state of nature. Whatever war may have done to precipitate the creation of civil society, or whatever contribution monarchy may have made to the origins of government, the essential foundation of civil society is common consent, and the power of government is a trust from the people. Thus Hobbes institutes force as the guardian of reason in the person of an absolute sovereign above the law; Locke holds force in abeyance with the threat of rebellion to insure that reason prevails in keeping the executive as well as the legislative subject to the law.

Their theories of rights are correspondingly opposed: Hobbes' being conventionalist, Locke's naturalist. Hobbes denies any validity to rights in the state of nature: the right to life is futile; liberty is reciprocally thwarted; property is unknown. In the commonwealth, though, the absolute sovereign protects the lives of everyone by holding them at his sufferance; liberty hides in private life and the silence of the law; property is allocated by the sovereign as he deems fit. Locke, on the other hand, derives rights from the state of nature, where he thinks life, liberty, and property are as much duties as rights, having a capacity for self-limitation as well as mutual reinforcement. Civil society is established, therefore, to have a community in which the bounds of these rights can be specified by law, impartial judges can settle disputes about them amicably, and effective enforcement of judicial decisions becomes practicable. Whereas Hobbes has a positivist conception of rights, making them the product of the commonwealth and indeed the prerogative of the sovereign, Locke has a rationalist conception of them, as intrinsic to and inalienable from human nature.

Does this contrast between Hobbes' conventionalism and Locke's naturalism imply that a social contract foundation for rights is necessarily authoritarian while a natural law foundation for rights must be liberal? Neither history nor logic imposes such a conclusion. Within a liberal nation like our own, the legal realism that is the heir to Hobbes' positivism has expanded the number and the range of rights through legislative action and judicial review. By contrast, natural law, albeit not necessarily from a Lockean perspective, has often been invoked to justify slavery, prohibit trade unions, and deny women's rights. Yet in a natural law foundation of rights there is an inherent power lacking in a social contract foundation. Only from a naturalist perspective can there be any appeal against the rectitude of constitutional provisions themselves or the authority of government officials in the performance of their duties. The realism and enforceability of conventional rights are counterbalanced, therefore, by the critical and transcendental appeal of natural rights. Without a natural basis for rights it is hard to see how there could be any distinction between morality and legality, how there could ever be constitutional moments in which a people rises up to suspend normal politics and refound a nation. More importantly, what standards can a people point to when they constitute a new nation, what standards can nations appeal to when they are in conflict with one another, if not rights implicit in human nature itself?

Yet both natural law and social contract have a role to play if a theory of rights is to be practical as well as sound. More attention must be paid to Hobbes' presumption that rights are based upon need—the overriding need to protect the right to life in the face of violence, which seems as endemic to civil society as it did to his version of the state of nature. This insight must be redeemed without incurring the liability in Hobbes' political theory of allowing power to subvert the very notion of right by substituting the structural violence of absolute sovereignty for the incidental violence of occasional crime, to the disregard of civil rights, dissent, and resistance to oppression. Likewise, the rational bases must be discovered, or recovered, for Locke's presumption that rights are natural to human beings, apart from any constitutional validation and in contrast to the identification of rights with the prerogatives of a power elite. This insight must be exploited without adopting a crude interpretation of Locke's theory of property rights—one that would dehumanize the very notion of right by telescoping life and liberty into property, instead of gauging the function of property by the needs of human development. A critical appropriation of the fundamental insights of Hobbes and Locke might well reveal more of complementarity than of contradiction between their two theories, while it might also enhance the rationality and the realism of discourse about human rights.

* *Professor of Philosophy, Ramapo College of New Jersey*

# Notes

1. For a report on the 1993 United Nations World Conference on Human Rights, see "A Rights Meeting, but Don't Mention the Wronged," *The New York Times*, 14 June 1993.

2. Bruce Ackerman, *We the People 1: Foundations* (Cambridge: Belknap Press of Harvard University Press, 1991); Gordon Wood, *The Radicalism of the American Revolution* (New York: Alfred A. Knopf, 1992); J.C.D. Clark, *The Language of Liberty, 1660–1832: Political Discourse and Social Dynamics in the Anglo-American World* (Cambridge: Cambridge University Press, 1994); See also Bernard Bailyn, ed., *The Debate on the Constitution: Federalist and Anti-Federalist Speeches, Articles and Letters During the Struggle over Ratification*, 2 vol. (New York: Library of America, 1994).

3. Ackerman, *We the People,* 7–16.

4. Ackerman, *We the People,* 16–33.

5. Richard Hofstadter, ed., *Great Issues in American History: A Documentary Record,* 2 vol. (New York: Vintage Books, 1958) 1:26–31, 46–52, 70–74.

6. Garry Wills, *Inventing America: Jefferson's Declaration of Independence* (Garden City NY: Doubleday, 1978), 167–255; Clark, *Language of Liberty,* 129–40, 176.

7. Hofstadter, *Great Issues,* 1:75–110.

8. Wood, *American Revolution,* 229–369.

9. Ackerman, *We the People,* 58–162. The civil rights movement, from Brown v. Board of Education in 1954 to the Civil Rights Acts of 1964, would also appear to be a moment of this kind, although Ackerman ignores it, while the Reagan presidency, which he does cite as a potential constitutional moment, has not had a similar ground-breaking impact.

10. Hofstadter, *Great Issues,* 1:103–07.

11. Charles A. Beard, *An Economic Interpretation of the Constitution of the United States,* new intro. (1913; New York: Macmillan, 1935) 17–18, 73–188.

12. Louis Hartz, *The Liberal Tradition in America: An Interpretation of American Political thought since the Revolution* (New York: Harcourt, Brace & World, 1955), 350–86.

13. Wood, *American Revolution.*

14. Clinton Rossiter, *Seedtime of the Republic: The Origin of the American Tradition of Political Liberty* (New York: Harcourt Brace, 1953), 142, 214–15.

15. John Diggins, *The Lost Soul of American Politics: Virtue, Self-Interest, and the Foundations of Liberalism* (New York: Basic Books, 1984), 67–68, 76–94.

16. Bernard Bailyn, *The Ideological Origins of the American Revolution* (Cambridge: Belknap Press of Harvard University Press, 1967), ix, 19–21, 34–39, 94–159, 283; idem, *The Origins of American Politics* (New York: Alfred Knopf, 1970), viii, 11–58; J.G.A. Pocock, *The Machiavellian Moment: Florentine Political Thought and the Atlantic Tradition* (Princeton: Princeton University Press, 1975), 467, see 427–40, 525–50; Gordon Wood, *The Creation of the American Republic, 1776–1787* (New York: W.W. Norton, 1972), 11–28, 49–70, and *passim.*

17. Wills, *Inventing America,* for the Declaration of Independence, and *Explaining America* (Garden City NY: Doubleday, 1981), for the Constitution.

18. Clark, *Language of Liberty,* chs. 3 and 4.

19. Edward S. Morgan, *The Birth of the Republic, 1763–89,* rev. ed. (Chicago: University of Chicago Press, 1977); Jack P. Greene, *Pursuits of Happiness: The Social Development of Early Modern British America and the Formation of American Culture* (Chapel Hill: University of North Carolina Press, 1988).

20. Thomas L. Pangle, *The Spirit of Modern Republicanism: The Moral Vision of the American Founders and the Philosophy of Locke* (Chicago and London: University of Chicago Press, 1988).

21. Citations, by chapter and page number within parentheses in the text, will be to Thomas Hobbes, *Leviathan,* ed. Richard Tuck, Cambridge Texts in the History of Political Thought (Cambridge: Cambridge University Press, 1991). That the point of Hobbes' political philosophy was to legitimate absolute sovereignty is a commonplace of Hobbesian scholarship, both among those who deny the cogency of the argument, like Jean Hampton, *Hobbes and the Social Contract Tradition* (Cambridge: Cambridge University Press, 1986), 3, ch. 4, and those who endorse it, like Deborah Baumgold, *Hobbes' Political theory,* (Cambridge: Cambridge University

Press, 1988), 10–15, 56–79.

22. Hampton, *Social Contract Tradition,* argues convincingly that Hobbes thinks shortsightedness (ch. 3), rather than either passion or reason by itself (ch.), is to blame for the interminable conflicts of the state of nature.

23. Hampton, *Social Contract Tradition,* 122–23, 126–27; Baumgold, *Hobbes' Political Theory,* 49.

24. This is not to adopt Hampton's interpretation in *Social Contract Tradition*, ch. 4, that Hobbes' conception of sovereignty by institution virtually collapses into sovereignty by acquisition because of the inconceivability of the former succeeding without a posse powerful enough to punish any potential violators of the social contract.

25. Baumgold, *Hobbes' Political Theory,* 37–55.

26. I reject the "orthodox paradigm" or "official interpretation" of Hobbes, exemplified perhaps most effectively in Hampton, *Social Contract Theory*. Hampton begs the question of the irrationality of absolute sovereignty (189); mistakenly assumes Hobbes is arguing for the individual self-interestedness of contracting for such a regime (167–88); and both misses the point and misinterprets Hobbes in contending his argument is invalid (and probably unsound as well) because rational individuals would not compact to alienate their right of self-defense if their object is self-preservation (190–97) but would (as Hobbes, in fact, allows) rebel against a tyrant threatening their lives (197–207). I agree, rather, with Baumgold, in *Hobbes' Political Theory*, that absolute sovereignty can conceivably be a rational choice (56–79) and that Hobbes is arguing it is preferable for ordinary people if the only alternative is to become embroiled in civil wars ignited by internecine elite conflicts (ch. 7). But I reject the assumption Baumgold shares with Hampton that Hobbes is arguing for a constitutional foundation of absolute sovereignty to avert the threat of losing a war, for I take Hobbes to be counseling the rationality of an *ex post facto* ratification of the historically normal foundation of states by right of conquest.

27. See Richard Tuck, *Natural Rights Theories: Their Origin and Development* (Cambridge: Cambridge University Press, 1979), 125–32.

28. References to the *Second Treatise of Government* will be to John Locke, *Two Treatises of Government,* ed. Peter Laslett, Student Edition (Cambridge: Cambridge University Press, 1988). They will be found within parentheses in the text, according to paragraph and, usually, line numbers; e.g. ((2:1–3; 24), with the exception of when entire chapters are indicated by 'ch.' and number; e.g. (ch. 9). References to Laslett's introduction will be in the endnotes.

29. Laslett, *Two Treatises,* 45–66; Richard Ashcraft, *Revolutionary Politics & Locke's* Two Treatises of Government (Princeton: Princeton University Press, 1986), chs. 7, 8, and 11; idem, *Locke's* Two Treatises of Government (London: Allen & Unwin, 1987), ch. 1.

30. Ashcraft, *Revolutionary Politics,* ch. 1.

31. Ashcraft, *Revolutionary Politics,* ch. 3; Ashcraft, *Two Treasises*, ch. 2.

32. Ashcraft, *Two Treasises*, 143–47.

33. Ashcraft, *Two Treasises*, 126–27.

34. See Ashcraft, *Two Treasises*, 107.

35. Ashcraft, *Two Treasises*, 198.

36. See Ashcraft, *Two Treasises*, 171–75, for a careful argument that Locke intended to include among the property-owners establishing civil society not just the landed gentry, but everyone with a stake in life.

37. The entire *First Treatise* is a refutation of Filmer's attempt to identify power with monarchy, to define monarchy as patriarchy, to trace patriarchy to Adam, and thus to claim a divine right of kingship. See also Ashcraft, *Two Treasises*, chs. 3–4.

38. This is contrary to Ashcraft, in Two Treatises, 115, where he argues that Locke did not allow for civil society without the simultaneous formation of a government.

39. Ashcraft, *Two Treasises*, 224: "Suffice it to say that if what is, in fact, a complexly structured work could be reduced to a single simple sentence it would be that the people always have an absolute right to defend themselves by force against the actions of a tyrant."

40. This is contrary to Ashcraft, *Two Treasises*, 216–18, in which he argues, consistently with his interpretation of the simultaneous origin of society and government, that the dissolution of the government returns the people to the state of nature.

# Chapter 9:
# Restitution, Retribution, Political Justice and The Rule of Law

Michel Rosenfeld*

## Revolution, Justice According to Law and the Need to Go Beyond

Violent revolution effectively simplifies the work of justice, by marking a sharp rupture between *ancien* and *nouveau régime*, and by providing a murky interim period fit for settling old accounts and for dismantling old power structures that stand in the way of the new order. Otherwise, justice's requisite backward glance would have to extend, in principle, to the beginning of history. This, moreover, would be compounded today, by justice's necessary extension farther into the future as a consequence of our increasing capacity to seriously threaten the vital interests of future generations.

Though they may at first seem as odd bedfellows, law like violent revolution, can also contribute to making justice's work more manageable. By reducing justice to justice according law one can avoid the uncertainties and disputes bound to surround justice beyond law in any contemporary pluralist setting.[1] In the face of significant disagreement concerning religion and ethics, attempts to harmonize justice according to law and justice beyond law could well dangerously polarize society. But violent revolution and justice according to law can combine to facilitate the work of justice, by obviating the need to address any claim to justice that stretches beyond law or that relates back past the revolution.[2]

As the recent collapse of the former Soviet empire demonstrates, however, not all radical, systemic changes occur in the context of violent revolution. Moreover, as indicated by many painful historical experiences in the twentieth century — ranging from Nazi and Stalinist atrocities technically conforming to law to *de jure* racial segregation in the United States — justice cannot always be confined in good conscience to justice according to law. Thus, the insufficiencies of justice according to law make it imperative to look to justice beyond law, including to political justice. Also, in light of the recent peaceful transitions to democracy carried out in certain former socialist countries, it is apparent that justice cannot simply ignore the actions of the previous regimes. Indeed, failures in the course of these transitions to restore property expropriated under socialism to their previous owners, and to punish or ban from public life those responsible for serious abuses under the past regime, have provoked intense calls for justice. And, in particular for restitution and retribution.

Restitution and retribution in the context of transitions from socialism to democracy afford a privileged vantage point to examine some of the most vexing problems confronting the scope and limitations of justice in contemporary settings. Not only do restitution and retribution stand at the crossroads between political justice and justice according to law, but also they must extend both backward and forward beyond the horizon of any single regime. Furthermore, restitution and retribution cannot be achieved independently of distributive, compensatory and procedural justice and yet they appear to undermine rather than to complement these forms of justice.[3] Paradoxically, restitution and retribution seem at once to depend on comprehensive justice and to preclude its achievement.

In what follows, I examine restitution and retribution and defend the thesis that in a pluralistic society comprehensive justice is at once necessary and impossible. Furthermore, I argue that the impossibility of justice should not be a cause for despair, but an occasion to renew the call for justice and to fuel its relentless pursuit. Because justice is impossible, we should constantly strive for its best possible approximation. And consistent with that there can be no categorical determination of the legitimacy of restitution and retribution. As we shall see, such a determination can only be properly made in context and from the perspective of comprehensive justice. For the former socialist countries of East Central Europe that means, I argue, that *some* restitution and *some* retribution may be justified.

Part II, places the problem of restitution and retribution in the context of the recent transitions from socialism to democracy in East Central Europe, indicates how this problem relates to other concerns of justice, and assesses some of the solutions proposed thus far. Part III, presents the case for comprehensive justice through an examination of the links between restitution, retribution distributive justice, compensatory justice and procedural justice. Finally, Part IV draws on the insights developed in Part III to buttress the claim that some restitution and retribution seems justified in contexts such as those of the recent East Central European transitions to democracy.

## Justice, Restitution, Retribution and East Central European Transitions to Democracy

The East Central European transitions to democracy provide a unique setting for considering questions of justice because they gave rise to a large number of complex and unsettling backward-looking and forward-looking issues. First, these new democracies had to deal not only with a forty year legacy of repressive and brutal socialism, but also with prior unresolved injustices perpetrated by the Nazi occupier or by local governments in the hands of Nazi sympathizers. To give but one typical example, take the case of Jewish property expropriated by the Nazis, then obtained by a local citizen in the interim period between the end of World War Two and the communist takeover of the late 1940's, and finally expropriated again by the socialist state. Second, in terms of the future, these transitions have had to deal with the thorny problems associated with transforming a socialist economy into a market economy, and with developing fair and efficient programs of privatization of state owned property. Moreover, these backward and forward looking issues are for the most part inextricably intertwined, thus exacerbating the potential for conflicts. For example, from a backward looking perspective, restitution of property to one who suffered expropriation by the socialist state might loom as highly desirable. But from a forward looking perspective, such restitution could well prove inefficient when compared to privatization favoring ex members of the socialist *Nomenklatura* who may well be best equipped to manage business enterprises.

Even if we remain exclusively within a backward-looking perspective, we encounter a wide array of different issues, which make principled and legitimate solutions both difficult and elusive. Thus, the acts under socialism which arguably call for some kind of compensation, restitution or retribution cover the gamut from outright murder and torture to treason, intimidation, the destruction of reputation, suppression of freedom of expression and freedom of conscience, religious persecution, arbitrary denials of opportunities, spying on and surveillance of ordinary citizens, and uncompensated expropriations of private property. Moreover, some but, by no means all, of the above acts were illegal under prevalent socialist laws. Furthermore there were acts, such as the killings and torture that took place in the aftermath of the Hungarian Revolution of 1956, which were illegal when committed but were not prosecuted due to the Communist Party's control over the legal enforcement apparatus of the state.[4]

From the standpoint of justice according to law, there is an important difference between past acts that were legal when committed and those that were illegal and, between illegal acts that are still punishable (because the statute of limitations has not yet expired and because the socialist law enforcement authorities have not decided not to prosecute) and those are not. Strictly speaking, acts that were legal when committed are beyond the reach of justice according to law as well as are illegal acts which have not been prosecuted pursuant to a legally permissible exercise of prosecutorial discretion or because of expiration of the relevant statute of limitations. To overcome the hurdle imposed by unjust laws or by politically tainted decisions not to prosecute, it may be necessary to appeal to political justice. Political justice, however, is problematic in that it puts current democratic governments committed to the rule of law in the paradoxical position of having to depart from it to redress past abuses of it.

Claims for restitution or damages for communist expropriations of private property raise another difficult theoretical problem that seems to have received little attention.[5] Discussions of restitution generally seem to assume that communist expropriations of private property amounted to wrongs properly calling for compensation or restitution. This assumption is reinforced, moreover, by the perception that current regimes are pursuing the *restoration* of the pre-communist institutional commitment to private property. Upon reflection, however, it is arguable that communist expropriations were not wrongs under then prevailing distributive norms, but rather legitimate acts in pursuit of the communist conception of the good.[6] Indeed, in and of themselves, expropriations of private property, which may be defended on Marxian, egalitarian or utilitarian grounds, do not necessarily amount to wrongs. Although unacceptable under libertarian conceptions of justice, nationalizations of the means of production and redistributions of property — which in varying degrees have been quite common in Western democracies[7]

— need not be regarded as inherent evils. In short, to the extent that communist expropriations can be plausibly viewed as failed but honest attempts to achieve a morally defensible conception of distributive justice, arguably they caused certain *harms*, but not necessarily any *wrongs*. And consistent with this, it unclear that the current regime would be justified to impose its own conception of the good or of distributive justice (and/or those of pre-communist regimes), when dealing with claims for restitution or compensation arising out of communist expropriations.

Another thorny problem relates to claims for retribution and raises issues of both procedural and substantive justice. In cases of murder or torture, retribution mainly raises procedural issues, as locating and convicting the culprits becomes increasingly difficult with the passage of time. In cases involving collaborators and informers who spied on their neighbors and who contributed to perpetrate the communist state's campaign of repression, fear and intimidation against its citizens, however, these procedural issues may well be overshadowed by difficult substantive issues.

A good example of these difficulties is provided by the controversy concerning "lustration" in (the then) Czechoslovakia.[8] After the Soviet invasion of 1968, Czechoslovakia's secret police systematically infiltrated the daily lives of citizens thorough a massive network of informers. Informers were by and large recruited through blackmail, and virtually everyone was subject to blackmail as many ordinary and necessary transactions had been rendered illegal.[9] Informers, moreover, caused harm as the information they provided was used to harass and embarrass citizens as well as to ruin careers. Also, the use of informers was so pervasive that people had reason to be suspicious of even their closest friends. It is therefore understandable that the victims of informers were ready for some kind of retribution, and lustration seemed appropriate as a way to expose former informers and to insure their exclusion from influential positions in the new democracy.[10]

Upon further consideration, lustration presented vexing problems as not all informers were equally culpable. Some had volunteered and received money or favors for their services whereas others only collaborated to save their families. Some provided information that led to ruining lives and careers, but others only furnished information which they believed to be harmless.[11] Moreover, in the atmosphere of repression and fear that permeated through the entire body politic, it is arguable that a vast majority of informers should not be judged by ordinary criteria for acts committed under extraordinary circumstances.

Restitution[12] may be regarded as a special case of compensatory justice. In the paradigmatic case of compensatory justice, the wrongdoer's illegitimate gain is equivalent to the loss suffered by the victim as a consequence of the wrong. In such case, the requisite compensation would at once eliminate the wrongdoer's gain and the victim's loss, putting both of them in the position in which they would have been but for the wrong. Moreover, particularly if compensation is to take place shortly after commission of the wrong, restitution may well amount to the best alternative in the paradigmatic case. For example, if a thief steals an heirloom from a victim, prompt restitution of that heirloom to the victim would seem best suited to satisfy compensatory justice.

Compensatory justice, however, does not require restitution; it only requires compensation equivalent to the victim's loss and the wrongdoer's gain. Furthermore, with the passage of time restitution may not even be equivalent to compensation. Indeed, compensation is supposed to put the victim *at the time of compensation* in the position in which she or he would have been *at that time* but for the wrong. Take for example, the case where a thief steals a valuable painting from an art dealer and keeps it for several years. Suppose further that cognizant of the fluctuations of the art market, the dealer would have undoubtedly exchanged the stolen painting during the course of those years for property which would now command a higher price. In that case, the value of restitution would clearly be lower than that of compensation, and it would clearly seem in the interests of the victim to opt for the latter.

There are also cases, on the other hand, where restitution would seem preferable to compensation. For example, where the personal emotional value of an item far exceeds its market value, a victim would be better off with restitution than with compensation. In addition, opting for restitution may obviate the need to extend compensation to all the members of what would otherwise amount to a similarly situated group of victims. Thus, in the context of the transition from socialism to democracy, restitution of expropriated real estate could be stressed so as to avoid the prospect of having to compensate all citizens for all the wrongs which they suffered under communism.

As compared to compensation which — at least in its paradigmatic case — is equally oriented towards wrongdoer and victim, restitution is more victim oriented whereas retribution is more wrongdoer oriented. Undoubtedly, retribution has roots in revenge, but there is also clearly much more to it than that. For example, retribution can play an important forward-looking role, by preventing past wrongdoers who have attained influential positions from enjoying great distributive advantages under the new regime. Furthermore, retribution may have a deterrent effect, by signaling to would be wrongdoers that the acquiescence of the current regime is no safeguard against future accountability. Also, even though retribution is oriented towards wrongdoers, it can have a positive effect on victims by publicly acknowledging their suffering and the systematic violations of their inherent dignity, thus symbolically effacing their degradation and simultaneously affirming their intrinsic worth.

Jon Elster has been a particularly forceful advocate against restitution and retribution in East Central Europe.[13] In essence, Elster's argument sketches an all or nothing position. Partial restitution and retribution, according to Elster, do not yield partial justice. They exacerbate injustice. Restitution is unjust as it favors former property owners over other victims. This is particularly objectionable to Ester who regards wrongful deprivations of educational and employment opportunities as likely to have caused greater harm than wrongful confiscations of property. Elster, moreover, considers partial retribution unjust, not only because it is exceedingly difficult to assess relative culpability in terms of the vicissitudes of daily existence under the yoke of the socialist state, but also because available historical records tend to corroborate the misdeeds of relatively minor wrongdoers while remaining largely silent concerning those most responsible for the mistreatment of the citizenry. Thus, Elster objects retribution on both substantive and procedural grounds.

George Sher disagrees with Elster's view of restitution, based on a distinction that he draws between the consequences of wrongful deprivations of property and those of wrongful denials of opportunities.[14] According to Sher, the general measure of compensatory justice should be adjusted for certain acts and omissions of the victim during the time period that extends between the injury and its compensation. Specifically, Sher is concerned that we not assume gratuitously that the victim would have pursued an opportunity had it not been wrongfully denied. Sher also believes that we should not disregard the victim's actual behavior to the extent that it belies that the victim would have taken advantage of the wrongfully denied opportunity. Consistent with this, the longer the time span between injury and compensation, the weaker the justification for compensation is likely to be. For example, if someone was just wrongfully deprived of an opportunity to attend a medical school, the case for compensation would be very strong. If, however, someone had been thus wrongfully deprived twenty years ago, the case for compensation would be much weaker, as there would be significant doubts that the person in question would have completed medical school, established a successful practice and remained in that practice until the present.

Unlike claims for compensation relating to deprivations of opportunities, claims for restitution are much less likely, according to Sher, to be fraught with uncertainty. Thus, if a farm has been in the hands of the same family for several generations prior to communist expropriation, it seems quite likely that the family in question would still own the farm absent such expropriation. Accordingly, Sher maintains that restitution of expropriated property is justifiable in as much as it is much less likely for property rights than for opportunity rights to be squandered by acts or omissions of victims.

Stephen Holmes proposes yet another justification for restitution.[15] Even if restitution is not morally justified or efficient, Holmes argues that it is nevertheless politically desirable in East Central Europe, because it legitimates the privatization of property which had been expropriated by the communists. From a purely backward-looking perspective, restitution may be unjust because it discriminates among past victims. From a purely forward-looking perspective, on the other hand, restitution is likely to be inefficient, to the extent that it would not put property in the hands of those best suited to exploit it for the common good. As a bridge linking the pre-communist past to the post-communist future, however, restitution is pivotal in its affirmation of the sanctity of private property and its consequent repudiation of the socialist vision. Moreover, the legitimacy and urgency of restitution can be magnified by treating the recent transitions to democracy as restorations rather than revolutions. Indeed, from the standpoint of a restoration not only must the post-communist future find firm roots in the pre-communist past, but the communist experience must be reduced to a mere passing aberration.

The communist experience can also be cast as aberrant through the use of retribution. Building on Ruti Teitel's notion of "transitional reparatory justice"[16] — according to which reparations in the course of the transition to democracy are designed to reinstate the fundamental rights and inherent dignity of the victims of the communist state — it seems plausible to justify retribution as a powerful tool of reparatory justice. Even if retribution is confined to publicizing past wrongs and making public the identity of past wrongdoers, it tends to restore the dignity of past victims by acknowledging that their suffering resulted from unacceptable misdeeds rather than from the unfortunate consequences of failed policies. Moreover, to the extent that retribution blocks the access of past wrongdoers to coveted benefits in the new democracies, it contributes to eliminating wrongfully obtained advantages and to establishing a clean slate.

On balance, many arguments can be advanced for and against restitution and retribution in the context of the East Central European transitions to democracy. Moreover, some of these arguments seem tailored to the particular circumstances of these transitions, while others do not. To be in a better position to sort out these arguments, however, it is first necessary to look into the relationship between restitution, retribution and comprehensive justice.

## Restitution, Retribution and Comprehensive Justice

Different forms of justice, such as distributive and compensatory justice, are often depicted as being entirely independent from one another.[17] Distributive justice, moreover, is primarily forward-looking whereas compensatory justice is backward- looking. Paradigmatically, compensatory justice seeks to restore a disrupted equilibrium between two persons, a wrongdoer and a victim, by placing both of them in the position in which they would have been absent the disruption.[18] Accordingly, compensatory justice seems to operate completely independently form distributive justice. Let us assume, for example, that distributive justice requires all benefits and burdens to be apportioned according to utilitarian principles. Let us assume further that a destitute mother of several hungry children steals a loaf of bread from a well fed millionaire. From the standpoint of distributive justice, there definitely seems to be greater utility in letting the mother keep the bread to feed her children than in insisting that she return it to its lawful owner. From the standpoint of compensatory justice, however, such a return seems clearly called for as the optimal means to eradicate the disruption caused by the theft.

Upon closer examination, compensatory justice cannot operate independently from distributive justice. The apparent independence between the two turns out to be purely a matter of *form*, which cannot be sustained at the level of *substance*. As a matter of form, the paradigm of compensation only requires two people and a disruption susceptible of erasure. Identifying such a "disruption" and locating the "baseline" upon which the "equilibrium" upset by the disruption is set, however, cannot be accomplished without reliance on substantive distributive principles. For instance, a small merchant that is run out of business presumably suffers the same *harm* whether this is due to theft or to competition by a much larger and more powerful business enterprise. Nevertheless, many would agree that theft is a compensable *wrong* whereas financial ruin as a consequence of lawfully conducted competition is not. Underlying this distinction, moreover, is a commitment to the proposition that the distributive outcomes of a free market economy are just (or at least not unjust). Accordingly, one can only sort out harms that amount to disruptions from those that do not, on the basis of contestable substantive distributive norms.[19]

Securing a baseline upon which an equilibrium susceptible of disruption may be established also requires recourse to substantive distributive norms. In a complex universe of social interaction, there are uninterrupted dynamic processes that constantly alter the total configuration of holdings and of intersubjective transactions. Without markers shaped by distributive norms, it is thus not possible to set baselines. For example, even if there is a consensus that theft is a compensable wrong, theft from a thief may not be deemed to justify compensation (at least with respect to the victim). Moreover, the relationship between baseline and distributive norms is particularly salient in cases involving changes in the prevailing principles of distributive justice. Assume, for example, that denials of opportunities to enter into market transactions are currently treated as compensable wrongs, but that they were considered justified under bona fide socialist distributive norms. Today, therefore, such denials of opportunities would certainly count as disruptions calling for compensation. But what is the proper baseline for such disruptions? Could it extend into the past to a time before the transition from socialism to democracy? Or should the change in prevailing distributive norms be deemed an impregnable barrier precluding any such baseline prior to the transition?

More generally, what counts as a disruption, in the context of compensatory justice, depends to a significant extent on the characteristics of the state of affairs that is construed as a baseline. At the highest levels of abstraction, one can distinguish between two contrasting types of baseline: one of them may be referred to as the "atomistic-individualist" baseline; the other as the "communitarian" baseline. Under the atomistic-individualist approach, the baseline emerges as a static universe of largely self-sufficient individuals who remain entirely independent from each other. These individuals, moreover, strictly refrain from interfering with one another based on their adherence to a regime of purely negative rights and duties.[20] Compensable disruptions under this type of baseline include, above all, departures from the status quo involving violations of negative rights. At the root of the communitarian type of baseline, on the other hand, is a dynamic community of persons mutually dedicated to the pursuit of welfare and solidarity through a collective undertaking secured through an elaborate network of positive rights and duties. Consistent with this communitarian baseline, compensable disruptions would arise not only form interference with another's rights, but also as a consequence of failing to intervene to further the well-being of others. Thus, whereas under the atomistic-individualist baseline failure to rescue a person in danger would not amount to a compensable disruption, under the communitarian baseline it clearly would.

Underlying the atomistic-individualist and the communitarian perspectives are not only different principles of distributive justice but also different conceptions of the good. From the atomistic-individualist perspective, the process of distribution generated by a free market economy is deemed to be just, and the good is defined in terms of satisfying the individual's needs, wants and preferences. From the communitarian perspective, on the other hand, distributive justice requires constraining or superseding market outcomes, and the good is conceived much more in terms of achieving solidarity and satisfying collective interests than in terms of promoting individualistic pursuits.

Consistent with the preceding analysis, compensatory norms cannot ultimately become independent from distributive norms, and both of them must necessarily be linked to contestable conceptions of the good. As a consequence of this, it seems preferable to approach questions of justice from consequence of this, it seems preferable to approach questions of justice from the unified standpoint of comprehensive justice than from the separate vantage point of each of the different forms of justice. Comprehensive justice encompasses all the forms of justice, including compensatory, distributive, restitutive, retributive and procedural justice. Moreover, what sets apart one conception of comprehensive justice from another are not the forms of justice but the different conceptions of the good upon which these competing conceptions are respectively grounded.

Actual handling of questions of justice is likely to be piecemeal rather than comprehensive. Accordingly, comprehensive justice should be regarded as analytic and critical tool of reconstructive theory.[21] In actual practice, for instance, whereas both compensatory and distributive justice require commitment to contestable substantive norms, the same group of actors may appeal to mutually inconsistent norms according to whether they are dealing with compensatory or distributive issues. Thus, it is possible to embrace a utilitarian principle of distributive justice and at the same time maintain that theft is a compensable wrong regardless of the utilitarian consequences of such compensations. In that case, a libertarian conception of the good informs compensatory justice while a utilitarian conception is reserved for distributive justice. In contrast to such actual practices, however, comprehensive justice requires adopting a single conception of the good, e.g., utilitarian or libertarian, and constructing a picture of how all the different forms of justice would relate to one another provided they were all consistently based on the same conception of the good.

Comprehensive justice is necessary as a means to establish consistent norms for the resolution of intersubjective conflicts. Comprehensive justice, however, is also impossible to the extent that it sets an ideal which cannot be met as the different requirements of the various forms of justice that it encompasses cannot be fully reconciled. By seeking to integrate backward-looking and forward-looking concerns, comprehensive justice allows for drawing more flexible and more permeable boundaries between different forms of justice. But even with this increased flexibility, the diverse forms of justice ultimately prove to have an irreducible core, and that makes it impossible to reconcile all the demands of justice.

Consistent with comprehensive justice, distributive justice should be understood in its broadest meaning as encompassing both the processes and products of distributions resulting from the workings of social, political or economic forces. This broad understanding conflicts with certain contemporary theories of distributive justice, such as that of Robert Nozick.[22] Nozick excludes market distributions from the scope of distributive justice, thus treating such distributions as if they were natural. Such exclusion, while convenient from a libertarian standpoint, should be rejected, however, to the extent that it unduly privileges one system of distribution above all others. Even if the ultimate *product* of a free market economy remains beyond the control of economic actors, the *process* of market distribution is within the control of human agents as much as any other means of allocating the benefits and burdens stemming from social, political or economic interaction. In this respect, the market is analogous to a lottery. In a fairly conducted lottery, no one can determine in advance who will receive the benefits to be apportioned by the lottery. Nevertheless, it is entirely within the control of a relevant group of social actors to decide whether to use a lottery or other means to apportion such benefits. And since neither markets nor lotteries are "natural" processes, it makes perfect sense to ask whether they result in distributively just outcomes.[23]

As broad as the definition of distributive justice is under comprehensive justice, it does not extend to truly natural distributions. Thus, for example an earthquake may certainly impose "distributive" burdens among those affected, but it does not properly come within the sweep of distributive justice to the extent that it lies completely beyond the control of human agents. In as much as it is within the power of human agents to deal with the consequences of natural distributions, however, claims in relation to such consequences are properly included within the scope of distributive justice. Accordingly, whereas it would make little sense to claim that the destruction of one's home by an earthquake is distributively unjust; it would be perfectly acceptable to claim that it would be distributively just for society to provide the means to rebuild homes destroyed by earthquakes; or, that government rebuilding one's neighbor's home destroyed in an earthquake but not one's own, is distributively unjust.

To obtain a better grasp of compensatory justice under comprehensive justice, two important points must be addressed. The first concerns the handling of cases that depart from the paradigm of compensation; the second relates to the treatment of conflicts between compensatory and distributive justice in cases in which both are encompassed within the same set of substantive norms.

As already mentioned, in the paradigm case of compensation, the wrongdoer's gain is equal to the victim's loss, so that compensation wipes both of them out simultaneously. But what if the victim's loss is greater than the wrongdoer's gain? Or vice-versa? Or if the wrongdoer is no longer in a position to provide compensation? Or, finally, if the victim is no longer in a position to receive compensation? Answers to these questions vary. Under American tort law, for example, wrongdoers — even those who have acted negligently rather than willfully — are generally obligated to compensate their victims for all the injuries arising as the reasonably foreseeable consequences of the wrong.[24] On the other hand, certain scholars have refused to extend the reach of compensatory justice significantly beyond the paradigm.[25]

Most of these line drawing problems can be satisfactorily solved or avoided by subsuming compensatory justice under comprehensive justice. Regardless of where the line is drawn, compensatory justice has essentially two distinct purposes: wiping out the wrongdoer's illicit gain and making up for the victim's unjustified loss. In the paradigm case, both these purposes can be satisfied through a single act of compensation going directly from the wrongdoer to the victim. But even in other cases, the wrongdoer should be not more *entitled* to his or her illicit gain, and the victim should not be deemed to have a less legitimate claim to compensation. In other words, the *bases* for compensation remain the same whether or not one departs from the paradigm case. The problem created by departures from the paradigm case boils down, therefore, to one of *asymmetry* between wrongdoer and victim in terms of the consequences of the wrong.

The problems posed for compensatory justice by asymmetries between wrongdoer and victim can often be resolved by means of recourse to other forms of justice. For example, where the wrongdoer's gain amounts to less than the victim's loss, it may still be just to require the wrongdoer to compensate the victim for the latter's entire loss. From the victim's standpoint, such compensation would be fully justified under compensatory justice. From the wrongdoer's standpoint, on the other hand, only that portion of the compensation which corresponds to his or her actual gain as a consequence of the wrong would comport with the dictates of compensatory justice. Nonetheless, it might still be just to make the wrongdoer responsible for the difference between the victim's loss and his or her gain, if exacting that difference from the wrongdoer could be justified under distributive or retributive justice. Thus, many wrongs do not have zero sum consequences, but result instead in a net loss. Imposing the burden of such loss on the wrongdoer rather than on the victim or on society at large, certainly seems defensible under plausible principles of distributive justice. Similarly, exacting the equivalent to the victim's excess loss from the wrongdoer may be justified under retributive justice. Indeed, in as much as it is the victim's loss rather than the wrongdoer's gain which supplies the proper measure of retributive justice, forcing the wrongdoer to assume the excess loss satisfies retributive justice. Furthermore, to the extent that retribution requires depriving a wrongdoer of all wrongful gains, retributive justice justifies stripping a wrongdoer of his or her entire gain even if that gain far exceeds the victim's loss. In the latter case, how the excess gain extracted from the wrongdoer ought to be disposed of would be a matter of distributive justice. Hence, the victim would only be entitled to such excess if that proved to be distributively just.

Focusing on the conflict between compensatory and distributive justice in cases in which they are both encompassed within the same substantive norms is particularly important because it reveals the limits of justice and of the permeability of forms of justice. To illustrate this conflict, take the following simple example. Suppose that distributive justice requires allocating scarce jobs to the most qualified candidates. Consistent with this distributive principle, compensatory justice requires compensating someone who was refused a job for which he or she had proved to be the most qualified candidate. Suppose further, that the adequate measure of compensation, under these circumstances, is to provide the victim with the wrongfully denied job or some equivalent job. And, finally, assume that in the overwhelming majority of cases, the most qualified candidates who secure highly competitive jobs are not terminated by their employers for lack of adequate performance on the job.

With this in mind, consider the following scenario. A proves to be the most qualified candidate for job J in year one, but the employer awards J to B who is clearly less qualified than A. B quits after a year on the job, so that a new competition is held for J in year two. A competes again in year two, but loses out to C. Now C is clearly entitled, under the applicable principle of distributive justice, to J in year two, but A is equally entitled to J at that time, under the applicable principle of compensatory justice. Since only one person can be awarded J, then (assuming that the employer in question has no other job equivalent to J to offer) either compensatory or distributive justice may be satisfied but not both. Furthermore, this example clearly indicates that compensations have distributive effects.

Whether A or C should get J in year two cannot be decided within the ambit of either distributive or compensatory justice. This could be decided, however, within the broader perspective of comprehensive justice. For instance, Alan Goldman has argued that in cases similar to the one discussed above, compensation should be given priority over conflicting distributive imperatives, for otherwise valid distributive norms could be consistently violated with impunity.[26] Even if all such conflicts between compensatory and distributive justice could be satisfactorily resolved under the aegis of comprehensive justice, however, *complete* justice would still be impossible to achieve. Also, no matter how much more flexible the boundaries between them may become when gaged from the broad perspective of comprehensive justice, compensatory and distributive justice would still at bottom remain two distinct and irreducible forms of justice.

Although compensatory justice is essentially backward-looking and distributive justice forward-looking, neither one of the two is, for the most part, exclusively oriented in one direction. Compensatory justice must not only be projected into the past, from the time of compensation to the time of the wrong, but it must also complete the same journey in the opposite direction. Indeed, compensatory justice must travel from the date of the wrong in the direction of the future, to construct what might have been but for the wrong — an operation that is crucial for purposes of establishing the proper measure of compensation. Whereas, strictly speaking, the work of compensatory justice ends at the time of actual compensation, the consequences of its construction of what might have been may well extend farther in to the future. Thus, in constructing the counterfactual establishing the measure of compensation, compensatory justice must avoid the excesses of undercompensation and overcompensation, to prevent adverse retributive or distributive consequences subsequent to compensation.

On the other hand, while distributive justice focuses on future distributions, it must sometimes account for past distributions, or look backward into the past in the course of fashioning apt vehicles for just distributions. For example, Rawls argues for fair equality of opportunity, in the context of the principles of distributive justice which he advocates.[27] According to Rawls, fair equality of opportunity requires that "those with similar abilities and skills should have similar life chances...irrespective of the income class to which they are born".[28] Consistent with this, implementing fair equality of opportunity requires looking to past income discrepancies, so as to be able to devise measures — such as remedial education — designed to eradicate those advantages in the competition for scarce employment positions that are attributable to past disparities in wealth. In other words, discrepancies in income are not "wrongs", but their effect on the competition for scarce benefits must be countered much as the consequences of wrongs under compensatory justice. Thus, although for different reasons, distributive justice must on occasion look to the past just as compensatory justice is bound to do.

## Just Procedures and Pure Procedural Justice

Even where appropriate distributive, compensatory restitutive and retributive norms are firmly in place, justice cannot be achieved in the absence of just procedures. Thus, for instance, assuming a consensus that theft ought to be punished under retributive justice, if criminal trials for theft resulted more often than not in conviction of the innocent, such trials would clearly promote injustice rather than advance the cause of comprehensive justice. Following Rawls, one can divide procedural justice into two basic types. The first type requires both an independent criterion of distributive, compensatory, restitutive or retributive justice to determine what would count as a just outcome and a procedure designed to lead to such a just outcome. The second type, on the other hand, which leads to what Rawls calls "pure procedural justice," does not require for its operation any reference to an independent criterion of substantive justice. Instead, as Rawls sees it, in the context of pure procedural justice, any outcome is just, provided only that a fair procedure was followed.[29]

Rawls draws a further distinction, within the first type of procedural justice, between "perfect" and "imperfect" procedural justice.[30] If the procedure adopted to pursue the outcome prescribed by the relevant criterion of substantive justice assures that outcome, than we have perfect procedural justice; if it does not, then we have imperfect procedural justice. Moreover, justice according to law, by and large, goes hand in hand with imperfect procedural justice. Indeed, both the civil and the criminal trial, indispensable tools of any modern scheme based on justice according to law, are prime examples of imperfect procedural justice.[31]

Two important consequences follows from the inevitable dependence of justice according to law on imperfect procedural justice. First, even if justice according to law were in perfect harmony with universally embraced norms of justice beyond law, it could not guarantee just outcomes. In other words, the very need to rely on imperfect procedural justice is sufficient to make complete justice impossible. Second, the very concept of imperfect procedural justice runs counter to any notion that justice boils down to an all or nothing proposition. And, if one is willing to accept that procedures ought to be evaluated in terms of whether they are more or less just, then it is fair to inquire how imperfect a procedure may be before it should be rejected as unjust. Thus, whereas the criminal trial under the adversary system of justice is an imperfect means to ascertain the innocence or guilt of the accused, it can be defended as procedurally just to the extent that it leads to the just outcome in a large majority of cases, and that — all other things beings equal — no less imperfect alternative is available. In general, imperfect procedures should at least be more likely than not to produce just outcomes, and not be reasonably replaceable by relatively less imperfect procedures. Beyond that, however, where the line should be drawn between acceptable and unacceptable imperfect procedures depends on contextual considerations which should be gaged in terms of the multifaceted concerns falling within the scope of comprehensive justice.

In as much as pure procedural justice does not require assessing a procedure in terms of any particular outcome, it is apparently immune to procedural imperfections. In the context of pure procedural justice, the focus is on process rather than on product or outcome. Thus, if *any* distribution flowing from the operation of a free market economy were deemed to be just, then such economy would produce pure procedural (distributive) justice. And, in the absence of any tampering with market processes, who actually benefits most or least from the workings of the market economy would be indifferent from the standpoint of justice.

Pure procedural justice may well close the gap between procedure and outcome, but it cannot overcome the impossibility of justice. Pure procedural justice makes the process paramount, but whether any particular process is deemed to be just depends on adherence to contestable substantive norms. For example, there is no consensus that a market economy is *inherently* just, and while libertarians may vigorously argue that it is, utilitarians and egalitarians may just as energetically claim that it is not. Moreover, even in case of a consensus on substantive norms, pure procedural justice would still produce less than full justice, from the perspective of comprehensive justice. In particular, any serious tampering with the relevant process resulting in long lasting consequences would pit the aims of compensatory justice against those of distributive justice. Suppose, for instance, that in the face of consensus on the justice of a market economy, a particular ethnic minority has been denied for several generations, through discriminatory laws, the right to own property. Obviously such discrimination amounts to a serious tampering with the integrity of market processes, and because of its long standing nature, simply repealing the offending laws would seem insufficient to eradicate its evil consequences. Indeed, the repeal of the discriminatory laws wold not put their victims in the position in which they would have been absent the imposition of such laws, but leave them with the accumulated disadvantages of years of denial of access to fair market competition. Accordingly, full compliance with the requirements of compensatory justice would entail at least some constraining or overriding of ordinary market processes.[32]

Because of its emphasis on process rather than on outcome, pure procedural justice renders the task of constructing the counterfactual required by compensatory justice more problematic. Indeed, it is, by and large, much less speculative to reconstruct what might have been but for a wrong on the basis of a given outcome than on that of a process consistent with a multiplicity of different outcomes. For instance, if someone was wrongfully denied a particular property several years ago, it would be fairly simple and very likely non controversial to arrive at the proper measure of compensation, based on knowledge concerning the rate of return over the relevant time frame for the kind of property involved. If, on the other hand, someone is wrongfully denied an opportunity to compete in the marketplace, it would be quite speculative to assume that but for this wrong he or she would have consistently succeeded or failed. But without some such assumption, it would not be possible to establish any coherent measure of compensation.

Because of greater uncertainties concerning the relevant counterfactuals, violations of process based distributive rights seem to be less attractive candidates for compensation than violations of outcome based distributive rights. Indeed, to the extent that compensations have distributive effects, as the uncertainty concerning the validity of measures of compensation increases, so does the likelihood of upsetting seemingly legitimate distributive rights. For example, suppose that an applicant who was wrongfully denied the opportunity to compete for a job is subsequently awarded that job as compensation for the wrong, even though that applicant could have only expected a decent chance of landing the job had he or she been allowed to compete for it in the first place. Under these circumstances, the person who actually won the competition for the job, but who does not get the job because of the compensation, would be giving up a hard earned distributive right on the mere chance that the compensated recipient might have actually been wrongfully deprived of the job and not only of an opportunity.

Upon further reflection, however, it is not true that the case for compensation becomes necessarily weaker with each increase in uncertainty concerning the relevant counterfactual. At least in the face of massive and pervasive tampering with a process based scheme of distribution, uncertainties surrounding the relevant counterfactuals seem to become much less objectionable. This is due, moreover, to the fact that in such cases existing distributions upon which putative compensations would impinge would themselves rest on highly shaky grounds. For example, if all women were wrongfully barred from competing from highly coveted jobs, the likelihood that the men actually holding such jobs would be in the same position but for discrimination against women would be much lower than if only a handful of women had been thus discriminated. Accordingly, in cases of massive and pervasive discrimination, the likelihood that compensations would upset *legitimate* distributive rights would seem no greater than in cases where the relevant counterfactual is much less speculative, but where entitlements to existing distributions can be much more firmly established. In sum, under comprehensive justice, the key question is not how uncertain is the validity of a particular measure of compensation, but rather how likely is it to upset legitimate distributive rights.

## The Conflict Between Political Justice and the Rule of Law

Comprehensive justice also casts useful light on the relationship between justice according to law and justice beyond law, in general, and that between political justice and adherence to the rule of law, in particular. Since even compensatory justice is dependent on contestable substantive norms, there can be no sharp divide between the realms of law, morals and politics. Moreover, at the prescriptive level, justice according to law cannot be systematically distinguished from justice beyond law in as much as they both necessarily express commitment to contestable substantive norms.[33] Notwithstanding the permeability of law to morals and politics and the affinities between justice according to law and justice beyond law, however, there is an important sense in which law and justice according to law remain irreducible at their core. And it is precisely because of this irreducible core that a strong emphasis on adherence to the rule of law and a healthy skepticism towards the legitimacy of political justice seem warranted.

In the context of a consensus on religious, moral and political values, justice according to law would be fully consistent and perfectly aligned with justice beyond law. In the absence of such a consensus, however, justice according to law becomes the antagonist of justice beyond law. Moreover, whereas this antagonism certainly constitutes a source of tension, it can also be exploited for constructive purposes. Although justice according to law can never achieve complete neutrality among conceptions of the good, it can hold together a pluralist society by minimizing interference with the pursuit of a broad range of diverse value preferences.[34] More specifically, justice according to law can function as a barrier that shields legal actors from the dictates of justice beyond law shaped by conceptions of the good which they find objectionable. To be sure, such a barrier can never be morally or politically neutral. Nevertheless, buttressed by suitable constitutional constraints and by a commitment to democratic lawmaking, justice according to law can furnish a sufficient barrier for most legal actors to ward off subjugation to unacceptable norms.

Although constantly buffeted by morals and politics and always subject to reconfiguration, at its core the rule of law carves out a protective shield comprising a two pronged means of exclusion. First, because of law's coercive power, a legal actor can cogently abide by legal norms while refusing to embrace the particular moral or political values that inform enforceable laws. Second, the rule of law can be used as a check against the rule of morals and against the sway of raw unmediated politics. For the rule of law to provide more than trivial means of exclusion, however, it cannot rest on *any* normative foundation or on a normative vacuum. For example, the rule of law of a fundamentalist theocracy might technically allow legal actors to refuse allegiance to religious norms enshrined in laws, but only within the innermost precincts of their own conscience. Furthermore, adherence to the rule of law framed by fundamentalist religion would certainly exclude most, if not all, other conceptions of the good, but would leave no room for the pursuit of alternative value preferences. Accordingly, for law's power of exclusion to remain meaningful, the rule of law must be founded on adherence to a particular set of substantive norms, namely those that inform pluralism.[35] In short, for the rule of law to provide the best possible shield against morals and politics and to afford the broadest possible scope for the pursuit of diverse value preferences, it must ultimately rest on the morals and politics of pluralism.

Although the rule of law and justice according to law cannot be purged of all politics, they remain distinguishable from political justice. Leaving aside the problem posed by blatantly political applications of justice according to law — such as when certain existing laws are only enforced against the political enemies of the regime — the main difference between legal and political justice boils down to the following: justice according to law can ultimately rely on appropriate legal norms already in place prior to, and effective at the time of, the occurrence of those events which give rise to the relevant claims for legal relief; political justice, on the other hand, is characterized by its inability to establish sufficient links with such pre-existing legal norms.

This difference may be clear in theory, but it seems quite murky in practice. This seems particularly true in the case of the common law with its incremental judicial elaboration of legal norms.[36] Moreover, in some cases, the distinction in question may well seem altogether untenable, such as, for instance, in the case of retroactive laws which are permissible in the United States, though confined to civil as opposed to criminal law.[37]

Notwithstanding these difficulties, the above mentioned distinction between legal and political justice can be cogently maintained, provided it is treated as a contextual rather than a formal distinction. Also this distinction should be ascertained form the standpoint of a plausible reconstruction initiated at the time of demand for relief and projected toward the past in search of suitable legal baseline and disruption. The aim of such reconstruction is to locate legal principles, standards and rules operative at the time of the events giving rise to a subsequent demand for relief which would support *ex ante* a reasonable expectation concerning the actual disposition of that demand for relief. Furthermore, such reasonable expectation need not necessarily be gaged in terms of the ultimate outcome of a particular demand, but may instead be justified in terms of an identifiable process compatible with such ultimate outcome. For example, particular outcomes may not be predictable in the context of common law adjudication, but knowledge of existing precedents and awareness of the processes and legal culture of a common law jurisdiction may suffice to reasonably anticipate a limited range of plausible outcomes. Similarly, familiarity with process may even bring, under appropriate circumstances, limited uses of retroactive laws within the scope of reasonable expectations of typical legal actors. Finally, from the standpoint of a contextual reconstruction such as that proposed here, the distinction between written laws and unwritten legal norms is by no means crucial. Indeed, in terms of shaping reasonable expectations, a well known unwritten legal standard deeply embedded in the legal culture would certainly loom as more powerful tool than an obscure written legal rule buried in the midst of a long and complex statutory text. In the last analysis, therefore, from the vantage point of contextual reconstruction, what distinguishes political justice from legal justice is that in the case of political justice it is not possible to establish a plausible unbroken chain of reasonable expectations, drawing on legal materials available at the time of the events giving rise to a claim for justice, and extending to the moment when justice is actually supposed to be dispensed.

On the basis of the preceding analysis, it becomes plain that justice is contextual, multifaceted, complex and always incomplete and partial but open to further perfection. Also, any given course of action is not simply likely to be just or unjust, but rather just in certain respects and unjust in others. Accordingly, the best that can be expected is a thorough evaluation from the standpoint of the various forms of justice subsumed under comprehensive justice, and a determination of whether a proposed course of action would, on balance, and in light of all the relevant circumstances, advance or set back the cause of justice. With this in mind, I now examine to what extent restitution and retribution might be justified under the circumstances of the East Central European transitions to democracy.

## Building Bridges Between Politics and Law: The Case for Some Restitution and Some Retribution in East Central Europe.

By considering restitution and retribution in terms of comprehensive justice, it is possible to cast a different light on the various claims that have arisen in relation to the East Central European transitions to democracy. Because the approach under comprehensive justice is contextual in nature, just resolutions of specific claims depend on taking proper account of all the relevant particular circumstances involved. My objective here, however, is not to suggest solutions to actual claims, but rather to focus on the interrelation between various forms of justice, using the East Central European transitions as rich and complex case study. With this mind, I only concentrate on the general features of the East Central European experience discussed above, but that should suffice to account for the various ways in which restitution and retribution relate to other forms of justice within the perspective of comprehensive justice.

Based on the analysis in Part III, neither Elster's all or nothing approach to restitution and retribution, nor Sher's defense of restitution above other forms of compensation will do. Given the ultimate impossibility of justice, Elster's conclusions seem unwarranted in the absence of proof that restitution and retribution exacerbate injustices rather than merely failing to promote justice evenly or uniformly. Similarly, Sher's defense of retribution looses much of its force, if the broad uncertainties concerning the accuracy of the counterfactual relating to wrongful denials of opportunities under communism are properly set against the dubious validity of the distributive "rights"[38] that emerged in the context of such denials. Thus, even if generally there is less uncertainty concerning wrongful deprivations of property than concerning wrongful denials of opportunities, that was arguably not the case with communist expropriations of private property and systematic denials of opportunities.

### The Case For Some Restitution

If wrongful denials of opportunities are set on the same footing as wrongful expropriations of property, purely compensatory justifications of restitution appear particularly problematic. More fundamentally, the case for compensatory restitution seems to collapse altogether, in the face of the assumption that communist expropriations were legitimate under *bona fide* socialist notions of distributive justice. Consistent with that assumption, expropriations of private property should be no more compensable than the collection of legally prescribed income taxes in Western democracies. Moreover, the fact that such expropriations would be compensable under currently operative standards of distributive justice, does not, standing alone, justify setting the relevant baseline prior to the time of the transition to democracy. Indeed, commitment to pluralism does not justify discarding the legitimacy of actions compatible with a plausible conception of distributive justice in the name of any other such plausible conception.

Pluralism, however, does set certain limits in the context of distributive justice. In particular, pluralism justifies the repudiation of distributive schemes to the extent that they are incompatible with an acceptable minimum of respect for inherent human dignity. The mere transfer of the means of production form private hands to those of the state for purposes of achieving a more egalitarian distribution of benefits and burdens certainly does not exceed the tolerable limits under pluralism. But if such transfer were carried out abusively, with contempt for human dignity, or excessively, through punitive confiscations bearing scant relationship to the control over the means of production, that would exceed the limits of pluralism.

To the extent that communist expropriations were abusive or excessive, socialist principles of distributive justice should be no bar to compensatory restitution. But assuming similar abuses and excesses in connection with communist denials of opportunities, then compensatory restitution wold only seem justified if those who wrongfully lost opportunities were also entitled to compensation. Otherwise, compensatory restitution would be unjust in as much it would promote unequal treatment among similarly wronged victims.

From the standpoint of distributive justice, restitution seems quite appealing in the context of the East Central European transitions to democracy. One of the most daunting tasks confronting such transitions is the implementation of a fair and efficient scheme of privatization of state held property. But any scheme of privatization that leaves too much discretion to the government in selecting the beneficiaries of privatization would smack of arbitrariness and favoritism, and thus clearly appear unfair. Accordingly, if for nothing else, restitution is attractive as a means to insulate privatization from the dangers of government favoritism. Also, consistent with Holmes' observations discussed above, restitution can add an important element of legitimacy to the new economic order. Because of communist expropriations and contempt towards private property rights, the proper functioning of the new order may well require a significant boost in confidence concerning the inviolability of private property rights. And what better way to convince the citizenry of the new order's commitment to property rights than to reach back to the pre-communist era in order, as much as possible, to restore the property rights trampled by the communist regime. In short, by reaching back to the pre-communist past, restitution creates an aura of legitimacy that allows the citizenry to approach their future much more confidently.

If restitution were efficient, then the distributive case for it would be very strong. But even assuming that it is, in and of itself, inefficient, its positive effects may still outweigh its negative ones, thus commending it as a distributive tool. In the latter case, however, restitution's principal worth would lie in its legitimating capacities, which suggests that distributive justice would be better served with some restitution than with restitution across the board. Indeed, if restitution is inefficient, then there ought to be no more restitution than necessary to reap its legitimating benefits. Furthermore, to place the new order on a just distributive footing, more than restitution would in all likelihood be required. If everyone is to get a fair shake and a boost in confidence, some positive measures toward those who were subjugated by the communists, but who were not property owners in the pre-communist era, would seem in order. Hence, some restitution combined with other means to boost the confidence of the citizenry might well loom as distributively just in the context of privatization and transition to a market economy.

Settling for some restitution raises a serious problem in as much as it opens the door for the perpetration of new injustices in the course of separating those eligible for restitution from the remainder of the former property owners. This problem can be minimized, however, by insuring that differences in treatment are based on the application of defensible principles. For example, restitution could be restricted to those who could combine a compensatory and a distributive claim to it. Or, it could be confined to certain classes of property, if that were justified in terms of efficiency or legitimacy. Thus, so long as it is circumscribed in a principled manner and used in conjunction with other compensatory and distributive tools, some restitution may well serve the aims of comprehensive justice in the context of the recent East Central European transitions to democracy.

## The Case For Some Retribution

In some respects, the case for retribution in East Central Europe seems more compelling than that for restitution. On the one hand, retribution touches on more bases of justice than restitution. In addition to spilling over into compensatory justice as it pertains to wrongdoers, and into distributive justice to the extent that it bolsters the sense of dignity of a much abused citizenry, retribution performs a punitive and deterrent function. On the other hand, the assumption that socialist expropriations of private property may be justified under a plausible conception of distributive justice, which significantly restricts the case for restitution, arguably has no effect on that for retribution. Indeed, none of the practices giving rise to claims for retribution appear to be justifiable under any plausible socialist conception of justice.

The case for retribution in East Central Europe, however, confronts several vexing substantive and procedural objections. Chief among these is one based on the conflict between the demands of retribution and those of adherence to the rule of law. For various reasons, many seemingly compelling claims for retribution cannot be satisfied without departing from adherence to the rule of law, as no remedy for such claims is currently available within the scope of justice according to law. Satisfaction of such claims would hence require recourse to political justice. But even if political justice were acceptable under certain circumstances, it would be most unfortunate for former communist nations to have to turn to political justice. Indeed, because of the communist state's pervasive flaunting of the rule of law, strict adherence to the rule of law looms as one of the fundamental pillars of the post-communist democracies. Thus, in terms of the overall integrity of justice in those new democracies, it seems preferable to give up retribution altogether than to compromise the rule of law.

Two other important objections, one substantive, the other procedural, are those raised by Elster. The substantive objection is that in some cases, such as those involving informers, the pervasive atmosphere of fear and repression maintained by the communist state makes it unfair to base determinations of culpability necessary for purposes of retribution on pre or post - communist standards of legitimate conduct. The procedural objection, on the other hand, is that record keeping under the communist state was such that proof of wrongdoing by relatively minor offenders is much more likely to be available than such proof against the worst offenders.

Based on the force of these three objections, it does not seem possible to make persuasive case for comprehensive retribution in East Central Europe. Nevertheless, a legitimate case for some retribution consistent with comprehensive justice can be made even in the face of these objections. Thus, to be justified, retribution must be consistent with the rule of law and justice according to law; be limited to conduct that remains clearly culpable even after due consideration of the distortions brought to bear by the communist state on ordinary norms of conduct; and must be made subject to appropriate procedural constraints to insure that acceptable standards of imperfect procedural justice are met.

A good example of how some retribution may well comport with the demands of comprehensive justice is provided by the Hungarian Constitutional Court's handling of the retroactivity law designed to make those guilty of murder and torture in the aftermath of 1956 Revolution punishable notwithstanding the expiration of the relevant statues of limitation.[39] In two publicized decisions in 1992 and 1993, the Constitutional Court held that it was unconstitutional to extend statues of limitations retroactively given the Hungarian constitution's commitment to the rule of law. Nevertheless, the Court sanctioned prosecution for those crimes that qualified as war crimes or crimes against humanity, as being consistent with justice according to law, in view of legal obligations undertaken by the communist government in Hungary upon becoming a signatory to certain international conventions, prior to the expiration of the relevant domestic statues of limitation.[40]

Even when punishment pursuant to standards of criminal responsibility is completely foreclosed by adherence to the rule of law, it may still be possible to justify some retribution within the scope of civil law. For example, compensatory retribution may be pursued thorough existing tort law, making those culpable responsible for civil damages to be awarded to their victims. Similarly, distributive retribution may be promoted through forward-looking laws rendering culpable individuals ineligible for certain benefits, such as highly coveted public offices. Thus, as these examples illustrate, as long as it is properly circumscribed and balanced, and supplemented by the promotion of other forms of justice, some retribution seems called for by comprehensive justice in the case of East Central Europe.

## Conclusion

The domain of justice is vast and unruly. It extends into the past as far as memory reaches, and into the future as far as our imagination allows. Justice is also impossible, not only because we can never sufficiently master memory and imagination, but also because we ultimately disagree about the good. Nevertheless, justice is necessary, and as proof of that we need only imagine how demoralizing it would be if we felt it to be completely pointless to ask for redress, in the name of justice, for the atrocities and abuses of Nazism or of Stalinist regimes in East Central Europe.

Justice may appear more manageable if we compartmentalize it into its various forms. But as the preceding analysis of restitution and retribution indicates, compartamentalization is more likely to lead to distortion and frustration than to success. Comprehensive justice, on the other hand, by allowing the various forms of justice to blend without giving up their core identity has proven more fruitful. To be sure, as the case for some restitution and some retribution in East Central Europe demonstrates, the successes of comprehensive justice can only be partial. But these successes must only be partial in the sense of calling for ever greater justice, and must avoid at all costs being partial in the sense of fostering more injustice than justice as a consequence of projecting too narrow a focus on their targets.

**Professor of Law, Benjamin N. Cardozo School of Law, Yeshiva University.*

# Notes

1. "Justice according to law is achieved when each person is treated in conformity with his or her legal entitlement. Justice [beyond] law, on the other hand, is the justice that makes it plausible to claim that a law is unjust (even if it is scrupulously applied in strict compliance with the entitlements which the law establishes)." Michel Rosenfeld, "Autopoiesis and Justice," 13 *Cardozo L. Rev.* 1681 (1992).

2. A revolution, even a violent one, is unlikely to extinguish all the legal entitlements originating in the *ancien régime,* but that would not alter the role of the revolution in limiting the temporal framework of justice. Indeed, in the context of a radical revolution leading to a fundamental reordering of a society's social and political institutions, any pre-existing legal entitlement that survives the revolution would best be conceived as dependent for its (continuing) existence on recognition by the new order.

3. See Jon Elster, "On Doing What One Can: An Argument Against Post-Communist Restitution and Retribution" 1 *East European Constitutional Review* n. 2, 15–17 (1992).

4. See "Special Report: Retroactivity Law Overturned in Hungary," 1 *East European Constitutional Review* n. 1, 7–8 (1992) and Krisztina Morvai, "Retroactive Justice Based on International Law: A Recent Decision By The Hungarian Constitutional Court," 3–4 *East European Constitutional Review* n. 4, n. 1, 32–34 (1993–94).

5. See "A Forum on Restitution," 2 *East European Constitutional Review* n. 3, 30–40 (1993).

6. I am disregarding, for purposes of this discussion, another factor which strongly reinforces the East Central European perception that communist were illegitimate. That factor is the role played by Soviet occupation and domination. See Shlomo Avineri's remarks in the *Forum on Restitution, supra* note 5.

7. One may object that expropriations in the West are not comparable to the extent that they legally or constitutionally call for just compensation. See, e.g., U.S. Constitution, Amendment V. Nevertheless, much welfare-state regulation which restricts the exercise of private property rights does not require any compensation and thus resembles uncompensated expropriations. See e.g. *Keystone Bituminous Coal Association* v. *De Benedictis*, 480 U.S. 470 (1987) (public welfare land use regulation prohibiting mining company from mining 27 million tons of coal located under its own property upheld by the U.S. Supreme Court).

8. "Lustration" comes from the Latin term *lustrum*, "meaning a purifying sacrifice. Today, lustration refers to the examination of records seized from the secret police to discover whether people in positions of authority had been, during the communist era, among the more than 100,000 collaborators secretly informing on their fellow citizens." Vojtech Cepl, "Ritual Sacrifices," 1 *East European Constitutional Review* n.1, 24 (1994).

9. *Id.*

10. *Id.*

11. *Id.*, at 25.

12. Restitution is "the return of something to the owner of it or to the person entitled to it..." *Black's Law Dictionary* 1477 (4th Ed., 1968).

13. See Jon Elster, "On Doing What One Can," 1 *East European Constitutional Review*, n. 2, 15–17 (1992).

14. See George Sher's remarks in the *Forum of Restitution, supra* note 5.

15. See Stephen Holmes' remarks in the *Forum on Restitution, supra* note 5.

16. See Ruti Teitel "Reparatory Justice" (work in progress) (on file with the author).

17. See, e.g., Ernest Weinrib, "Legal Formalism: On the Immanent Rationality of Law," 97 *Yale L.J.* 949, 980, 984 (1988) (Compensatory or corrective justice and distributive justice are irreducible, and hence particular juridical relations come either within the sweep of corrective justice or within that of distributive justice, but never within that of both). Weinrib's views are consistent with Aristotle's for whom distributive justice concerns the distribution of public goods by political authorities whereas corrective or compensatory justice applies to private transactions. See Aristotle, *Nicomachean Ethics*, Book V (D. Ross, transl. 1925).

18. For a more extended discussion of the relation between distributive and compensatory justice, see Michel Rosenfeld, *Affirmative Action and Justice: a Philosophical and Constitutional Inquiry* 29–41 (1991) and Michel Rosenfeld, "Deconstruction and Legal Interpretation: Conflict, Indeterminacy and the Temptations of the New Legal Formalism" in Drucilla Cornell, et al. eds. *Deconstruction and the Possibility of Justice* 152, 179–88 (1992). The present discussion draws upon these works and further elaborates certain points made there.

19. For example, one may contest the proposition that lawful competition does not give rise to compensable wrongs, by maintaining that free market outcomes are unjust, or that they are only not unjust in cases where there are no great disparities among competitors.

20. See Michel Rosenfeld, "Deconstruction and Legal Interpretation", *supra*, note 18, at 184–86.

21. Reconstructive theory establishes analytically useful models through completion and supplementation of empirical data with the aid of counterfactuals. See Michel Rosenfeld, "Law as Discourse: Bridging the Gap Between Democracy and Rights," 108 *Harvard L. Review* (1995) (Book Review) (Forthcoming).

22. See Robert Nozick, *Anarchy, State and Utopia* 149–82 (1974).

23. Implicit in moral condemnations of gambling are judgments that they are distributively unjust, either because they unduly burden those who can ill afford to gamble or because they reward luck rather than merit. See *Marrin* v. *Trout* 199 U.S. 212 (1905) (gambling is a public vice). See also Reuven Brenner and Gabrielle Brenner, *Gambling and Speculation: a Theory, a History and a Future of Some Human Decisions* 49–90 (1990).

24. See William L. Prosser, *Torts* § 1, § 43 (4th ed. *1971); Milwaukee and Saint Paul Railway Company* v. *Kellog*, 94 U.S. 469 (1876).

25. See, e. g., Jules Coleman, "Moral Theories of Torts: Their Scope and Limits. Part II", 2 *Law and Philosophy* 3 (1993).

26. See Alan Goldman, *Justice and Reverse Discrimination* 65–67 (1979).

27. See John Rawls, *a Theory of Justice* 83–89 (1971).

28. *Id.* at 73.

29. *Id.*, at 85–87.

30. *Id.*, at 85.

31. Significantly, Rawls chooses the criminal trial under the adversary system of justice prevalent in the United States to exemplify what he means by imperfect procedural justice. See, id, at 85.

32. See the example concerning employment discrimination *supra*, at 27–28.

33. In other words, whereas the normative force of law may ultimately stem from its pedigree and enforceability (consistent at least with legal positivism), the particular content of any given law is more likely to be justified under certain conceptions of justice beyond law than under others. Thus, a complete legal ban on abortion would obviously be much closer to the Catholic Church's conception of justice beyond law than to that of contemporary radical egalitarian feminists.

34. For a systematic account of law as furnishing the normative backbone of pluralistic democracy, see Jürgen Habermas, *Between Facts and Norms: Contributions to Discourse Theory of Law and Democracy* (The MIT Press, 1995) (forthcoming).

35. For an argument in support of the proposition that pluralism is ultimately grounded on substantive rather than merely process-based norms, see Michel Rosenfeld, "Autopoiesis and Justice", *supra* note 1, at 1695.

36. For a discussion of the dynamics of common law adjudication, see Michel Rosenfeld, "Deconstruction and Legal Interpretation," *supra* note 18, at 168–69.

37. The United States constitution prohibits retroactive criminal laws. See U.S. Constitution Article I, Sec. 9. This ban, however, does not extend to civil laws. See, e.g., *Calder* v. *Bull*, 3 U.S. 386 1798.

38. If one considers the entire communist system for allocating benefits and burdens to have been unprincipled and unjust, then it would be more accurate to speak of distributive "advantages" instead of "rights".

39. See authorities cited in note 4, *supra* and "Constitution Watch: Hungary," 3–4 *East European Constitutional Review* n.4, n.1 10–11 (1993–94).

40. *Id.*, at 10.

# Chapter 10:
# The Concept of Justice in Computer Managed Telecommunications


George Teschner*


## Technological Revolution

The essence of the computer revolution is not electronic. Computers could be designed from optical or hydraulic circuits through which the light or fluids move, instead of electricity. The real revolution is linguistic. The computer allows for natural and formal languages to be efficiently and economically encrypted into binary code. Binary code consists of 1's and 0's and every statement in literature and science can be translated into it. The significance of the binary code is that its analog in the machine is the on-off switch. The great technological achievement in electronics in the latter half of the twentieth century was the invention of the transistor and the integrated circuit. Current technology packs billions of switches per cubic inch. The state of each switch corresponds to a 1 or 0 in binary code and a sequence of 1's and 0's corresponds to a string of alpha-numeric signs. Strings of alpha-numeric signs are the balances in bank accounts, the plays of Shakespeare, the entries in card catalogs and online encyclopedias, or what, in other words, has come to be known as "information".

The encrypting of language into machine manipulable binary code is as revolutionary for the technology of written language as was the invention of movable type. Just as the printing press caused the disappearance of the medieval scriptorium, the storing, copying, searching, retrieving, and transmitting of digital texts is making the traditional technology of the printed book obsolete. The storage of electronic texts is reliable and economical. Paper is bulky and perishable and requires the huge cataloging and storage facility of the traditional library. The continuous shelving and unshelving of books are labor intensive. The storage of electronic texts takes little or no space. The cataloging, classification, copying, retrieving and searching of electronic texts are automated and instantaneous. The clear advantages of digitized over printed text are forcing the reconceptualizing of copyright law, property rights, and authorship. How will it affect concepts of fairness and justice? To answer this we must look at the digitization of communication, ask how digital communication is different from forms of communication that have existed historically, and how the conception of justice will be effected by communication technology.

## Communication Technology

There are parameters, such as bandwidth, audience size, and interactivity that are useful in comparing different kinds of communication media. Bandwidth is the amount of data that can be transmitted at any given time. A voice grade telephone line transmits 15,000 bits per second, whereas fiber optic transmits over a hundred megabits per second. By increasing the number of lines, for instance, by laying more cable, the bandwidth of electrical and optical transmission can be increased without limit. The bandwidth provided by the electromagnetic spectrum, the carrier of radio and television transmissions, is narrow by comparison.

Books and magazines can also be described in terms of bandwidth. The amount of information that can be printed and distributed in the form of pamphlets, news articles, books, magazines, etc. is limited only by the availability of printing presses and paper. Hence the bandwidth of print is, in principle, unlimited. Limitations arise out of social and economic factors not because of the physical nature of the medium.

Printed material that is transmitted and stored in the same form that it is read requires huge and expensive facilities for holding and accessing printed information. Transmission of printed data depends upon moving masses of paper. Transmitting data whose physical embodiment is paper is an exceedingly slow process compared with electrical and electromagnetic transmission.

Although, like TV and radio, print is capable of reaching large audiences, printed material does not allow for interactive communication. The medium of television and books gives the viewer or reader no opportunity to directly and immediately affect the nature of the information that is being sent. The audience size of books, television and radio is large, whereas the audience size for the typical telephone conversation is usually limited to one.

The communication parameters are bandwidth, interactivity, individualization of information, speed of transmission, and ease of access and storage. Individualization of information is important because the recipient may already possess the information, thereby, making it irrelevant, or the information may presuppose knowledge that the recipient lacks, making it incomprehensible. Even worse, lacking interaction, there may be the impression that communication has occurred when it has not. The familiar phrase "Do you copy?" or "Return Receipt" is interactive to the extent that the sender knows that the recipient has received the message, but there is no way of knowing in such limited feedback that the communicants mean the same thing by the same message. The style and content of the communication are largely a function of the audience - hence the difference between professional journals which are written for select audiences, and magazines written for the general public. Whole differences in genre can be traced back to whether or not the medium of communication allows for interaction and the customizing of the message to the audience. The speed of transmission and the economics of storage and reproduction in the case of television and radio are an advantage over print. However, accessing recorded audio and visual information is difficult compared to indexing textual information.

How does live public speaking or classroom lecture compare with above mediums? In these cases, the larger the audience, the less interactive and individualized the communication. The inverse ratio of audience size to interactivity, is not different for radio and television. Although, in a lecture, a member of the audience has the opportunity of giving the speaker feedback to affect what is being said, the interaction is limited and the limitation increases with the size of the audience. Applause, laughter, facial expressions, and the shuffling of the body may be the only cues the speaker has of the effect the words are having on the audience.

Immediacy is a measure of how near the receiver is to the original text. How many hands has the communication passed through before it has been received? With each exchange in the transmission, the original spoken or written text is interpreted and altered. The mediation of text through channels of communication is often done to reduce the size of the original text. In that case the function of mediation is summarizing and condensing. In a lecture, mediation can either take the form of exegesis with the original text being interpreted and translated into a language, i.e., a vocabulary and syntax, that is familiar to the audience. For noninteractive mass communication considerable mediation must occur in order for the original text to be effectively received by a general audience. Mediated communication removes the receiver from the text of the original message by levels of interpretation which make it impossible for the receiver to challenge the interpretation.

Immediacy also means proximity in time. In order for communication to have temporal immediacy there must be no break in the continuity of the meaning bestowing context. The environment of the communication must remain hermeneutically stable. Although letter writing is interactive, the length of the period of time between the sending and receiving of messages is so long that continuity of context is broken. Letters are always an interruption in the daily course of affairs. One never sends a letter and then does nothing until the letter is answered. The letter arrives in the middle of some other project. So an interruption must occur in order that the letter is read. The sense of continuity that a reader may feel in reading the correspondence between two writers is a privilege the writers themselves could not have.

Is there a form of communication that optimizes all communication parameters? It would have to have the following properties: 1. no limit on the audience size 2. be individualized, and not mediated by translation and interpretation by third parties, 3. interactive, and 4. have unlimited bandwidth. Since the number of exchanges would be large, there would have to be some form of automatically sorting and ordering the messages by sender, receiver, time and subject matter, that is, who sent it, to whom it was sent, when was it sent, and what was it about? The question, "What is it about?", in information science translates into key words and combinations of key words according to boolian formulas. "What is it about" is a genus with many subcategories that can be manipulated according to different logical strategies. This is where computer technology links up with communication technology, both digital, to produce a computerized communication system that combines the advantages of computerized databases with the speed and bandwidth of electrical-optical transmission. In the current language of communication technology such a revolutionary system of communication goes under the unpretentious name of "bulletin board." Human civilization has never before experienced this form of communication. It is mass communication that is individualized and interactive.

## The BBS Message as Enunciative Event

The appreciation of the bulletin board message as a legitimate genre requires overturning certain assumptions about the nature of language and language acquisition.

The distinction between the acquisition of knowledge and the acquisition of language skills blurs as soon we begin to question the familiar distinction between meaning and expression. If there is no meaning behind the expression, and meaning is nothing more than the use and function of an expression, then language is less the means of acquiring knowledge, and more the substance of what is acquired. There is no content apart from language that can be reached through language. Language and language practices are the entirety and the substance of what is communicated.

Traditional assumptions about the nature of language that separate meaning and expression diminish the importance of a highly social interactive environment, like that of the BBS, for acquiring the language practices that constitute expertise in a given field. Among these assumptions are, that words are accompanied by nonlinguistic entities, namely meanings, which give words their value without which words would be mere things. Another assumption is that the meanings exist in isolation from one another, or, in other words, that they are nonrelational, and that meanings are transcultural and universal.

In nonlinguistic skills, competence is rarely abstracted from performance. The belief that the *way* something is said is less important that *what* is said, and the image of language as a conduit through which knowledge and information pass, is dependent upon the assumption that the substance of language rests in something that is nonlinguistic. The result is diminishing the importance of the actual linguistic event and the interactive contexts in which ways of speaking and writing are learned. This is much less true in oral cultures where the enunciative event is very important. The retelling of a story and the repeating of speech is never merely a re-presentation, but is a new presentation and performance. The printed book, compared with messages on the BBS, gives the impression that the meaning of words exists independent of the context in which the words are used. We repeatedly entertain the superstition that meaning is in the text itself, and that knowledge is, for instance, contained in libraries. But the meaning of a word resides in an interactive event that occurs at a particular time and place between specific addressers and addressees. The inscriptions in books are their traces. Where the event of enunciation is important, the hermeneutic character of the act of reading and listening is revealed. The printed text is not the enunciative event but rather its effect. Reading is a process of reconstructing the event that produced it. A statement can change in its meaning depending on whether the statement is made in law, ethics, or psychology. But mentioning these fields does not come close to the specificity of context that would fix the meanings of the sentence. To approach that we would need to know answers to the questions, when, where, by whom, to whom, and why, in the sense of knowing what function the utterance performs. It is this sort of information that the message log on the BBS presents to the reader. Instead of being left with the impression that there is a substance that words express, that is distinct from the expression, we have the impression that the value of the word resides in the particular way in which it is used in the process of conversation. With the printed book such a context has vanished.

That there are meanings that are isolatable, independent of a specific context of discourse diminishes the hermeneutical and pedagogical value of linguistic interaction of the kind that is found on the BBS. The attachment, for example, of the names of the addressor and addressee, time and date, and classification according to subject matter, all of which are clues indicating context, would then appear incidental to the substance of the message. If language acquisition is interactive and contextual, then indicators of context are semantically significant. Who said what, when, are important determinates of the meaning of what is said. Other parameters that determine meaning, for example, are whether the message is a reply to a previous message or whether a message is the beginning of a thread of messages that have branched to other topics. Such information, on the BBS, is immediately and instantaneously accessible in a way that is not possible in other communication and instructional mediums. It is always possible to overcome the disadvantage of entering into the middle of a conversation by returning to the beginning of the message log. The message log is a labyrinth of message threads that can be thought of as passages through the total semantic fabric of meaning that constitutes what the message log is about. The message log can be reviewed chronologically or topically and each reading reveals different semantic patterns.

That the meaning of words has a transcultural and transcendental existence further reduces the importance of the interactive conversational event, the act of enunciation. The word 'enunciation' has connotations of speech, yet the bulletin board is a literary medium, that is inflective, which makes the event of enunciation important. The inflection is not the rising and lowering, contracting or prolonging of phonemes. Instead it is the manipulation of other parameters of the electronic message such as the length of the message, the context of messages in which the message has been placed, the length of the sentences, its placement in the rhythm of conversation, etc.

The more sensitivity to the contextual nature of meaning, the less likelihood that the meaning of a word will be seen as depending upon some extralinguistic reference to concrete or abstract objects. With an increased awareness of the different way words are used, the less likelihood there is of reification. With an awareness of what words do from context to context there is a consciousness of language as a complex system of external relationships rather an expression of internal states.

## Semiotic Coordinates of the Message

The units of "meaning," that is, the elementary objects of interpretation are not words but texts. A word by itself does not constitute an enunciative event. The word 'penalty' uttered alone is not merely ambiguous; it is nonsense, until it is placed within a text that is present either virtually or actually. It must become part of a system of signs that, in the language of the grammarian, would be said to constitute a complete thought. A sentence is a text in so far as it is an elementary unit of meaning and the signs that make it up achieve the value that they have in dependence upon one another. There are jigsaw puzzles for children where each piece contains a large enough part of the entire picture that the portion that is depicted in the puzzle piece, is recognizable. More difficult puzzles fragment the picture so that no object is recognizable in the puzzle piece. In a highly fragmented picture, the puzzle piece is analogous to the nonsense of the utterance of an individual word. In the case of a sentence, it may be unclear what other sentences are connected with it, yet by itself it clearly possesses potential meaning in so far as we are ready to place it in some discursive context. Such is the distinction between nonsense and ambiguity. Nonsense has no meaning, we have no clue to where it belongs. Ambiguity has a surplus of meanings or interpretations no one of which can be fixed. In the case of ambiguity, we are able to imagine many contrary contexts in which the ambiguous utterance could meaningfully be placed. In nonsense we can imagine none.

What does the distinction between nonsense and ambiguity have to do with the BBS message? Messages are replies or requests for replies. They are of a genre suited to an interactive form of discourse. Messages are interconnected. Intertextuality is clearly at work in the message log. The meaning of a message text is not something isolated from other message texts. A printed book, by contrast, appears to be separated within bound pages from other parts of the world. It is something that appears finished, complete and independent. We speak of the contents of printed texts as having perennial meaning that transcend its time, place and origin, its culture and historical epoch. The morning newspaper, by contrast, is a slice in time. It is an arbitrary cross section of the continuum of events. The paper on which it is printed, and its text, becomes trash by the time the day's sun has set. The printed book appears less of an event, than the contingency and transience of news print. For the printed text we need to be reminded of its intertextual and cultural dependencies. We experience meaning, in one case, as internal, and in the other case, as external to the text. In the printed book, disambiguation is a centripetal phenomenon moving in toward a center, toward the intention of the author, in the BBS message, disambiguation is a centrifugal phenomenon moving outward toward a circumference that is the entire message log.

It has been the character of literate culture to be biased toward writing genre whose meaning is internal and centripetal. The writing is not seen as an event that is dependent on the particular circumstances of the addressor and addressee. A message, in its specific formal characteristics, is more closely related to a letter than to a novel or essay. It is brief and aphoristic. However, this formal resemblance is not to be taken for granted. Although a letter is prosaic, a message can take as many forms as it seems fit to the users. We can find poems, notes, or essay-like messages. Messages can be as long as one word or longer than a few pages. It seems more appropriate, in the end, to consider a message as a "space" where the act of enunciation is performed, and only loosely as a literary genre, since it can take so many different forms. What unites messages, rather than a common form, is their event characteristics, their temporality rather than their textual structure and format.

It is not the physical shape of the message but its placement in the rhythm of events that constitutes it as part of the message log.

In sending the message, the user is asked several things, among which date, number of messages, reference, receiver, sender, subject, status (public or private), conference, help place the message in the appropriate context. The information constitutes an index which marks the position of the message in semantic space. It determines how hermeneutically active the particular message is with respect to other messages. All the "header" information, singularly or taken together, can be the source of a possible interpretation. This means, among other things that the value, i.e., the potential productivity, of the message depends, to various degrees, on the header information. The productivity of a message is the degree of influence that it has in the messages log. A highly productive message would therefore receive many replies and produce branching into different topic areas. A particular message could be so productive that it may require creating a new conference with a new category of message.

The message log is a dialogical medium that discourages the solitary monologue. Messages are events occurring between addressers and addressees. Silent writing, e.g., a diary or journal, like silent speech, talking\writing to oneself, are special features belonging to literate cultures with advanced writing and printing technologies and are either unknown in oral societies or regarded as abnormalities. In oral societies, language is always an external phenomenon. Since the environment is dialogical and interactive, a user that "writes to and for him or herself" is an oddity. On the BBS, solitary thinking would amount to the absurdity of sending a message to oneself and listing it as private.

## Online Communication and Disputes over Justice

The most abstract definition of justice is "equals to equals and unequals to unequals." Aristotle distinguishes between numerical and proportional equality.[1] When we speak of people being treated fairly, we mean not that every person gets the same amount to the same degree, but rather that each receives the same proportionally. The proportion, for example, could be according to need or contribution. We could claim that those who are sick should receive more than those who are well, because they have greater need. So the principle of unequals to unequals, when applied in this situation, results in those who are well receiving less than those who are ill. However, if it is contribution that is considered, and it is distribution and contribution that are expected to be in proportion, then those who are ill would receive less than those who are well. In either case there is agreement that equals should be given to equals and unequals to unequals, but what is in dispute is whether it is need or contribution that is going to be included in the equivalence. Furthermore those who are sick and those who are well may be unequal as far as health and sickness are concerned, but equal with respect to such things as age, geographical location, and social position. If such factors as these are considered in establishing equivalence and difference, then whether well or ill the same amount would be distributed to each.

The same abstract principle of justice can yield two contradictory propositions in application. Aristotle, observes that "men agree that justice in the abstract is proportion."[2] Then we may ask, " What is the cause of dispute over matters of justice?" Aristotle's explanation is that we make the mistake of thinking that things that are equal in one respect are equal in all respects. So in our example, disputes would arise when need and contribution were considered exclusive of the other. Aristotle, for example, accounts for the oligarchical conception of justice by saying that it is based on the notion that inequality in respect to property is taken to be inequality in all respects. The source of dispute is not the abstract principle of justice, but taking the part as the whole. Compensation in wages can depend on the hours worked, seniority, education, etc. Although everyone agrees that equals should go to equals and unequals to unequals, what the particulars are that are going to be compared, in the formula of equality and inequality, are in dispute.

We can distinguish broadly between two kinds of discourse, one the abstract language of agreement, and the other the concrete language of dispute. The first is the language of law and the second is the language of fact, in which are found descriptions of the world in the language of the vernacular. The first is the product of either statutes or court decisions and is the result of some form of agreement either among legislators, jurors or judges. Agreement on the abstract principle of justice of equals to equals and unequals to unequals is vacuous. Substantive law is the application of this principle to the situation and the circumstance. It is in the language of the law that the abstract principle of justice is applied. What the language of law achieves and establishes is fixing an equivalence between dissimilar things and events. It is like the equivalence created when two different kinds of objects are assigned the same monetary value. There is agreement that for things of equivalent value, the same amount of money should be paid, in other words equals for equals, but there is disagreement over whether or not two things are of equivalent value. To say that a rug costs the same amount of money as two pairs of shoes is to establish an equivalence, but there would likely be disagreement because of countless factors that would make one person accept the equivalence and another reject it. Disputes arise because we take things that are equal in one respect to be equal in all respects. For example, wages are determined by many factors, such as seniority, time on task, education, the quantity and quality of the work. Those who focus on seniority alone would argue that those who have been in employment longer should receive higher wages, whereas those who focus on education alone might argue that those who have a better education should receive the greater wage. Two different perspectives pick out different features of the same object when determining equality and inequality. The bargaining that occurs between the buyer and the seller over price is a monetary code used for determining equivalence between a variety of different objects. Instead of asking how many shoes an overcoat is equivalent to, we ask how much does it cost. What is a fair price is another way of asking whether the items of the exchange are equivalent.

Those who establish such monetary equivalences, or in other words set prices, aim at equivalences that are likely to meet with agreement in the market place. Compensatory and punitive justice establish equivalences between dissimilar things. How much is the loss of a limb or the loss of reputation worth? We have recourse to the language of law and the formal procedures and rituals of the court to establish such equivalences. It is only by treating dissimilar things as the same that the universal agreement that exists with regard to the principle of equality and inequality, can be brought to bear upon what is particular and situational.

However, to speak of the abstract principle of equality and inequality and inequality and the particularity of fact statements is to appeal to a logocentric paradigm that obscures insight into the linguistic dynamics of bulletin board communication. The distinction that is being made is actually hermeneutical. What we have called abstract statements, the statements of law, are statements that are open to wide interpretation in application. We have, for instance, laws that guarantee freedom of speech, but what is to count as speech? Not yelling "fire" in a crowded movie theater; not carrying signs that support the enemy during time of war? Here is the tension between law and its application, between the general language of law and particular language of fact, situation, and circumstance.

The language of law is written and universal, the language of fact is oral and situational.

We ask how does the discursive environment of the bulletin board effect agreement and disagreement in matters of justice? Would our concept of fairness change in an environment in which people are communicating electronically and where such communication has become an integral part of their life?

The unique characteristic of the BBS as a communication medium is that it is mass communication that is interactive and individualized. Interactivity allows the bilateral mapping of different language practices onto one another in ways that communication, such as television, newspaper, and radio cannot achieve. Interactivity involves feedback between the sender and receiver of signs and sign systems. Through paraphrasing, parties to a communication can approach agreement over what constitutes a well-formed expression. Stipulative definitions, functioning like contracts, stabilize the linguistic practices used by the communicants.

In the environment of the bulletin board there is a greater likelihood of agreement and fairness. Why? We reason by first affirming again, Aristotle's observation that there is universal agreement with respect to the principle of equality and inequality- the principle of justice. The principle of justice, upon which all are said to agree, is stated at a level abstractness and universality approaching that of mathematics and logic. However, the principle, by itself, yields little of practical value, since in disputes, the items that are exchanged are not strictly speaking unqualifiedly equal.

Paraphrasing is a good example of a kind of linguistic exchange that seeks to determine equivalence. In communication that is not interactive the speaker has no way of knowing whether or not the audience means the same thing by the words that the speaker has used. In a more interactive environment, the speaker can request a statement that the listener judges equivalent to that which the speaker uttered. And just as in bargaining over the price of an item of exchange, various paraphrases can be sent and received until both parties agree upon a single statement that they judge to be equivalent to the original.

One set of language practices is mapped onto another. In the environment of the BBS, the messages that are exchanged can be made public so that the parties in communication also are aware of the possibility of other situations and contexts, i.e., hermeneutical perspectives that could change the meaning of the messages. The BBS is an open hermeneutic environment in which there are an unlimited number of addressers and addresses all who could interact in determining the meaning of what is said. Instead of autocratic speech that is incapable of resolving the proliferation of hermeneutic possibilities for all communicants, the BBS allows for the dynamics of communication exchange to approach uniform standards of linguistic practice. The uniformity however is not merely agreement over vacuous abstractions such as Aristotle's principle of justice, but concrete agreement born of the give and take of messages and replies which combine the enunciative specificity of oral communication with the degree of universality and formality found in written text.

**Professor of Philosophy, Christopher Newport College.*

# Notes

1. Aristotle, *Politics*, Book V, Chapter 1, 1301.

2. *Ibid.* p.1302.

# Index